THE
INSIDER
THREAT

THE INSIDER THREAT

HOW THE **DEEP STATE** UNDERMINES AMERICA FROM WITHIN

ADAM LOVINGER

New York • London

First American edition published in 2024 by Encounter Books,
an activity of Encounter for Culture and Education, Inc.,
a nonprofit, tax-exempt corporation.
Encounter Books website address: www.encounterbooks.com

Manufactured in the United States and printed on
acid-free paper. The paper used in this publication meets
the minimum requirements of ANSI/NISO Z39.48-1992
(R 1997) (*Permanence of Paper*).

FIRST AMERICAN EDITION

LIBRARY OF CONGRESS CATALOGING-IN-PUBLICATION DATA IS AVAILABLE

Information for this title can be found at the Library of Congress
website under the following ISBN 9781641774314 and LCCN 2024032762.

To EMR

CONTENTS

CHAPTER 1

DISCOVERING THE DEEP STATE

In framing a government which is to be administered by men over men, the great difficulty lies in this: you must first enable the government to control the governed; and in the next place oblige it to control itself.

— JAMES MADISON[1]

The electronic file I found on a Pentagon computer one rainy morning in September 2017 seemed to have materialized overnight, out of nowhere. Adrenaline pumping, I clicked it open. A deluge of sub-files plunged me into a vast digital underworld. What my eyes beheld, but my mind struggled to comprehend, was that here before me was a secret and detailed how-to manual on destroying one's bureaucratic enemies, tailored just for me. Where had it come from? Who had put it there? Who had given me access to it? Was it some kind of trap?

A few months before that discovery, my career was ascendant. For the past dozen years, I had held prestigious posts in the Office of the Secretary of Defense and U.S. National Security Council (NSC). I had lectured at esteemed defense forums in Europe and Asia and was going into my fourth year of teaching graduate students at Georgetown University.

That all blew up after the new U.S. national security advisor, Lieutenant General (Ret.) Michael T. Flynn, brought me in to work for him at the White House. First, my Top Secret/Sensitive Compartmented Information (TS/SCI) security clearance was suspended, making me ineligible to work in the Pentagon or White House, facts which were immediately (and illegally) leaked to the press. After that I was marched off to a nondescript Defense Department facility in northern Virginia, where a gaggle of personnel and security officers kept me under surveillance.

My steady stream of invitations to teach strategy to military officers, serve on prestigious panels, and deliver lectures dried up overnight. My crime? In the course of doing my job, which was to ensure the U.S. had strategies to win its wars in Iraq and Afghanistan and strategic competitions with China, Russia, and Iran, a shadowy network of hyper-empowered bureaucrats had decided they didn't want me doing that.

I wasn't the only one. Many who went to work for the Trump White House were driven out for nebulous reasons. A colleague who discovered how former National Security Advisor Susan Rice was "unmasking" Trump campaign staff was fired. Others who figured out how members of the Trump team were being targeted were themselves picked off one by one based on demonstrable lies. The point was to get rid of all of us quickly, with maximum damage to our careers and reputations.

Older and wiser mentors—former senior officials with experience working in the Pentagon, NSC, State Department, and Central Intelligence Agency—had warned me about the so-called "Deep State," or what the *New York Times* describes as a "network of civilian and military officials who control or undermine democratically elected governments."[2] The most ruthless members of this cabal, I was told, were concentrated in the Senior Executive Service of the U.S. national security, intelligence, and law enforcement bureaucracies.[3]

At first, I dismissed their warnings of a vast criminal conspiracy perpetrated by senior bureaucrats. Surely, any organized scheme to subvert U.S. law and obstruct federal process would be checked and balanced by other governmental officials. No, I was told: Deep State operatives are free to ignore the facts and law with impunity. This was, I thought, an absurd fantasy. "Your grip on reality is slipping, my friend," I told one mentor I knew well enough to speak to bluntly. He replied that I was mistaken. I stared back in disbelief. "You'll have to learn the hard way," he said.

Quietly racing against the clock, for several days I arrived at work early and left late in order to print off the entire Deep State playbook from my DoD computer. In the weeks that followed my discovery, I digested its contents.

The playbook explained the workings of the Pentagon's top strategist, James H. Baker, Director of the Office of Net Assessment (ONA). Baker's actions had been mysterious to me. One month after he had my security clearance suspended, he dispatched a subordinate to draft a "memorandum to file" on my boss at the White House National Security Council, alleging that he had mishandled classified information. The law states that such reports must be forwarded to security authorities for investigation. But, as Baker would later testify under oath, he never did that. Rather, he kept the memorandum for himself—surely to be used, should he so wish, as bureaucratic blackmail. If my NSC boss tried to protect me, Baker could threaten him with that memo or use it to suspend his security clearance.

A long-time friend who had worked at the Central Intelligence Agency told me that Deep State initiation rites mirror those of drug gangs. To join their ranks, a new recruit must commit a crime. That incriminating information serves as an insurance policy for higher-ups to enforce obedience.

A few months after furnishing his memorandum on my NSC boss to Baker, Baker's subordinate was appointed to the Senior Executive Service—making him the rough equivalent of a one-star general in the Pentagon hierarchy.

The playbook I encountered comes with instructions, templates, and pre-populated forms. Baker deployed one such form after a key U.S. ally reported that Baker was responsible for a leak of that country's classified information. Baker's actions, a senior foreign official complained, had resulted in a "life or death" threat to his country's war ships in the Western Pacific Ocean.

Baker's response followed the playbook to a T. He pretended to launch an investigation into the source of the leak. But in actuality, as he made clear in a secret "purposes and uses" section of that form, Baker just investigated me. He then passed that document off to top Pentagon officials who, before signing it, deleted Baker's incriminating admission.[4] Apparently, they were fine with Baker scapegoating a colleague for his own misconduct.

The edited form was then used to launch what the playbook calls "administrative due process." Devoid of any actual due process, this consists of employing battalions of taxpayer-funded lawyers, personnel experts, security clearance adjudicators, administrative law judges, special counsels, and inspectors general to overwhelm their hapless victim. Their job is to use baseless investigations, devoid of facts, law, and justice, to hound and crush anyone who dares to expose the Deep State for the threat it poses to the Republic.

Even the Freedom of Information Act (FOIA), a federal statute designed to shed light on secretive government processes, has been weaponized by the Deep State to do the opposite of its statutory purpose. Its operatives employ FOIA to ensure that their crimes never see the light of day and they are never held to account. In my case, FOIA was used to cover up the fact that I became the target of five progressively more invasive investigations lacking any legal predicate whatsoever. What is more, FOIA was used to conceal the fact that those launching these investigations were themselves implicated in the very crimes they pretended to investigate.

Those who question the independence or objectivity of such illegal investigations are accused of obstructing justice. The ensuing confusion buys Deep State operatives the time they need to cover their tracks, seize their victim's information, and destroy the records needed by those victims to mount their defense, prove their innocence, and offer suggestions to agency leadership for structural reforms.

The playbook instructs its users to charge those who resist with "insubordination" and to portray their efforts to defend themselves as evidence of "divided loyalties." Law-abiding officials are smeared as "insider threats," stripped of their security clearances, then hurled into an interminable and costly administrative process in which the facts and law are irrelevant.

By the time our victim realizes that he has fallen into a trap, and that all these "investigations," "hearings," and "appeals" are little more than a cruel joke, it is too late. His savings have been depleted fighting an unwinnable battle, and his friends and supporters have moved on, their patience and sympathy worn thin from hearing about a truth so much stranger than fiction that they begin to question his credibility.

After completing their weaponized investigations, Deep State operatives reward themselves with medals and promotions. Their cloying self-praise is yet another perverse mockery, a celebration of their impunity to break U.S. law. "If we can get away with this, just think about what we can do to you," is the message these actions send to the rest of the federal workforce.

In my case, dozens of Senior Executive Service members, including the deputy secretary of defense, the DoD general counsel, the acting DoD inspector general, and hordes of their willing subordinates, worked in concert to construct a web of falsehoods, subvert the federal investigative process, strip me of my Top Secret/SCI security clearance, smear my reputation, and fire me from my job. How they pulled it off was all spelled out in the playbook.

CHAPTER 2

THE OFFICE OF NET ASSESSMENT

The famous city planner of Washington, DC, Pierre Charles L'Enfant, served alongside General George Washington in the U.S. War of Independence. The role of France had proved decisive in assuring American victory. But the new country was weak and needed time to regroup before the next onslaught, so Washington turned to physical spectacle. He commissioned L'Enfant to present the United States to the world as a classical power worthy of the Roman Republic.

The site chosen for Washington's "Federal City" was a swamp across the Potomac River from his beloved Mount Vernon plantation. Washington drained that swamp to build his paean to republican government. In the 1940s the Pentagon was built atop a former hobo encampment and decommissioned airfield across the river.

The five-sided, five-ringed, five-storied Pentagon building was inspired by the other sixty-eight "star forts"[1] that by 1865 guarded the maritime gateway to the nation's capital. It was designed to cast a spell on visitors. Those approaching it find their postures elongated and senses dilated. Even boisterous packs of school children are hushed into decorous solemnity.

Protocol dictates that foreign dignitaries enter the fortress from the river entrance, where they are treated to a spectacular, panoramic view of monumental Washington bathed in a sea of white marble. In the vestibule of the gray stone behemoth, the foreign visitor is welcomed by framed photographs of smiling four-star combatant commanders, each a testament to America's unrivaled power projection capacity and global primacy.

Though a military fortress, the Pentagon is filled with art. Framed in gold, portraits of secretaries of defense and chairmen of the joint chiefs of staff peer down from its walls in triumph and tragedy. Featured prominently in one hallway and painted in a stark realist style on the heels of the 1991 Gulf War is a portrait of Dick Cheney. Confident and victorious, he meets our gaze with following, unblinking eyes. Off to the side and hung somewhat crookedly is an abstracted, even surrealist Robert Strange McNamara, who peers off into the distance, avoiding eye contact. McNamara was not the last defense secretary to conduct a decades-long conflict without a coherent strategy.

•   •   •

In 2002, after only six months into Operation Enduring Freedom, Secretary of Defense Donald H. Rumsfeld lamented, "We are never going to get the U.S. military out of Afghanistan." The following year, he wrote in a memo, "I have no visibility into who the bad guys are. We are woefully deficient in human intelligence."[2]

Seven years into the Obama administration, in 2015, the president's "Afghanistan war czar," Lieutenant General Douglas Lute, repeated that refrain to an interviewer: "We were devoid of a fundamental understanding of Afghanistan—we didn't know what we were doing.... What are we trying to do here? We didn't have the foggiest notion of what we were undertaking.... If the American people knew the magnitude of this dysfunction.... Who will say this was in vain?"[3]

Those questions remained unanswered six years later, as the Biden administration in August 2021 evacuated Kabul ignominiously after twenty years of aimless war, the longest in U.S. history.

Beginning in 2001, when U.S. forces first entered Afghanistan, the Pentagon deployed more than 775,000 U.S. troops to that war zone, 30,000 of whom were deployed no less than five times. For the Iraq and Afghanistan wars combined, almost 7,000 U.S. troops were killed and more than 50,000 wounded. Many more were psychologically scarred. The total dead from those two wars, which cost the American taxpayer roughly $8 trillion, is estimated at 515,000, over half of them civilians.

"Lessons Learned" reports, produced by DoD 's special inspectors general for Iraq and Afghan reconstruction, concluded what had become clear to me by 2006: Pentagon leadership had never bothered to craft a coherent strategy to win the Global War on Terror, much less the peace.

In graduate school, I studied how the Roman and British empires made one strategic blunder after another. I learned that great powers are "complex systems," and thus are subject to "cascading failures" and rapid collapse. This phenomenon is known as the "Seneca effect," after Roman philosopher Lucius Annaeus Seneca, who in a letter to his friend Lucilius, observed how "increases are of sluggish growth, but the way to ruin is rapid."[4] The DoD's glaring lack of strategy in conducting its wars in Iraq and Afghanistan, echoing the decline of great empires past, compelled me to seek out DoD's highest-level strategy office. It turned out to be just down the hall from my office on the third floor of the Pentagon's A-ring.

•   •   •

In 2004, when I was hired by the Office of the Secretary of Defense as an associate deputy general counsel for international affairs, I had never heard of the Office of Net Assessment. ONA had originated in the early 1970s, during what many historians consider the nadir of American self-confidence. This was an era that saw the birth of OPEC, growing gas lines across the country, stagflation, and recession. With the U.S. military under fire at home and bogged down in the jungles of Indochina, the USSR had the wind at its back. Moscow leveraged that strategic momentum to field a new generation of nuclear weapons, achieve strategic parity and even surpass the U.S., and grow Soviet spheres of influence throughout the developing world.

A key vulnerability that the Kremlin exploited was the tendency of America's leaders to launch and prosecute wars without even rudimentary strategies for success. In 1973, to ensure that a war like Vietnam would never happen again, Defense Secretary James R. Schlesinger brought Andrew W. Marshall over from the U.S. National Security Council at the White House to lead ONA at DoD.

Over the course of three meetings in his cavernous Pentagon office, Marshall patiently explained ONA's history and craft to me. Its roots lie deep in the NSC, where Henry A. Kissinger had brought Marshall from the RAND Corporation in 1971. Unlike intelligence assessments, net assessments are long term, looking twenty to thirty years into the future. Their purpose is to inform not just national security strategy, but grand strategy.

It should be noted that net assessments themselves are not strategies. Rather, they are crafted to inform strategy development by providing critical context. Focusing on relative, as opposed to absolute, power (hence the "net" in net assessment), they are multidisciplinary analyses of American strengths and weaknesses compared to those of our competitors. Using those assessments, competitive strategies are crafted to shape the long-term competition in our favor.

One day in late summer 2006, after I expressed my frustrations with the lack of strategies to win our wars in Iraq and Afghanistan, Marshall ended our meeting by telling me, "well, it sounds like I should hire you." This was music to my ears.

The highly classified net assessments of the 1970s and '80s, some with the marginalia of various secretaries of defense still visible on their well-thumbed pages, run well over one hundred pages in length. Each focused on the enduring predispositions and vulnerabilities of the Soviet Union, including Moscow's strategic fears. ONA analysts had assessed that Soviet leaders cared foremost about their personal survival. Therefore, at great expense to their country, they had built a vast network of underground bunkers to protect themselves.

Armed with that knowledge, the Reagan administration deployed Pershing 2 missiles to West Germany. The fact that they could kill the Soviet leadership before they could get to the safety of their bunkers was then messaged to Moscow. That repositioning of forces made those bunkers strategically irrelevant. Purloined documents from the Soviet archives suggest that ONA accurately assessed our adversary's predispositions. Reagan-era policies to reinstate the MX missile and the B-1 bomber programs and develop the Strategic Defense Initiative all shaped Soviet behavior as intended.

Over the following decade I learned that parts of the U.S. national security bureaucracy and the intelligence community resented ONA. Culturally, the office had a reputation as aloof and Ivy League. We had our own (hideous) necktie. Deputy Director David Epstein was a Cornell graduate with a PhD in Government from Harvard. I was one of two civilian analysts. The other was Harold Rhode.

With a PhD from Columbia in Ottoman history, Rhode is a brilliant orientalist, as he would have been called before that word was transformed into a slur by the literary critic Edward Said. Fluent in nearly a dozen languages, including Farsi, Arabic, Turkish, and Hebrew, Rhode was the star protégé of Princeton University professor Bernard Lewis, whom the *New York Times* had crowned "the doyen of Middle Eastern studies."[5]

Marshall, known affectionately as "Yoda" after the Jedi master of *Star Wars*, had studied economics and math at the University of

Chicago. He was taciturn and cryptic, and some mistook his long silences for standoffishness. I believe he was just shy.

ONA was resented for other reasons. One of these was the fact that almost no one in the Pentagon understood what net assessment was. Part of the problem is that most universities refrain from teaching it, even at the postgraduate level, as it is based on the old-fashioned conception of a multidisciplinary liberal arts that has been abandoned in favor of the specialization and quantification of the social sciences. At a minimum, net assessment requires comparing and synthesizing the most strategically significant military, technological, economic, cultural, demographic, and geopolitical components of the long-term strategic competition between the U.S. and our adversaries.

Another source of friction is that net assessments focus on future contingencies, which, by definition, are educated guesses. By contrast, the Pentagon lives and breathes certainty in the form of numbers, charts, and graphs—not because these tools most accurately reflect reality, but because they are simple, concrete, and look good on Power Point presentations. From my experience working on Iraq and Afghanistan, I concluded that the Pentagon becomes obsessed with metricizing wars to hide the fact that we are losing them. Disconnected from culture and history, leaders use metrics—the number of schools built, the miles of road laid down, and so forth—to construct the illusion of success, buy time, and obscure the reasons for failure on their watch, before moving on to their next assignment.

"Every data point was altered to present the best picture possible," is how U.S. Army Colonel Bob Crowley described the reporting on Afghanistan. Surveys, Crowley discovered, "were totally unreliable but reinforced that everything we were doing was right and we became a self-licking ice cream cone."[6]

Something similar seems to have have happened at the Pentagon under Secretary of Defense Robert McNamara. Using systems analysis that he had imported to DoD from his time as president of the Ford Motor Company, he metricized the Vietnam war, reducing it to body counts and other misleading measures of success.

But there was another reason for the friction between ONA and the rest of the Pentagon bureaucracy, and this was ONA's reputation for engaging with politically incorrect truths. By September 11, 2001, the strictures of "political correctness"—later, "wokeness"—had fully migrated from the academy to the U.S. national security bureaucracy.

When the United States was attacked by a foe whose leadership invariably claimed to draw its legitimacy from a religion, that culturally based "enduring predisposition" required one to generalize. But leveraging the Islamism of Al-Qaeda, ISIS, or the Taliban for strategic advantage in a net assessment subjected ONA to charges of "racism," so the subject became off limits.

As the U.S. began targeting Al-Qaeda positions in Afghanistan in October 2001, then–Deputy Secretary of State Richard Armitage stunned his Pakistani counterparts by telling them "for you and us, history starts today."[7] Years later, the Bush administration's ahistorical and culturally neutral approach to those conflicts in the Muslim world remained entrenched. "Whether you call them ISIS or ISIL, I refuse to call them the Islamic State, because they are neither Islamic [n]or a state," said Hillary Clinton.[8] Of course, that was exactly how those Islamist fighters saw themselves.

Just as it had in Vietnam decades before, the strategic consequences of those intellectual blinders and that self-deception all but ensured America's defeat in Iraq and Afghanistan.

On September 1, 2021, U.S. Special Forces interpreter Baktash Ahabi published an assessment of what followed from America's culturally ignorant approach to foreign policy. By "building roads, schools and governing institutions—in an effort to 'win hearts and minds'—without first figuring out what values animate those hearts and what ideas fill those minds," Ahabi wrote, the U.S.

government "wound up acting in ways that would ultimately alienate everyday Afghans."[9] One report by DoD's Office of the Special Inspector General for Afghanistan Reconstruction (SIGAR) echoed Ahabi's assessment:

> We found the stabilization strategy and the programs used to achieve it, were not properly tailored to the Afghan context, and successes in stabilizing Afghan districts rarely lasted longer than the physical presence of coalition troops and civilians.[10]

But admonitions of that kind were ignored. Ahabi concluded that the failure to take culture seriously and use that knowledge to craft and execute U.S. national security strategy had resulted in "self-inflicted damage caused by a failure to understand the enemy of the day."[11] According to Craig Whitlock's December 2019 analysis of the SIGAR papers in the *Washington Post*,

> Obama's strategy was also destined to fail. U.S., NATO and Afghan officials told government interviewers that it tried to accomplish too much, too quickly, and depended on an Afghan government that was corrupt and dysfunctional.
>
> Worse, they said, Obama tried to set artificial dates for ending the war before it was over. All the Taliban had to do was wait him out.[12]

"Sooner or later a false belief bumps up against solid reality, usually on the battlefield," George Orwell wrote over half a century ago.[13] But, as Bob Crowley recounted in a SIGAR interview, that warning was not heeded: "There were a number of faulty assumptions in the strategy: Afghanistan is ready for democracy overnight, the population will support the government in a short time frame, more of everything is better."[14]

Whitlock continued: "While the Taliban was easy to demonize because of its brutality and religious fanaticism, the investment proved too large and [corruption was too] ingrained in Afghan society to eradicate."[15] But corruption is a two-way street. Because government defense contractors are in the business of war, they are incentivized to perpetuate the conflicts that drive demand for their goods and services. That often, though not always, makes their interests diametrically opposed to those of the United States. As Whitlock lamented:

> Since 2001, Washington has spent more on nation-building in Afghanistan than in any country ever, allocating $133 billion for reconstruction, aid programs and the Afghan security forces. Adjusted for inflation, that is more than the United States spent in Western Europe with the Marshall Plan after World War II....
>
> [Economists described] an array of mistakes committed again and again over 18 years—haphazard planning, misguided policies, bureaucratic feuding....
>
> Much of the money, they said, ended up in the pockets of overpriced contractors or corrupt Afghan officials, while U.S.-financed schools, clinics and roads fell into disrepair, if they were built at all.[16]

As Whitlock reported in his 2021 book, *The Afghanistan Papers: A Secret History of the War*, for twenty years the Pentagon had engaged in an "unspoken conspiracy to mask the truth"[17] about Afghanistan. What is more, when the *Washington Post* tried to see the Pentagon's "Lessons Learned" reports on Afghanistan, Deep State operatives in the DoD Office of Inspector General (DoD OIG) dragged their feet. As Colbert I. King of the *Washington Post* would observe, they also concealed U.S. Government evidence and deceived the American people:

What in the world should be done about senior U.S. officials who failed to tell the truth about the war in Afghanistan, making rosy pronouncements they knew to be false and hiding unmistakable evidence the war had become unwinnable? ...

They lied about the Afghanistan war. They painted rosy pictures over ugly truths, and they hid "unmistakable evidence the war had become unwinnable" even as U.S. tax dollars were being stolen and American bodies fell to the ground.[18]

Members of the Senior Executive Services (SES) in the U.S. national security bureaucracy and Senior Intelligence Service (SIS) of the IC are never held to account for these offenses. That impunity normalizes malfeasance within the ranks of the "leaders" entrusted with sending young men and women to fight America's wars in foreign lands.

A LEGENDARY OFFICE IN DECLINE

When I joined ONA in 2006, the Pentagon was led by Secretary of Defense Donald Rumsfeld. He and Marshall had been friends since the time they held their same jobs in the Ford administration. Rumsfeld respected Marshall's brilliance. Having studied DoD operations and mistakes during the hiatus between his two tours as secretary of defense, Rumsfeld returned to the Pentagon in 2001, ready to re-organize U.S. military operations according to rigorous national security strategies.

Rumsfeld had many years of experience running big corporations, so he was under no illusions about the resistance defense contractors would mount against a "transformation" of the U.S. military. Though very different personalities, both Rumsfeld and Marshall agreed this mission had to come first. They planned to cut outdated concepts of operations and legacy weapons systems—such as the Crusader artillery system and the RAH-66 Comanche armed reconnaissance helicopter—and replace them with relevant ones.

Following the end of the Cold War, Marshall turned his focus to the U.S.-China strategic competition. To broadcast his view that the People's Republic of China (PRC) posed the greatest threat to U.S. interests, Rumsfeld put on a show of lunching in the Pentagon's Navy Mess with Marshall. That was unusual because both mean ordinarily ate lunch at their desks. Richard Perle, Marshall's friend and Reagan's assistant secretary of defense, said it was a clear bureaucratic signal: "It went all over the building that Andy was back."

The bedrock of their partnership was a shared conviction about America's proper role in the world. Born in 1921 in Detroit to a stonemason father and homemaker mother, Marshall received a medical deferment during World War II because of a heart murmur. An avid student of international relations, Marshall lived the adage that "power abhors a vacuum." He witnessed how the victorious democracies of World War I had lost the peace through isolationism, which Nazi Germany and Imperial Japan interpreted as weakness. Marshall's generation bore the brunt of that leadership failure

An ONA colleague once told me that on a side trip taken to the American cemetery near Normandy Beach in France, the famously reserved Marshall let down his guard to quietly sob at the grave of an American soldier who had died liberating Europe from tyranny. As they left the cemetery, Marshall gently placed his fingers on the marble headstone of that fallen soldier and whispered, "Thank you."

For the "Greatest Generation," the unmistakable lesson of the rivers of American blood spilled in World War II was that the world's democracies had to believe in themselves, draw strength from their liberal convictions, and play a global leadership role. As Ronald Reagan put it, "Winston Churchill, in negotiating with the Soviets, observed that they respect only strength and resolve in their dealings with other nations. That's why we've moved to reconstruct our national defenses. We intend to keep the peace. We will also keep our freedom."[19]

To safeguard that freedom long term, America needed serious national security strategies informed by context-driven net assessments. This was not "imperialism." The resultant *Pax Americana* reduced war through deterrence. Under the U.S.-led world order, battle deaths dropped from a high of about 2,013 per 1 million people in 1942 to 12 per 1 million people by the year 2016.[20]

Following Al-Qaeda's September 11, 2001, attack on America, ONA became a bureaucratic backwater. Having focused its energies on the worthy topics of Defense Transformation and China since the end of the Cold War, the office had completed no net assessments on the Middle East and Central Asia. This meant that ONA had nothing to contribute to America's War on Terror. I knew none of this when I joined the office in 2006.

Marshall's diminished stature under his friend Rumsfeld wounded his pride. He blamed "the political class" as being "not up to the task." Marshall had a point, but it was a poor excuse. Done right, net assessments focus on the enduring characteristics of U.S. strategic competitions long term, are designed to stand the test of time, and can be adjusted to changing circumstances. Their continued production was imperative for those occasions when the "political class" births a strategically minded leader determined to prevent America from entering wars blindly, losing, and following in the footsteps of other once-great powers. Instead, Marshall turned his attention to training a next generation of strategists, for which I am a forever grateful beneficiary. But it didn't make up for the fact that under Bush, Obama, Trump, and Biden ONA produced no net assessments to inform America's wars in Afghanistan or Iraq.

CHAPTER 3

THE OBAMA DOCTRINE

*A nation can survive its fools, and even the ambitious. But it cannot
survive treason from within. An enemy at the gates is less formidable, for he is known and carries his banner openly. But the traitor
moves amongst those within the gate freely, his sly whispers rustling
through all the alleys, heard in the very halls of government itself.*
—MARCUS TULLIUS CICERO[1]

Upon entering the White House, Obama knew little about foreign
policy. As a student at Harvard Law School, he had concluded
that "America is a racist society."[2] Domestically, he supported race-
based preferences that shifted resources and opportunities to address
social grievances and adjust power dynamics between racial and
ethnic groups. Extrapolating that worldview to foreign policy, Obama
viewed the United States, and the West more generally, as oppressors
that had unjustly subjugated and exploited the non-Western world.

In 2009, the newly inaugurated President Obama crossed several
continents to address those global grievances. On June 4 of that year,
from the podium of Cairo University, he expanded on his earlier
confession that "we have not been perfect"[3] and apology for "our own
darker periods of our history," given to the Turkish parliament two
months before. In Egypt, he disclosed his view of Israel, analogiz-
ing the plight of Palestinians to that of South African blacks under
apartheid and slaves in the antebellum American South. According
to Obama, Palestinians "endure the daily humiliations—large and
small—that come with occupation." Israel was responsible for their
"pain of dislocation."[4]

In that address, Obama carefully avoided any mention of Israel as the biblical homeland of the Jewish people. He also glossed over the history of Islamic imperialism that emerged much later from the Arabian Peninsula. For Obama, none of that mattered.

In his eyes, Israel was irredeemably guilty because it was created by Europeans, for Europeans, as a Holocaust sympathy sop. First the Crusaders, then the British Empire, then Israel forced the region's darker-skinned natives to pay the price for Western imperialism. Dennis Ross, Obama's Middle East advisor, explained his boss's approach to imposing "equity" on the Israel-Palestine conflict: "President Obama, seeing the Israelis as the stronger party and the Palestinians as the weaker one, put the onus on Israel."[5]

At a press conference at the majestic Palais de la Musique et des Congrès in Strasbourg, France, Obama said that America "has shown arrogance and been dismissive, even derisive"[6] to foreign peoples, and that the United States was no more exceptional than other nations.[7] Obama delivered that address, which seemed designed to invalidate the post–World War II global order that hundreds of thousands of Americans had fought and died to create and safeguard, from the very soil American soldiers liberated from tyranny twice in the last century.

•   •   •

The purpose of the president's "Apology Tour" was to win American support for his foreign policy agenda. The "Obama Doctrine," as that agenda came to be known, would superimpose a race-based grievance politics paradigm onto international relations. In the name of "equity" and to correct past wrongs, Obama would adopt a strategy to intentionally erode U.S. and Western power, and augment that of non-Western countries.

But in the wake of the new president's Apology Tour, national polling found that ordinary Americans were patriotic, proud of their country, and repulsed by his vision for a weakened and contrite America. The Chicago Council on Global Affairs consistently finds that Americans, from all political stripes and both sides of the aisle, want U.S. presidents to lead, not seek penance, and will not accept a doctrine that humbles and enfeebles America relative to other world powers.[8]

The new president's job approval rating plummeted sharply.[9] "If all countries are 'exceptional,'" observed James Kirchick of the *New Republic*, in reference to Obama's Strasbourg address, "then none are, and to claim otherwise robs the word, and the idea of American exceptionalism, of any meaning."[10]

Addressing the global leadership vacuum created by the the Obama presidency, polls found that support for U.S. international leadership was higher than at any time since Chicago Council Survey began nearly fifty years before.[11] But the American people's distaste for his eponymous doctrine would not stop Obama. If he could not implement it directly, he would do so indirectly.

For the centerpiece of the Obama Doctrine, he would resurrect from the dead an outmoded approach to foreign policy—"balance of power" politics—and make it central to his foreign policy vision. This was essentially a rebranding operation, a good example of what Thomas Sowell has described as Obama's inimitable skill as a politician:

> Barack Obama's political genius is his ability to say things that will sound good to people who have not followed the issues in any detail—regardless of how obviously fraudulent what he says may be to those who have.[12]

Obama knew that balance of power politics would "sound good to people" because of its long and illustrious European pedigree. At the 1815 Congress of Vienna, Count Klemens von Metternich, the Foreign Minister of the Austrian Empire, used balance of power as his rationale for the Concert of Europe, the agreement among

European aristocrats who, after vanquishing Napoleon Bonaparte's France, would meet periodically to adjust and restrain the worst excesses of European power politics.

Further, balance of power politics was not alien to the American experience. It earned a place in the U.S. foreign policy tradition after Henry A. Kissinger, national security advisor and secretary of state in the Nixon and Ford administrations, imported it from Europe to America. He wielded it as a means to stabilize global order at a time of deep divisions in America over the downward spiral of U.S. involvement in Vietnam and the rise of Soviet power relative to that of America.

Kissinger assessed that a foreign policy aimed at balancing Soviet power would give America the breathing room it needed to reconstitute its battered economy and national defense. *Détente*, as this version of that policy came to be known, accomplished what Nixon and his successors had set out to do. But it was a temporary fix, not a long-term solution to the problem.

About a decade later, President Ronald Reagan would discard balance of power politics on the grounds that it was the preserve of an anemic America. This shift of policy was captured vividly in June of 1988, when Reagan ascended a podium before the Brandenburg Gate in a divided Germany and implored the Soviet leader, "Mr. Gorbachev, tear down this wall." By then, the Reagan Doctrine's policy of "peace through strength" had inverted the 1970s-era U.S.-USSR power differential in America's favor. In 1989 the Berlin Wall crumbled. Two years later, the Soviet Union collapsed into the dustbin of history.

With the end of the Cold War, something approaching a new bipartisan U.S. foreign policy consensus had developed.

U.S. preeminence, represented by strategically located military bases spanning the globe, shielded U.S. allies and partners under an American security umbrella. That primacy broadcast American resolve, deterred threats to the rules-based liberal global order, defused what defense analysts call the "security dilemma," and kept the peace. In the words of Madeleine Albright, President Bill's Clinton's secretary of state, America was the "indispensable nation,"[13] buttressing the cause of liberalism against authoritarianism.

•   •   •

After the fallout from his disastrous "Apology Tour" showed him that the American people would not accept a U.S. president degrading their country from foreign soil, much less relinquishing U.S. power to other countries to achieve a balance of power, Obama shifted his strategy. He would eschew open discussion and debate about his long-term plans for America.

Only after the fact would Hillary Clinton, Obama's former secretary of state, describe their top-down approach: "I don't believe you change hearts. You change laws, you change allocation of resources, you change the way systems operate."[14] By then, that lesson had been her political lodestar for nearly half a century.

"We had a fundamental disagreement. He [Saul Alinsky, Clinton's college mentor] believed you could change the system only from outside. I didn't," she wrote in her 2003 autobiography, *Living History*. "...my decision was an expression of my belief that the system could be changed from within."[15]

As Harvard- and Yale-educated lawyers steeped in the philosophical foundations and history of the U.S. constitutional order, Obama and Clinton knew that secretive policymaking, removed from the refiner's fire of open discourse and debate, was alien and abhorrent to the American political tradition. "For if Men are to be precluded from offering their Sentiments on a matter, which may involve the most serious and alarming consequences," George Washington warned in a 1783 address to officers of the Continental

Army, "reason is of no use to us; the freedom of Speech may be taken away, and, dumb and silent we may be led, like sheep, to the Slaughter."[16]

Similarly, John F. Kennedy warned his fellow Americans in April 1961 that

> [w]ithout debate, without criticism, no Administration and no country can succeed—and no republic can survive.... [Americans] decided long ago that the dangers of excessive and unwarranted concealment of pertinent facts far outweighed the dangers cited to justify it. Even today, there is little value in opposing the threat of a closed society by imitating its arbitrary restrictions. Even today, there is little value in ensuring the survival of our nation if our traditions do not survive with it.[17]

From my role at the Pentagon, I had a front-row seat to how the Obama administration abandoned U.S. primacy, dismantled the *Pax Americana* that upheld the liberal global order, and mobilized a secret army of hyper-empowered bureaucrats to implement the Obama Doctrine by stealth from within.

CHAPTER 4

TRANSFORMATION FROM WITHIN

Under Marshall, the *raison d'être* of the Pentagon's Office of Net Assessment was to ensure U.S. primacy. Because that was anathema to his eponymous doctrine, Obama tried to disband ONA in 2011 and again in 2013. On both occasions Congress put up a spirited defense. But the onslaught was far from over.

One dark winter day in 2014, Marshall summoned me to his office to discuss my annual "performance plan." Though his door was open, I knocked, as I invariably did. He looked up from his book expressionlessly, then gestured that I should sit down on an overstuffed leather chair opposite his own. Books and papers stacked precariously on all sides seemed to envelop us both in a protective cocoon.

At the time of our meeting, Marshall was ninety-three years old. He had created the discipline of net assessment from scratch and had led ONA for over forty years.

"Adam, I'm changing your performance plan. I want you to figure out where the national security strategy process has broken down and come up with a plan to fix it."

By then I had worked in the Office of the Secretary of Defense for over a decade. Marshall's directive was more expansive, complicated, and important than anything he had ever asked me to do before. It also showed me that Marshall was not going to abandon ONA's mission without a fight. The fact that he wanted me on his side in that battle was one of the greatest honors of my life.

"Sir, there is nothing I would rather do than that."

"I've asked Mike Pillsbury to help you and he's agreed. He helped Reagan roll back the Soviets in Afghanistan. He knows what to do," he said.

With that I left Marshall's office, happier than I had ever been in my eight years in ONA.

•   •   •

An expert on Chinese military strategy, Dr. Michael P. Pillsbury was at the time one of ONA's longest serving advisors. He and Marshall had first met during the Nixon administration. Since 1971, Pillsbury had worked for Marshall directly, sometimes as a Pentagon civil servant, but most of the time as an outside consultant or volunteer.

Pillsbury had authored some of the office's most important assessments over the course of his four-decades-long relationship with the office, and he mentored generations of ONA civilian and military staff alike. In between those activities, he had served as a high-level political appointee in Republican administrations. Under President Reagan, he was the assistant deputy undersecretary of defense. From that perch, he played a key role in equipping the Afghan mujahadeen with weapons to expel Soviet forces from Central Asia. Yet despite his occasional high-level appointments, Pillsbury always returned to his professional "home" in ONA.[1]

•   •   •

Around the time Marshall gave me my new marching orders, the Obama administration stopped trying to disband the Office of Net

Assessment. Instead, as Obama was doing at the time throughout the U.S. national security, intelligence, and law enforcement bureaucracies, he would remove those who disagreed with his ambition to erode Western power to the benefit of non-Western countries, and replace them with loyalists.

Soon after the 2014 holiday season, Deputy Secretary of Defense Robert O. Work set about removing Andrew W. Marshall, ONA's one and only director since its founding in 1973. That Work, a retired Marine colonel and former undersecretary of the U.S. Navy, forced Marshall to retire is not widely known. I have learned that even many of Marshall's long-time friends are under the mistaken impression that Marshall stepped down voluntarily.

Like most bureaucratic hit jobs, Marshall's expulsion from the Pentagon was a hasty affair. The idea was to get it done quickly and install a malleable placeholder. Andrew D. May, ONA's Associate Director, fit the bill.

Quick-witted and congenial, May exudes boyish charm and conducts himself with ease. He has a reputation of being a kind mentor to the next generation of national security professionals, of going the extra mile to lend a helping hand.

Yet May was malleable because he was compromised. Government evidence indicates that he was hired and promoted based not on merit, but fraud.[2] In 2005, May drafted the official DoD job description that would be used to hire him. It mirrored his professional credentials precisely. Five years later, he repeated that fraud with his appointment to serve as Associate Deputy Director of ONA.[3] He was not alone.

In May 2015, James H. Baker took over the ONA directorship as Marshall's permanent replacement. Like Andrew May, Baker was compromised—by design. Deep State operatives never promote anyone to hold a consequential position in the Senior Executive Service or Senior Intelligence Service without first generating a blackmail file on them.

Long-time ONA staff were baffled by Baker's lack of professional qualifications for the job. He had spent his U.S. Air Force (USAF) career not in some high-level strategy position, or even as a pilot, but in aircraft maintenance.

As Baker told it, one day Chairman of the Joint Chiefs of Staff, Admiral Michael Mullen, plucked him out of obscurity to serve as his strategy advisor—the job he held immediately before taking the helm of ONA. While a former maintenance officer advising the Chairman was one thing, directing ONA—the Pentagon's highest-level strategy office—was quite another.[4]

Baker made that leap by massaging his resume to meet the position's requirements, particularly the mandatory technical qualification to have "demonstrated experience in the development and coordination of net assessments."[5] Baker wrote on his application that he had "drafted documents which lay out net assessments of the United States military and its allies versus its adversaries," "co-led all ten of the [Chairmen of the Joint Chiefs of Staff] Strategic Seminar Series, which produced net assessments," and "drafted the Chairman's memorandum to the President and the Secretary laying out insights and conclusions: our net assessment of U.S. military potential now and in the future, weighed against the most likely strategy and capabilities of our opponents."[6]

Each of ONA's two dozen or so Top Secret net assessments completed under Marshall's directorship took about a year to finish and typically ran over one hundred pages long, with multiple annexes containing various calculations. Even viewed in the most charitable light, Baker's breezy meeting summaries of "day-long" conferences were not net assessments. Baker later conceded that he knew what he wrote was false because, in his words, "net assessments are very difficult projects and can take years to produce."[7]

As one former Pentagon official remarked, what Baker wrote on his application for ONA's top job was like claiming he had written a peer-reviewed book when in fact he had only written an op-ed. But Baker's ability to produce net assessments, it soon became clear, was of no real interest to Obama.

There was another oddity in Baker's hiring: before his appointment to ONA's top job, Deputy Secretary of Defense Work broke with over forty years of precedent by turning the ONA director billet from a political appointment into a theoretically nonpolitical civil-service position. That transformation, which came with civil-service job protections, indicated that Work saw Baker playing a critical role in a long-term strategy. This was hinted at in a *Defense News* article at the time, which characterized Baker's hire as "part of a wave of new Pentagon personnel moves in recent days, senior-level officials who will outlast President Obama's final term in office."[8]

Two years later, Tufts University Professor Michael Glennon summed up the cumulative effect of eight years of such "personnel moves":

> A de facto directorate of several hundred managers sitting atop dozens of military, diplomatic, intelligence, and law enforcement agencies, from the Department of Homeland Security to the National Reconnaissance Office, has come to dominate national security policy, displacing the authority not only of Congress but of the courts and the presidency as well.[9]

The following year, while promoting his book *Higher Loyalty*, former FBI Director James Comey described the purpose of what Glennon called a "double government," but what is more commonly called the "Deep State," to a New York City audience:

> There is a deep state in this sense. There is a collection of people, CIA, NSA, FBI [and] in the United States military services who

care passionately about getting it right, who care passionately about the values we try to talk about.[10]

During the lead-up to the 2016 presidential election, I learned first hand what Comey meant by "values."

•　　•　　•

Soon after assuming the directorship in May 2015, James H. Baker made it clear that his top priority was building what he called "connective tissue" between ONA and the Central Intelligence Agency. That was odd. ONA was CIA's client. Like the U.S. Government's other sixteen or so intelligence agencies, CIA provided intelligence products to the office.

If ONA officials had questions about a CIA product or believed it was deficient, we could arrange a meeting at Langley or the Pentagon and try to get to the bottom of the matter. But that relationship hardly passed as "connective tissue," a term which suggested somehow conjoining ONA and Agency operations to work in tandem.

On November 14, 2016, Baker clarified his meaning. On that day, Baker called me at the Pentagon from the road. His daughter was visiting colleges, and Baker was performing his fatherly duty as chauffeur.

"Adam, you should know that some friends at CIA have concerns about Michael Pillsbury. A while back they gave me a security file on him, and based on its contents I'm not at all optimistic that we can elevate his clearance to SCI," Baker said.

"Sir, you got a security file from CIA on Pillsbury?"

"Yes, that's correct."

I couldn't believe that Baker was saying that on an open line. CIA's legal authority is strictly relegated to conducting foreign espionage and operations *outside* the continental United States. Keeping a security file on a U.S. citizen permanently residing stateside is the purview of FBI, not CIA.

Two years later, Baker would testify under oath that the CIA file was part of his due diligence. He was about to elevate Pillsbury's security clearance, learned of the file, and was "curious" to see what was in it. But that made no sense.

For one thing, DoD had its own security clearance–adjudication procedure. An outside agency, especially the CIA, had no jurisdiction over that process whatsoever. What is more, Baker was not a security professional, and was thus forbidden from tampering with that process.

But what concerned me most was that by the time Baker had called me at the Pentagon from the road, Pillsbury was not a government official.

"Sir, Pillsbury is a private citizen. Did he give you permission to access that file?"

"No."

"Sir, CIA has nothing to do with this. This is done by DIA [Defense Intelligence Agency] officers seconded to WHS. Accessing a CIA file on Pillsbury is almost surely a criminal violation of his Privacy Act rights. That could get the office in a lot of trouble," I said.

There was a long silence, with some muffled talking in the background.

"OK. I'll put Pillsbury forward and try to get him SCI."

With that, Baker hung up.

Ultimately, CIA had no credible "dirt" on Pillsbury. DoD did its own security clearance check on him, and he was cleared in about four days—record time. That was no surprise to anyone. By then Pillsbury had worked with ONA for nearly half a century and already had a Top Secret clearance when Baker elevated it further to TS/SCI.

As I rode the metro home from the Pentagon that evening, I thought back to what I had said to Baker on that phone call and regretted it. Not because of the content, which was true. Rather, in my surprise at Baker's admission about getting a CIA file on Pillsbury without his permission, I had momentarily forgotten that his teenage daughter was seated next to him in the car when I said that Baker's violation of Pillsbury's Privacy Act–protected rights was a criminal offense.

CHAPTER 5

A NUCLEAR IRAN WOULD "MORE FAIRLY REBALANCE AMERICAN INFLUENCE"

During his 2009 Apology Tour, Obama hinted that his plan was to cut Israel down to size. But he concealed that ambition by pretending to seek Middle East peace. While all U.S. presidents since Israel's founding have tried to make peace between the Jewish state and its neighbors, Obama's approach was novel. He would do so by creating a Sunni-Shia balance of power. "The competition between the Saudis and the Iranians," Obama would spell out in 2016, "requires us to say...that they need to find an effective way to share the neighborhood and institute some sort of cold peace."[1]

It fell to Obama's Middle East advisor, Robert Malley, to clarify his boss's strategic thinking. The "ultimate goal" of the Obama administration's Middle East policy was to create "a more stable balance of power" in the region.[2] But that made no sense to most students of geopolitics and Islam.

As the president and his foreign policy advisors knew all too well, Muslims in the Middle East tend to form long-term alliances and partnerships based on sect. Sunnis constitute the vast majority of Muslims world wide, about 90 percent, whereas Shi'ites constitute a minority of about 10 percent. Shi'ite Iran is a large part of that one-to-nine minority, making any U.S.-led plan to balance Sunni with Shia power wildly impractical on its face. But that didn't matter to Obama, because that wasn't his true plan.

"THE AMERICANS SAY THEY STOPPED IRAN FROM ACQUIRING A NUCLEAR WEAPON. THEY KNOW IT IS NOT TRUE."

One important facet of Obama's balance of power strategy was the Joint Comprehensive Plan of Action (JCPOA), an agreement between China, France, Germany, Iran, Russia, the United Kingdom, the EU, and the United States. Obama supported that agreement, also known as the "Iran Deal,"[3] not on the grounds that it would restrain Iran's nuclear-weapons program, but because he knew it did just the opposite.

Since 1979, "death to America" has served as the Iranian regime's de facto motto. Nevertheless, the Iran Deal contained what came to be called "sunset clauses." Just as the sun disappears over the horizon, those limiting provisions were designed to expire after a set period. At that point, all the substantive restrictions on Iran's nuclear program would vanish. Once that happened, the world's greatest state sponsor of terror, which had killed and maimed thousands of U.S. and allied troops in Iraq and elsewhere with explosively formed projectiles (EFPs) or improvised explosive devices (IEDs), was free to develop a fully fledged, internationally sanctioned, industrial-scale nuclear weapons program.

In the calculus of the Reverend Jeremiah Wright, Obama's former pastor and spiritual mentor, that was fair and just. Wright considered the 9/11 terrorist attacks against America legitimate payback:

We bombed Hiroshima, we bombed Nagasaki, and we nuked far more than the thousands in New York and the Pentagon, and we never batted an eye ... and now we are indignant, because the stuff we have done overseas is now brought back into our own front yards. America's chickens are coming home to roost.[4]

A week after finalizing the JCPOA, Iran's Supreme Leader, Ayatollah Ali Khamenei, exposed the president's "signature foreign policy initiative"[5] for the fraud that Iran analysts in DoD knew it was from the beginning: "The Americans say they stopped Iran from acquiring a nuclear weapon. They know it is not true." In that same speech Khamenei declared what was known among Pentagon Iran analysts, but concealed from the American people: "Even after this deal, our policy toward the arrogant U.S. will not change."[6]

THE "NUCLEAR DEAL WOULD ALSO MORE FAIRLY REBALANCE AMERICAN INFLUENCE"

For both Tehran and the Obama administration, the Iran Deal's principal targets were Israel and the United States. In July 2015, Iranian Foreign Minister Mohammad Javad Zarif boasted that "this nuclear agreement puts the Zionist regime in an irrecoverable danger."[7]

Three months before that announcement, retired Chairman of the Joint Chiefs of Staff Admiral Mike Mullen wrote that the Iran "nuclear deal would also *more fairly rebalance American influence.* We need to re-examine all of the relationships we enjoy in the region.... Détente with Iran might better balance our efforts across the sectarian divide."[8]

Baker, who had served as Mullen's top strategist on the Joint Staff before rising to lead ONA, explained the Obama Doctrine in a speech to a foreign audience: "Iran may, if it chooses, 'safely' possess a nuclear weapon" on the grounds that nuclear weapons "offer Iran only limited use in reshaping the power dynamics in the region."[9] Baker assured his audience that the Middle East "region dominates Iran in every dimension of power, even though lack of Sunni cooperation severely hampers effectiveness."[10]

Baker, Mullen, and Obama all knew that Iran's aggression would only increase once the JCPOA's sunset clauses expired and Tehran was free to develop nuclear weapons. What is more, at the time, all of these men knew something that ordinary Americans did not.

In May 2011, U.S. Special Forces had seized files from Osama bin Laden's Pakistan compound. They contained detailed Iran-Al-Qaeda joint operational-planning documents for attacks on civilian targets throughout Europe with chemical and biological weapons. The strategic objective of that operation, according to those Iran-Al-Qaeda materials, was to reignite another post–9/11 holy war between the Islamic world and the West.

Should that happen, Baker, Mullen and Obama all knew that Washington was required under Article 5 of the North Atlantic Treaty to treat an attack on any NATO ally as an attack on America. They also knew that an Iranian nuclear arsenal would clip America's capacity to do so. But overall, Baker assured his foreign audience, the Iran Deal, with its "sunset clauses" paving the way for Tehran's possession of nuclear weapons, constituted a "significant and selective common gain."[11]

In November 2022, the United Nations International Atomic Energy Agency (IAEA) reported that Tehran, while negotiating the JCPOA in bad faith, had been operating a parallel clandestine nuclear program. The purpose of that report was to announce that Iran had already achieved "nuclear breakout," meaning Tehran had enriched enough uranium for at least one nuclear weapon.[12]

The IAEA had not previously detected that secret nuclear program because, as reported by the Associated Press on August 19, 2015, the IAEA had agreed to a secret side deal that permitted the Iranian regime to inspect its own nuclear sites and report on its own compliance with the JCPOA back to the IAEA. According to the AP report, that arrangement:

diverges from normal inspections procedures between the IAEA and a member country by essentially ceding the agency's investigative authority to Iran. It allows Tehran to employ its own experts and equipment in the search for evidence for activities that it has consistently denied—trying to develop nuclear weapons.[13]

Three months after Mullen acknowledged that the true purpose of the Iran Deal was to balance American power, Khamenei offered up his interpretation of what the JCPOA meant for America. Perhaps so that his message would not be lost on the illiterate, Iran's leader tweeted an image of Barack Obama holding a pistol to his own temple.[14] But the Iran Deal was a "cornerstone"[15] of the Obama Doctrine and a "prize foreign policy win."[16]

"OBAMA, OBAMA, ARE YOU WITH THEM OR WITH US?"

But the greatest resistance to Obama's détente with Iran came not from Europe, Israel, or the Sunni Muslim world, but from the Iranian people themselves. In June 2009, in the wake of rigged national elections, Iranian civilians had revolted against the regime. Video footage of the "Green Revolution" showed throngs of protesters flooding the streets of Tehran, only to be met by club-wielding paramilitary forces on motorcycles who chased and often beat them. Others were picked off by regime snipers firing high-powered rifles from the tops of apartment buildings. Regime collapse might well have occurred. If so, Israel's regional primacy would be ensured, dashing Obama's dream for a regional balance of power with Jerusalem's archrival.

O Ba Ma, written in the Persian alphabet, means "he is with us."[17] For this reason, on the streets of Tehran, the protesters chanted, "Obama, Obama, are you with them or with us?"[18] Obama's answer to that question echoing off the walls of Tehran's killing zones was to stand on the sidelines silently.

The regime interpreted accurately what Obama's show of no solidarity with the Iranian people meant. They could escalate their violent crackdown on the protesters with impunity. Which they did.

Only when the slaughter of innocents became too politically embarrassing did the president speak up to offer a scrap of human-rights window dressing. With lips pursed and in his most solemn baritone voice, Obama assured the Iranian people that he would "bear witness" to their slaughter.

But within the Pentagon it was known that Obama could have tipped the balance to the Iranian people, had he wanted. It was a lost opportunity for America to stand up for democracy, freedom, and the fundamental human rights of the Iranian people.

General Mohammad Ali Jafari, Iran's top commander of the Iranian Revolutionary Guard Corps, would later concede that the Green Revolution was a "greater danger for the system and the Islamic revolution" than the Iran-Iraq War.[19] That assessment was no anomaly. It was widely shared by all of Iran's top leaders, including Supreme Leader Ayatollah Ali Khamenei, who admitted in a 2013 interview that the civilian protesters had brought the regime to the "edge of the cliff."[20] In 2009, the fact that Iran was on the brink was known to Obama as well. But he preferred to suppress that intelligence and prop up the regime.

•   •   •

With the collapse of the Green Revolution, Obama tasked U.S. Secretary of State John Kerry with legitimizing the Iranian regime, destroying any chance for the Iranian people to throw off the yoke of tyranny. The morale of freedom-loving Iranians plummeted to new lows. The task for the Obama administration was now to ensure that the newly normalized Islamic Republic of Iran would be empowered and sustained long term.

To do that, the White House instructed Kerry to effectively suspend all inspections of Iran's nuclear sites, fast track the reeling and nearly bankrupt Iran into the global financial system, and shower the country with billions of dollars of foreign-held financial reserves. Iran analysts in the Pentagon knew that as soon as Tehran got those funds, they would be diverted.

Domestically, they were used to jump-start the regime's nuclear-capable-long-range-missile program. This was justified by Iranian Foreign Minister Mohammad Javad Zarif, who argued that "violating the arms and missiles embargo" of the United Nations "does not violate the nuclear agreement."[21] Beyond Iran's borders, Hezbollah's budget ballooned by 40 percent, expanding that terrorist group's sphere of influence throughout Syria, Yemen, the Gaza Strip, and Latin America.[22]

As a confidence-building measure, Americans and Iranians came together and set up the Iran Experts Initiative (IEI), under the auspices of Iran's Foreign Affairs Ministry. On May 14, 2014, Iran's Foreign Minister Zarif led the IEI's first meeting, which took place alongside JCPOA negotiations in Vienna's luxurious Palais Coburg hotel.

The IEI functioned, like the Iran Deal itself, as a joint Iran-U.S. effort to normalize the regime until the Iran Deal's "sunset clauses" could kick in. Its American members, three of whom would go on to join Biden's State Department in senior national security–sensitive positions, worked for Tehran.[23] One of them, Ariane Tabatabai, wrote articles and gave interviews to Iran's IRGC-sponsored Fars News Agency in support of Tehran's strategic interests.

Tabatabai took her direction from Foreign Minister Zarif's top advisor, Mostafa Zahrani, a member of the Islamic Revolutionary Guard Corps: "I would like to ask your opinion" wrote Tabatabai to Zahrani in June 2014, "and see if you think I should accept the invitation and go" on a trip to Israel.[24] The next month, she informed

Zahrani that she would be asking his advice on how to handle upcoming testimony she was presenting to the U.S. Congress on the nuclear deal. The committee hearing, she wrote, would be "a little difficult since [other witnesses] do not have favorable views on Iran."[25]

Like James H. Baker, who worked to embed Iran's strategic objectives within American policy and long-term strategy, Tabatabai would join the Office of the Secretary of Defense as a senior Biden administration official. Despite years of service to Tehran, she was appointed chief of staff for the assistant secretary of defense for special operations and low intensity conflict, a position that comes with a Top Secret/SCI security clearance. That was no anomaly.

Years earlier, Baker had declared that radical Islam was no longer a strategic threat to America. On May 19, 2016, Andrew D. May announced Baker's decision to eliminate the "contest with (and within) Radical Islam" from ONA's research agenda.[26] It stands to reason that if radical Islam was no longer a threat, neither were radical Islamists and their supporters, like Tabatabai.

Baker's and May's decision to ignore radical Islam was a return, full circle, to ONA's institutional failure prior to September 11, 2001. Even though radical Islamists had nearly destroyed ONA's office suite in the Pentagon on that day, ONA continued to refuse to conduct net assessments on radical Islam or the Global War on Terror. That dereliction of duty left U.S. military operations in Iraq and Afghanistan strategically blind for two decades.

These developments all advanced the Obama Doctrine's strategic purpose: to foreclose any possibility of regime change in Iran so as to prevent a free Iran from returning to its pre-1979 entente with the United States and Israel. If that happened, it would represent a triumph for "Western imperialism" that they could not permit.

The Iranian people learned the hard way that, while the Islamic Republic of Iran had stayed the same since 1980, America had radically transformed. The foreign policies of Obama and Reagan were not just incompatible. They were *diametrically opposed.*

Balancing the power between America and its enemies was nonsensical and immoral under Reagan's view of the world. Reagan's "forward strategy" was the opposite of Obama's preference for "offshore balancing"[27] from afar. Reagan's naval strategy, space-based Strategic Defense Initiative, and MX missile and B-1 bomber programs were about protecting the homeland, enveloping our democratic allies in a protective cocoon, and deterring America's enemies. They were definitely not about balancing power, leading from behind, standing on the sidelines, or waiting for the arc of history to complete its course.

While Obama transferred American and Western power to our enemies, Reagan, a man ridiculed as a buffoon by America's ruling class, summed up his eponymous doctrine as "We win and they lose. What do you think of that?"[28]

CHAPTER 6

SABOTAGING THE U.S.–JAPAN ALLIANCE

In May 2015, Baker placed Andrew D. May in charge of ONA's research agenda. "Well, that's ominous," a long-time advisor to Marshall told me.

"What do you mean?" I asked.

"You know, May is called 'Cashier' for a reason."

As ONA's first-ever direct hire ever from the defense industry, May was particularly solicitous of defense contractors. One, in particular, the Long Term Strategy Group (LTSG), a private, for-profit company, was special.

DoD evidence reveals that May in his official DoD capacity had helped create LTSG for a friend: Jacqueline Newmyer-Deal, who owned the company. On September 23, 2015, May praised LTSG's work product to ONA staff as "very good." And he transferred millions of taxpayer dollars annually to the contractor for an incessant stream of questionable work product.

None of LTSG's studies for ONA was peer reviewed. One of the contractor's reports rehashed the writings of popular author Malcolm Gladwell. Titled "On the Nature of Americans as a Warlike

People," it concluded that "educated American elites are anti-war compared to the rest of America."[1]

Other LTSG studies focused on issues entirely disconnected from the mission of the U.S. Department of Defense (DoD). For example, May and Baker paid LTSG $442,788 for a study on the "changing demographics in family structures in China."

In December 2018, Baker justified May's role in building a highly profitable company for a friend on the grounds of "institution building."[2] But May and Baker were not LTSG's only boosters.

A release of documents in 2016, extracted by government watchdog Judicial Watch under the Freedom of Information Act, showed that Newmyer-Deal had solicited government contracts from U.S. Secretary of State Hillary Clinton. Newmyer-Deal had met Chelsea Clinton at Sidwell Friends School. After Newmyer-Deal graduated from Harvard and Chelsea from Stanford, they attended Oxford University together. "Jackie and I are still best friends," said Chelsea. "She was in my wedding, and I was in hers."[3]

Between 2016 and 2019, LTSG was second only to the RAND Corporation as ONA's highest-paid contractor. While RAND had about 1,700 employees, LTSG had just twelve. To keep costs down and profits up, LTSG employed recent Harvard undergraduates to write its reports for ONA.

•　　•　　•

By October 17, 2016, it had become clear why Obama and Work had chosen Baker to lead ONA. To achieve a balance of power between the West and its strategic competitors, Baker intentionally subverted one of Washington's most important democratic allies.

On that day, while having lunch with Baker in the Pentagon's Navy Mess, I told him I was worried about ONA's management of a classified project with the government of Japan, conducted by LTSG, called the "Task Force on Enhancing the Japan-U.S. Alliance."

"As the only lawyer in ONA, I feel it's my duty to tell you that LTSG is employing [name of alleged Chinese spy] on the Task Force," I said.

At the time, it was widely known in the office that the individual in question was a suspected Chinese spy and the subject of multiple FBI investigations.

"So, what is your concern?" Baker asked.

"Sir, we should at least tell the Japanese that the FBI keeps investigating him on that suspicion. If we don't, that's a betrayal of the Japanese."

I knew that telling Baker what I thought about that potential counterintelligence threat was going to make him uncomfortable, and maybe feel threatened himself. But it was my duty to tell him; there was no way around it.

A few days before our lunch, Commander Anthony L. Russell (USCG), the "action officer" who was responsible for the Task Force's day-to-day operations, had told me that the suspected Chinese agent was responsible for setting up the Task Force, and that while he lacked a U.S. security clearance, May and Baker thought it was OK to let him sit in on nearly all the classified Task Force meetings.

I first thought that this might have been just gross negligence. But in reviewing some of the Task Force documents, I learned that May, Baker, and Russell were knowingly deceiving the Japanese government. They did that, among other ways, by representing in writing to Tokyo that the alleged Chinese spy was actually a "U.S. Representative." That falsehood was so carefully crafted that it seemed designed to put the Japanese officials at ease, so they might more freely share their nation's classified secrets with the suspected enemy agent.[4]

Like everyone in ONA, Baker knew that the alleged Chinese spy had no security clearance, LTSG as a company had no Facility Security Clearance, and its contractors lacked security clearances. U.S. Government evidence would later show that LTSG employees had photocopied classified documents at a public copy shop in downtown Washington, DC, carried classified information home from meetings in the Pentagon and government buildings in Tokyo, taken it on commercial jets, and downloaded it onto their private devices.[5]

I expected Baker to respond to my concern responsibly. That would have meant immediately suspending the Task Force, informing the Japanese what had happened, ordering a "spill assessment" to discover the extent of the compromise, gathering up all of Tokyo's stray classified materials, and ordering a full investigation. But none of that happened.

Instead, as he sat across from me at lunch, the normally calm and collected Baker turned red, exhaled loudly, and shook his head from side to side disappointedly. Glaring at me in between bites of navy bean soup, he finished his lunch quickly and silently. We had walked to the mess together, but on our return to Pentagon 3A932, ONA's office suite, he scurried on ahead of me.

"I can't believe you said that," Mike Pillsbury told me later that day after I recounted my lunch with Baker.

"What do you mean? That's my job. I'm the only lawyer in ONA and I needed to tell him that he's undermining U.S. national security."

"You have zero emotional intelligence," Pillsbury said.

"I don't care about Baker's emotions," I said. "He's my boss, he's doing something illegal. If I don't tell him that, he'll continue to subvert the U.S.-Japan alliance."

"Adam, you don't understand."

Pillsbury, my senior by a generation, intimated that in my relationship with Baker I had crossed some invisible Rubicon.

For the first dozen years of my time working in the Pentagon, I had felt entirely free to provide my honest legal opinion on any matter of significance whatsoever. So secure was I that the facts and law were all that mattered, I never even considered that I would suffer retaliation as a result of delivering truthful but unwelcome news to a superior.

While I remained fortified by my faith that doing my duty would protect me from Baker's retaliatory animus, on October 19, 2016, I drafted a memorandum to the file out of an abundance of caution. In that memo, I documented my counterintelligence disclosure to Baker. Based on the available evidence, I concluded that Baker and Andrew D. May had "betrayed the Japanese government, risking a serious diplomatic scandal between the U.S. and Japan."[6]

•   •   •

For the next month, Baker's behavior towards me was like nothing I had ever experienced from a boss. If I walked into a room, he walked out. If I passed him in any one of the Pentagon's seventeen miles of hallways, he would move to the other side of the hall and avoid eye contact.

Two weeks after my lunch with Baker, on November 9, 2016, half a dozen Japanese officials arrived at ONA's offices in the Pentagon for a Task Force meeting. The day before, Trump had won the general election against Hillary Clinton. Baker was, in his words, "not a happy camper."

I went to the Task Force meeting only to check and see if Baker had heeded my counterintelligence concerns. He had not. Seated there poring over Japanese classified information was the uncleared suspected enemy agent, taking notes.

Russell was dual-hatted as both the Task Force action officer and ONA's "security lead," meaning he was in charge of ensuring that ONA followed all security guidelines to protect Foreign Government Information. Under oath, Russell testified in December 2018 that the LTSG employees who lacked security clearances were "diligent," and there was nothing wrong with their taking hand-written notes of classified information and carrying them back to their offices and homes.[7]

On November 23, 2016, the Washington Free Beacon published an article written by defense reporter Bill Gertz titled "Japanese Intelligence Tells Pentagon China Engaged in Multi-Year Takeover Attempt of Senkaku Islands."[8] That piece contained Japanese clas-sified materials from two LTSG reports, but those reports, Gertz reported, lacked the required classification markings.

What worried Russell the most, however, was not the leak, but the fact that the existence of a secretive Task Force that seemed designed to undermine the U.S.-Japan alliance was now public knowledge. Russell's concern was well known inside ONA.

Everyone in the office knew that Baker was pouring fuel on a fierce bureaucratic turf war in Tokyo. Reports prepared by LTSG and Russell frequently commented on how the Task Force generated "noticeable tension" among Japanese agencies, reducing relations between them to "very brittle."

This was the alleged Chinese spy's idea, which Baker enthusi-astically endorsed. Specifically, for ONA's Japanese Government counterparty he had chosen not a high-level strategy office in the Japanese Ministry of Defense (MoD)—ONA's natural equivalent in Japanese government—but instead the Cabinet Intelligence Research Office (CIRO), an office that performs internal police functions in Japan.

In June 2016, I asked Task Force action officer Anthony L. Rus-sell, "why did ONA choose CIRO and not the MoD as the Penta-gon's Task Force counterparty?" His response was, "CIRO is run by Japanese aristocrats. They are the power behind the throne." That didn't sound right to me. When I ran that by some other Japanese officials, they laughed and said "that is absurd."

• • •

Two days after the leak, the Embassy of Japan issued Baker a démarche. A senior Japanese intelligence officer then informed Baker and Russell in writing that the publication by Gertz of their state secrets posed a "life or death" threat to Japanese warships in the Western Pacific.[9] Baker and Russell feigned concern.

In early February 2017, Baker flew to Tokyo on what he called his "mea culpa trip."[10] The official U.S. position was that the leak inflicted "serious harm to U.S. diplomatic efforts."[11] In Japan, Baker assured his Japanese interlocutors that he would safeguard their secrets and investigate the leak. But he was playing a double game.

Under U.S. law, after the leak, Baker, Russell, and May were required to report it to the DoD Office of Inspector General (OIG), whose job was to secure all stray classified materials on ONA's unclassified systems, conduct a "spill assessment," and determine the extent of the damage. That meant combing through LTSG's offices, the homes of their contractors, and the commercial copy shop where Newmyer-Deal wrote she had photocopied Japan's classified information.[12]

Following completion of the spill assessment, DoD OIG was required to conduct a full criminal investigation of the leak. But Baker, Bob Work, Barbara A. Westgate (director of Washington Headquarters Services [WHS]), Paul S. Koffsky (acting general counsel), and Glenn A. Fine (acting inspector general) made sure none of that happened.

Baker then carried with him to Tokyo on a commercial flight the very same classified reports that had been leaked to Gertz. He also continued to store Japanese secrets on ONA's *unclassified* computer system for ten months after he and Russell had promised to safeguard them. This made those secrets widely available to uncleared officials and contractors, ensuring maximum compromise of Tokyo's secrets.[13]

•   •   •

In December 2018, at the hearing on my appeal of the revocation of my security clearance before the Defense Office of Hearings and Appeals (DOHA), Baker testified under oath that his and May's mishandling of Japanese classified information had served a secret purpose. When the presiding administrative law judge asked Baker how sharing classified information with a suspected Chinese spy advanced the Task Force on Enhancing the Japan-U.S. Alliance, Baker said it was classified and asked to meet with him privately.

Obviously, Baker was playing chicken with Judge Foreman. The last thing Baker wanted was to have anyone look into his sharing a close ally's classified materials with a suspected enemy agent who lacked a security clearance of any kind. So, to head that off, Baker scared Foreman off with ominous warnings that he was on some secret mission that required violating U.S. law. The administrative law judge took the hint. So as not to embarrass Baker further by shining a light on Baker's latest subversion of U.S. interests, Foreman changed the subject. But that was too little, too late.

By then, everyone in that DOHA courtroom had seen ample evidence of Baker triangulating with America's enemies against U.S. allies. As Baker wrote to Deputy Secretary of Defense Work, thanks to them, "Japanese officials [could not] discount the possibility of the U.S. choosing to establish a new 'great power' relationship with China at the expense of Japan's national security interests and the alliance relationship."[14]

Government evidence revealed at DOHA also showed that Baker had told Pentagon leadership he "[didn't] believe in ANZUS," the Australia–New Zealand–United States mutual defense treaty,[15] and that in his capacity as the Pentagon's senior strategist, he had concluded that "primacy is clearly and increasingly costly...such as the defense of Taiwan and Israel."[16] That Baker would use the Task Force to undermine the U.S.-Japan alliance was simply the most recent feather in his cap, among many that he had earned for advancing the Obama Doctrine.

CHAPTER 7

TARGETING A PRESIDENTIAL TRANSITION TEAM

That James H. Baker would gather a CIA file on Michael P. Pillsbury was not wholly unexpected. Within weeks of Baker's taking the helm of ONA in May 2015, it had become obvious that his relationship with Pillsbury was headed over a cliff.

Culturally and ideologically, the two men could not have been more different. Pillsbury comes across as an American patrician and looks the part. He drove a convertible Jaguar and lived in an eighteenth-century mansion in Georgetown. His ancestors hailed from England, once walked the ramparts of Pillsbury Castle, and fought alongside George Washington in the American Revolutionary War. That lineage qualified him for membership in the Society of the Cincinnati, where he served on the Revolutionary War battlefields commission.

After his undergraduate studies at Stanford, while getting his PhD at Columbia, Pillsbury went to Taiwan to learn Mandarin Chinese. That began a lifelong commitment to mastering the language. In his late sixties, when I first met him, he would excuse himself from meetings to attend Chinese lessons.

Pillsbury is the only non-native Mandarin speaker I have met fluent enough to carry on technical military discussions in that dialect. During the Bush administration, he used those skills to translate for Secretary of Defense Rumsfeld during his meetings with PRC officials.

Pillsbury began advising Marshall in 1971, the year Henry Kissinger brought the latter over to the U.S. National Security Council from the RAND Corporation. When Secretary of Defense James R. Schlesinger joined the Pentagon and brought Marshall with him, Pillsbury came as well. He had been an ONA fixture since 1973.

As his 2015 *New York Times* bestseller *The Hundred Year Marathon* makes clear, Pillsbury is also a China hawk.[1] "Before the word became a slur, I was proud to call myself a neoconservative," he once told me. As Marshall was, Pillsbury is a resolute advocate for American primacy. Both men were appalled by Obama's policy of ceding America's strategic advantage to its enemies for the misguided purpose of creating a "balance of power."

Pillsbury is also a principled supporter of America's defensive commitments to Taiwan, Japan, and South Korea, so he was dismayed, though not surprised, to learn that Baker had knowingly shared Japanese classified information with a suspected Chinese spy and told a foreign audience that "primacy is clearly and increasingly costly... such as the defense of Taiwan."[2]

Baker conceded that he "needed" Pillsbury. But his ego also demanded deference from the ONA veteran. Like other sharp-elbowed bureaucrats who rise based on ruthlessness rather than talent, Baker was highly attuned to slights. After Pillsbury once referred to the former maintenance officer turned Pentagon grand strategist by his informal U.S. Air Force call sign "Maintenance," Baker responded icily that he was "a technologist."

Provoking further tensions in their relationship was the fact that Baker depended on Pillsbury to set up meetings he couldn't secure for himself. For example, fresh from a meeting of the LTSG Task Force on Enhancing the U.S.-Japan Alliance, Baker had Pillsbury introduce him to a female Chinese general in Singapore.

Baker also had Pillsbury draft his correspondence with foreign leaders. Those leaders would then respond to Pillsbury, not Baker. "Unfortunately, the director of the Indian integrated defense staff did not deign to reply to your letter in February," Pillsbury wrote indelicately in an email to Baker on July 1, 2016.

By then, Baker's conduct toward Pillsbury had become uncomfortably passive-aggressive, motivated by a palpable hatred. The unbalanced Baker-Pillsbury dynamic, fraught from the beginning, had reached a tipping point. That was when Baker set his trap.

•   •   •

Baker started directing me to use Pillsbury as a resource in ways that were illegal. One way was to include him on a project for which he lacked the required security clearance. Another was to have Pillsbury, a private citizen, conduct what the law calls the "inherently governmental function" of U.S. foreign relations.

At the time, I realized that none of this was right and objected to Baker. He accused me of insubordination. But if I agreed to break the law as Baker was demanding, he could use that against me. I had never encountered anyone like Baker in my entire life, so it took me a while to grasp what he was up to.

When I told Pillsbury what Baker was doing, he passed that information on to his long-time friend, Republican Senator Orrin Hatch of Utah. Hatch, who at the time was one of the Washington's most senior politicians and no naïf when it came to the schemes of wily bureaucrats, immediately scheduled a meeting with U.S. Secretary of Defense Ashton B. Carter at the Pentagon.

It was clear to all that, at best, Baker was playing bureaucratic games; at worst, he was a threat to U.S. national security. Secretary of Defense Carter stepped in and directed Baker to normalize Pillsbury's role in ONA as a subject-matter expert on Asia. In a dig directed at May and Baker, Carter complained that China "had long been neglected by our big strategic thinkers in the Pentagon."[3] Without embarrassing them directly by name, Carter was chastising May and Baker for the failure of ONA, which is called the Pentagon's "big think office," to produce net assessments for over a decade.

Since few people understood the potential of ONA better than Pillsbury, Carter told Baker that it was "necessary" to elevate Pillsbury's security clearance from Top Secret to TS/SCI and make him a U.S. official. Carter appointed Pillsbury to the position of "Special Government Employee." By then Pillsbury was a member of the Trump Presidential Transition Team (PTT).

On November 14, 2016, while driving with his daughter to visit prospective colleges, Baker told me that CIA had sent him a file containing dirt on Pillsbury. He said that the contents of that file were so unfavorable that it would be difficult to consummate Secretary Carter's directive. Nevertheless, a few hours after our call, Baker signed a three-page form that stated he was "satisfied" that "a favorable security/suitability determination ha[d] been rendered" for Pillsbury's TS/SCI clearance. It also stated that:

> This is an urgent request for the appointment of Dr. Pillsbury to the position of "expert/consultant" so he can continue to strengthen, and ensure continuity, of the U.S.-India Strategic Partnership as required by SECDEF.

Later that evening, I told Pillsbury about Baker accessing his CIA file. He winced.

"What did you tell him, precisely?" .

"That he was criminally violating your Privacy Act rights," I said.

"My God. You're worse than Typhoid Mary!"

He was referring to a turn-of-the-century Irish cook and "healthy carrier" of the bacterium that causes typhoid fever. She inadvertently infected dozens, without getting sick herself. Pillsbury was right to be concerned that Baker would target him. But I was no "healthy carrier" of Baker's retaliatory pathogens.

•　　•　　•

On January 11, 2017, nine days before the start of the Trump administration, three members of the NSC Presidential Transition Team called Baker in his Pentagon office to inform him that I would be leaving ONA to join the Trump administration's NSC. By then Baker was infamous at PTT headquarters. As the Pentagon PTT lead later told me, Baker had already illegally concealed ONA work product from her team. Baker did that by classifying *unclassified* ONA contractor reports.

Alerted to Baker's schemes, the NSC PTT leadership insisted on a conference call so there would be witnesses to what Baker told them about me.

"General Flynn wants Adam Lovinger to serve as his Senior Director for Strategic Assessments on the NSC," one member of the PTT said.

There was a long pause.

"That could be a problem," Baker said.

"How so?"

"Adam is currently under investigation for serious misconduct in the performance of his official duties. That investigation will be finished soon. Would General Flynn be willing to take someone else from my staff?"

"No, the general wants Adam."

There was another pause. Then Baker reluctantly agreed to release me to the NSC immediately.

What those who joined the Trump administration would soon realize was that they were not in power. The Deep State held the real power in the U.S. national security, intelligence, and law enforcement federal bureaucracies. Trump administration officials, even very senior ones, who could not be coopted by the Deep State to do its bidding and insisted on holding those bureaucracies accountable for following U.S. law, would have their careers and reputations destroyed.[4]

Two days later, on January 13, 2017, Russell wrote to Baker that I posed a "professional threat" to them both:

> Sir, I was just asked by Adam Lovinger to walk out with him as he departed ONA for the day.... He indicated that he believed your treatment of Mike [Pillsbury, then on the Trump Presidential Transition Team], including inquiries to the CIA, were violations of the Privacy Act and the Hatch Act.... I took this as an explicit professional threat toward you and an implied one toward myself and I chose to not respond at all and simply turned and walked away. Immediately upon returning to the office I shared the contents of this conversation with Andrew May to ensure a witness to the events and my response, or lack thereof.[5]

Russell's reference to "inquiries to the CIA" related to Baker's gathering a security file on Pillsbury. His reference to the Hatch

Act, a federal statute that forbids executive branch officials from engaging in political activity, related to Baker's use of CIA to gather dirt on Trump's Presidential Transition Team.

Thanks to the playbook, I learned later that hours after receiving the above email from Russell, Baker secretly filed an "Incident Report" in my security file (on what is called the "Joint Personnel Adjudication System" or "JPAS"). That began the process of stripping me of my Top Secret/SCI security clearance. That done, Russell drafted a memo placing me on "administrative leave."

Several days later, attorney James B. Vietti, a subordinate of WHS director Barbara Westgate, wrote me out of my ONA job description. That was May's idea: eight months later, when I found the playbook on my DoD computer, I learned that May had suggested that WHS "eliminate Adam's billet."

Baker then placed Russell in charge of investigating me. But Vietti feared that what Baker and Russell were doing was too obviously illegal. On paper, legal counsel is required to stop criminal subversion of DoD processes and correct for that abuse of authority. But Vietti seemed mainly concerned that Russell wasn't sufficiently covering up his own and others' misconduct.

On January 17, 2017, Vietti warned Russell that Baker's actions looked too much like "a 'go forth and find a justification to fire him [Lovinger]' sort of investigation."[6] The personnel lawyer then wrote to Russell: "It looks like you're trying to interfere with or hinder his [Lovinger's] advancement in some way and that the email [to the NSC] would be sent after [Lovinger] complained that Baker had violated the Hatch Act."

Despite all these behind-the-curtain efforts to derail my secondment to the NSC, on January 20, 2017, I departed by Secret Service van from the Presidential Transition Team headquarters at 18th and E Street, NW, passing through the heavy black-steel gates of the White House, and officially assumed my position as senior director for strategic assessments at the U.S. National Security Council.

THE U.S. NATIONAL SECURITY COUNCIL

In Washington, proximity to power is everything. The magnificent federal buildings of DC, and the self-importance they inspire, infect almost everyone who walks their halls. Just days earlier I had been a civil servant in a Pentagon cubicle. Overnight my working environment became a suite of historically furnished offices in the majestic Eisenhower Executive Office Building (EEOB) on the corner of 17th Street and Pennsylvania Avenue.

Constructed in 1888 in the French Second Empire style, the EEOB has gracious eighteen-foot ceilings, black-and-white-checkered marble floors, and sumptuous, historically pristine period rooms. Many of the office suites have ornate marble fireplaces. In its early years the building housed the Departments of State, Army, and Navy all under one roof. Today the Navy and State Department libraries are iron-latticed oases of quiet calm.

My third-floor office was separated from the West Wing of the White House by West Executive Avenue; it was only a five-minute jaunt to the second-floor National Security Advisor's Office, White House Situation Room, and Navy Mess. For the first time in my career, I was assigned an executive assistant and had staff reporting to me. My new job put me in the U.S. Government pecking order a little higher than an assistant secretary; I was the civilian equivalent of a three-star flag officer (that is, lieutenant general or vice admiral). But I was under no illusions. As the Founders had intended, like everyone else in the White House, even the president, I was a temporary worker, and wonderfully expendable.

•   •   •

Incoming National Security Advisor Michael T. Flynn was appalled to learn that ONA had done no net assessments for the entirety of the Obama administration. To correct that deficit, my job on the NSC was to, in Flynn's words, "do ONA's job for it."

As I contemplated my new duties, I reflected on how my mentor and legendary first boss in ONA, Andrew W. Marshall, had held a similar position when Henry Kissinger brought him to the White House from the RAND Corporation in 1971.

Both Marshall and I had been tasked by national security advisors with guiding America's strategic recovery from "forever wars," and building or rebuilding the Pentagon's and NSC's capacity to craft and execute net assessment–informed national security strategies. Those strategies were necessary to inject more logic into our alliances and partnerships and ensure that all strategic initiatives coming out of the White House were mutually reinforcing.

But crafting strategies to end America's directionless wars also posed a strategic threat to the Deep State–contractor nexus, which had become invested in perpetuating those wars as long as possible. A week later, I met with Flynn and several other NSC staff in his West Wing office to discuss the president's Iran policy. As the meeting ended, Flynn asked me to stay behind.

"Baker has some serious concerns about you," he said gravely.

That sent a cold chill down my spine. Flynn then smiled and broke into a laugh.

"You must be doing something right," he said.

While my relief was growing exponentially by the millisecond, I still had no idea what he was talking about.

"Just like Obama warned Trump not to hire me, Jim Baker warned me not to hire you!"

Flynn was referring to a November 10, 2016, meeting between Obama and Trump. During that White House meeting, despite all the weighty world issues the outgoing president might have raised with Trump, Obama seemed monomaniacally fixated on Flynn, telling Trump not to appoint Flynn as his national security advisor.[7]

All told, Trump was beseeched three times on three separate occasions (later by National Security Advisor Susan Rice and FBI Director James Comey) not to hire Flynn. Though each of those messages had an unmistakable "or else" quality, Trump brushed them all off. If anything, these fervent objections made it clear to Trump that Flynn was the right man for the job.

• • •

On the heels of the 9/11 terrorist attacks, Michael T. Flynn had been appointed director of intelligence at the Joint Task Force 180 in Afghanistan. That was followed by a steady stream of promotions to Commander of the 111th Military Intelligence Brigade (2002–2004), then to Director of Intelligence for each of the Joint Special Operations Commands (2004–2007). Prestigious appointments to the U.S. Central Command (2007–2008), U.S. Joint Staff (2008–2009), and International Security Assistance Force in Afghanistan (2009–2010) followed.

From those positions of leadership, Flynn revolutionized U.S. counterinsurgency doctrine. As he would later detail in *Fixing Intel: A Blueprint for Making Intelligence Relevant in Afghanistan* (2010), which he coauthored with Matt Pottinger and Paul D. Batchelor, the U.S. military's existing intelligence processes were not just broken, but self-defeating.[8]

Intelligence gathered in the field was sent back to the U.S. for analysis. This was cumbersome and untimely, and it led to poor analysis, because the analysts charged with analyzing the information from afar lacked the local knowhow to accurately interpret what they were looking at.

Flynn recommended several changes. To get actionable intelligence, U.S. forces had to win the trust of locals. That meant decamping from the safety of fortified bases and armored vehicles to live among the Afghan people. That showed the local population that Americans had skin in the game. He also shortened the analysis-operations cycle by cutting out Washington and conducting tactical intelligence assessments in the field. Those changes resulted in radical improvements in mission outcomes.

But they also posed a direct threat to the connective tissue binding for-profit contractors to U.S. national security and intelligence agencies. By the second year of the Obama administration, that nexus had achieved institutional capture of the entire enterprise. It became a major force driving the course of the wars in Iraq and Afghanistan.

In July 2012, Flynn became the eighteenth Director of the Defense Intelligence Agency (DIA). As he recounted to me years later, before assuming that role he studied ten years of DoD Inspector General audits of DIA's expenditures of billions of U.S. taxpayer dollars. None of those audits was "clean." For an entire decade, at least, DIA had failed to properly account for its contractor expenditures.

Seeking to root out that corruption and dysfunction, Flynn did what ordinary Americans expect from their leaders. He demanded transparency. "Right now," Flynn said during a speech on September 12, 2013,

> we are conducting DIA's first-ever full audit of the agency's capabilities, and I have launched a special Task Force that is laser-focused on examining and analyzing DIA's reliance on

contracting to make sure we are spending our money as wisely as possible. I take the mandate to cut waste very seriously, and I also want to make sure we are putting our money into the right places where our attention will have to be focused on the various crossroads, and ultimately, strategic turns that we will have to negotiate in the future.[9]

In August 2014, Obama forced Flynn to "retire," despite the fact that Flynn was regarded as the "best intelligence officer for the past twenty years," in the words of NSA head Admiral Rogers.[10] Retired four-star general Barry McCaffrey concurred, calling Flynn "the best intelligence officer of his generation."[11]

•   •   •

What I didn't know at the time of my early February 2017 meeting with Flynn was that FBI Director Comey had already ambushed and fabricated a "process foul" against him. That was recorded in writing by Assistant Director of Counterintelligence Bill Priestap: "What is our goal? Truth/Admission or to get him to lie, so we can prosecute him or get him fired?"[12] Similarly, around the same time, the actions of Baker's subordinate Commander Anthony L. Russell appeared, in the words of WHS attorney James Vietti, like "a 'go forth and find a justification to fire him [Lovinger]' sort of investigation."[13]

As I exited Flynn's West Wing office he said, "Adam, see what Baker is doing to you as a badge of honor."

"What do you mean, sir?"

"You were doing your job; Baker wasn't, and isn't. You make him look bad."

What neither of us fully realized at that moment, however, was that when our respective bosses failed to heed their threats, Obama and Baker marked us as "insider threats." With that, the Deep State set out to weaponize federal authorities, smear our reputations, and destroy our careers.

CHAPTER 8

"SHOW ME THE MAN, AND I WILL FIND YOU THE CRIME"[1]

Either the Constitution matters and must be followed... or it is simply
a piece of parchment on display at the National Archives.
—*Texas v. Pennsylvania* (2020)

It was not long after the November 2016 leak of Japanese classified information from the Task Force on Enhancing the Japan-U.S. Alliance to Washington Free Beacon reporter Bill Gertz that a group of DoD Senior Executive Service members conspired to cover for themselves by blaming me for that leak. Their motives were straightforward.

Because neither May nor Baker had been qualified for his job, they were indebted to those who placed them in those roles. May repaid his sponsor by helping set up the Long Term Strategy Group, the defense contractor owned and run by Chelsea Clinton's best friend, Jackie Newmyer-Deal. May would funnel LTSG tens of millions of dollars while ignoring the fact that its employees lacked the security clearances required to perform the work he assigned them. A proper investigation into the leak of Japanese classified information threatened to expose that lucrative racket.

The leak also incriminated Washington Headquarters Services Director Barbara A. Westgate personally, and WHS organizationally.

67

Westgate oversaw an army of 125,000 employees who performed a wide range of executive, legislative, and judicial functions at DoD. Among its duties, WHS was in charge of ONA's "contracting" and "security management" duties. This included ensuring that LTSG contractors had the required security clearances to handle classified information, which they did not.

Deputy Secretary of Defense Robert O. Work had plucked Westgate out of retirement and appointed her to lead WHS in the run-up to the 2016 presidential election. For an office as important as WHS, it was customary for a vacancy during such transitional periods to be filled by the existing number-two official as acting head, before the new presidential administration would put in its own leader.

Pulling somebody out of retirement was a clear sign that the hire was politically motivated. Operatives in the last stages of their careers are particularly useful, because at that point they have little to lose. That makes them freer to break the law. Often these actions translate to generous post-retirement contracts with the federal government.

Acting DoD Inspector General Glenn A. Fine had also been appointed in the waning days of the Obama administration. After the leak, he and his deputy, Marguerite C. Garrison, were required by law to complete a "spill assessment" and a criminal investigation into the source of the leak. But they refused, even after the government of Japan formally notified DoD that the ongoing leak posed a "life or death" threat to Japanese warships.[2]

Since such a "spill assessment" never took place, Japanese classified information continued to be mishandled for at least ten months after the discovery of the leak. Fine and Garrison were ultimately notified on four[3] separate occasions of the severity of the leak and the fact that a suspected Chinese spy was involved. But by then, Fine was dealing with the public fallout over his role in targeting then-candidate Trump's foreign policy advisor, Lieutenant General (Ret.) Michael T. Flynn.

According to a declassified Department of Justice (DoJ) report, Peter Strzok and Fine met with James Baker on September 30, 2016. Most press accounts assume that the "James Baker" in question is former FBI general counsel James A. Baker, not ONA lead James H. Baker. But James A. Baker told a mutual acquaintance of mine that he was not at that meeting, and the FBI has no records of his joining that Strzok-Fine rendezvous.

• • •

The operational job to scapegoat me for the leak fell to ONA's Baker and his security chief, Anthony L. Russell. They did that by launching a series of progressively more invasive investigations that claimed to investigate the source of the leak of Japanese classified information, but which in actuality only investigated me.

As their predicate for those investigations, Baker and Russell claimed there were "verbatim quotes" in the Washington Free Beacon article that only a person who attended a November 9, 2016, meeting in the Pentagon could have known.

That was their original claim. But when they were asked which "verbatim quotes" from that meeting had made it into the news article, Baker and Russell could not get their stories straight. Baker changed his story and said the leaked information had come from a meeting in October 2015 in Tokyo that he and Russell had attended (and I had not). But Russell said that the leak had to have been an "inside job" from the meeting I had attended in November 2016. In Russell's telling, Baker hadn't attended the October 2015 meeting in Tokyo. Baker's travel records for that meeting, and his Tokyo trip report, were then introduced as government evidence.[4] Russell's version of events collapsed under scrutiny.

There had been over a dozen private-sector contractors and U.S. and Japanese officials at both classified meetings, many of whom lacked security clearances.

Foremost among those who should have been investigated for leaking to the press was the alleged Chinese spy, who, unfathomably, had been tasked with setting up the Task Force in the first place. Under oath, Russell testified that the alleged enemy agent had attended all of the Task Force's classified meetings but one. If he was indeed a spy for the PRC, this person would have had a significant interest in undermining Japan's national security by compromising its military secrets.

I had no motive to leak anything to Gertz. At the time, I was a twelve-year veteran of the Pentagon and on the cusp of a coveted appointment to a senior position on the NSC. I had the highest-level security clearance, an unblemished professional record, and a pristine security file. But it is difficult to prove a negative.

On December 12, 2017, I wrote to Gertz. "I am being fired from the civil service because of the false charge that I leaked sensitive information to you," I told him. "I respectfully request your assistance, Mr. Gertz, in issuing a sworn affidavit attesting that I did not leak any internal ONA documents to you, ever."[5] An hour later Gertz issued his response, "I respectfully decline."[6]

I recounted Gertz's response to my neighbor who lives two blocks away from me in Chevy Chase, Maryland. Defense strategist Dr. Edward Luttwak was born in Romania. Forced to flee with his family from the Nazis, Luttwak knew tyranny when he saw it. He called up Gertz, and the two men spoke. Luttwak then compiled an account of their conversation. In a sworn affidavit on November 6, 2018, Luttwak wrote,

> I called Mr. Gertz...to tell him that I was quite certain in my mind that Adam Lovinger was not the source of the unauthorized disclosure [to Gertz]: I knew him to be much too disciplined for such a gross violation of confidentiality that could damage a critical

alliance relationship. Mr. Gerz [*sic*] replied in words that I do not recall but which I interpreted as clearly exculpatory, whereupon I asked him to state as much, i.e., [t]hat Adam Lovinger was not the source of the disclosure he had published.... Mr. Gertz politely refused, citing... that exculpating one possible source would open him to requests for further exculpations till the exposure of the true source by a process of elimination, thereby preventing him from protecting his sources.... I regretfully accepted his explanation.

•   •   •

U.S. law requires that classified leaks of Foreign Government Information by Pentagon officials must be conducted by professional criminal investigators attached to the DoD Office of Inspector General. Instead, Deputy Secretary of Defense Work chose Jennifer C. Walsh.

On January 12, 2017, Walsh emailed me for the first time. She wrote that she was a Russia analyst, that she worked at the U.S. National Defense University, and that Deputy Secretary of Defense Robert O. Work had directed her to investigate ONA's leak of Japanese classified information.

After consulting with several national security lawyers, it was obvious to me that Walsh was usurping DoD OIG's authority. So I asked Baker under what legal authority Walsh was operating. He responded by email the following week: "Ms. Walsh's authority flows from the Deputy's [Work's] office, WHS and OGC [the Office of General Counsel]. Please comply swiftly and fully with her requests." That was all a lawyer needed to know that Baker and Work were subverting the federal investigative process.

Following Baker's incriminating admission, I called Walsh. She was friendly and professional.

"I'm conducting an inquiry into the leak of the Japanese government's classified information that was published by Bill Gertz last November," she said.

"That doesn't sound right to me. I'm pretty sure a leak of classified Foreign Government Information is a criminal matter. Are you a criminal investigator?"

"No, I'm not."

"A lawyer?"

"No, I'm a Russia analyst. I work on policy."

"Ms. Walsh, this investigation seems highly illegal. You should really pass this on to the DoD Office of Inspector General so they can do a proper investigation."

After a long pause, during which I suspect Walsh grasped that she was being used to criminally subvert DoD's investigative authorities, Walsh croaked, with an audible lump in her throat, "I'll get back to you," and hung up.

In Walsh's investigative appointment letter, Work had listed ONA's Baker and Russell as leak suspects.[7] The official point of the investigation was to identify the source of the leak of Japanese classified information. But that was not the objective as Baker saw it, which he carelessly left a written record of, and I was able to obtain by sheer accident from the playbook.[8]

Though Baker himself was a named leak suspect, Work, along with WHS Director Westgate and acting DoD General Counsel Paul Koffsky, put him in charge of naming the other leak suspects and investigating the leak. That "investigation" had to be a rush job. The reason for this was that a Japanese intelligence officer had told Baker that Tokyo was suspending the Task Force until there was, in his words, a "significant update (such as arrest, or at least, identification of the leak perpetrators)."[9]

In February 2017, before the investigation had been conducted, Baker flew to Tokyo and gave his report on its findings. As I discovered in the playbook, Russell had drafted "talking points" on the investigation's conclusion for Baker to present to the government of Japan: they had identified "one of our [that is, ONA's] civilian employees" about whom Baker and Russell had "found extensive evidence of misconduct along several lines of activity." Me, in other words. During later administrative proceedings, Sean Bigley, my lawyer, introduced the "talking points" that Russell had drafted and Baker had delivered in Tokyo. Russell denied drafting them, saying, "This is not my statement."[10]

"It came off your share drive," Bigley said,[11] after which Russell changed his story: "So the talking points, there's a good chance that I may have wrote [*sic*] it."[12]

Under oath, Russell explained why he and Baker had fingered me to the government of Japan as the leaker of their classified information, before any investigation had been conducted:

> So I will tell you that I would have been able to make those same statements [in the talking points about Lovinger's guilt] based on my hypothesis before an investigation was even formed based on my familiarity with all of the events that transpired. So if...[the] investigation was able to substantiate those, then we're simply restating—the hypothesis had been proven.[13]

•   •   •

Deputy Secretary of Defense Work curried favor with Chelsea Clinton's best friend and gave her lucrative defense contracts, all of which violated laws regarding fraud, waste, abuse, security clearances, and the handling of classified information. Work had forced out Andrew W. Marshall and then appointed James Baker, who was unqualified to lead ONA, to do his bidding. Baker did what Work asked of him. In return, Work nominated Baker for a prestigious medal.

In an elaborate ceremony in January 2017, hosted in Pentagon Room 3E944, the sumptuous office suite of the Deputy, Work read out a solemn citation for a "FY2017 Meritorious Executive Presidential Rank Award Nomination," which Baker would later officially receive with some delay, in 2021.

In the citation, Work praised Baker's role in a variety of bilateral initiatives involving U.S. allies. Official DoD evidence reveals that Baker had written that encomium to himself, then given it to Work to read aloud before the entire ONA office staff. The whole event was surreal.

Everyone knew that Baker had earlier proposed to Pentagon leadership that America abandon Taiwan, Israel, and the Australia–New Zealand–United States mutual defense treaty. Stunned ONA staff shuffled out of Work's office. In the hallway on our way back to ONA's office, an officer who had witnessed that ceremony murmured loud enough for me to hear, "I hate this place."

Turning to that officer, who had earned medals for valor on the battlefields of Iraq and Afghanistan, I asked, "What do you mean?"

We were in the light-filled inner A-ring of the Pentagon. Stopping in front of one of its floor-to-ceiling windows, we both looked out onto the central courtyard and its leafless trees.

"Don't you see what just happened? Work just gave Baker a get-out-of-jail-free-card."

"What?"

"By putting those lies in the citation for Baker's award, he sanitizes it, he makes it official."

"I don't understand."

"By making the lie the basis for Baker's award, the Pentagon's reputation is now on the line. If someone ever challenges that citation, or exposes those lies, that would raise doubts about all DoD awards. That would be a nightmare for the department, so they'll go to the mat to defend it, to cover the whole thing up."

•   •   •

The last I heard from Walsh was on February 10, 2017, at 11:31 a.m.:

> Mr. Lovinger, I am in receipt of your Jan 24 email.... The Inquiry
> is ongoing, and has not been formally concluded at this time.
> You will be contacted if further information is needed from you.
> Sincerely, Jennifer Walsh[14]

My final email to Walsh was at 3:12 p.m., on February 20, 2017.
I sent it to memorialize our prior agreement that she would duly
report the Work-Baker-Westgate-Koffsky conspiracy to intentionally
usurp the DoD OIG investigative authority:

> Ms. Walsh,
> Please confirm that you forwarded to the DoD OIG all materials
> related to your investigation (including the sourcing of the com-
> plaint, the evidentiary basis of the allegations submitted to you,
> and the precise role played by James H. Baker and DEPSECDEF
> Work's office).
> Sincerely, Adam Lovinger[15]

Walsh did not reply to my email, but her report was comprehensive. Her official findings concluded that Work, Baker, Westgate,
and Koffsky had substituted a bogus investigation for the required
spill assessment and criminal investigation of the leak of classified
Foreign Government Information.

She had determined, in bold letters prominently displayed at
the beginning of her report, that the entire scheme must be turned
over to the DoD Office of Inspector General. Walsh's second
recommendation was for DoD to immediately fix the way ONA
was using the Long Term Strategy Group so that LTSG contractors stopped mishandling Tokyo's secrets, which threatened the
U.S.-Japan alliance.

Walsh did not explicitly address the fact that Baker was openly sharing Japanese classified information with the alleged Chinese spy. But she did write that Baker's and Russell's actions indicated that they were intentionally undermining the U.S.-Japan alliance. She wrote that Baker and Russell knew that LTSG contractors lacked security clearances and that those contractors had been mishandling Japanese classified information for over a year, in their offices, at their homes, and on commercial airliners traveling to and from Tokyo and Washington, and that LTSG contractors had used a commercial printing service to make multiple copies of that classified information.

Finally, Walsh noted that Russell and Baker had egregiously violated Tokyo's trust.[16]

Walsh's report told the DoD OIG's Glenn Fine and Marguerite Garrison what they already knew—that they had failed to safeguard Tokyo's secrets after the November 2016 leak. It had been their responsibility to ensure the completion of a spill assessment and criminal investigation. Walsh's report put them on notice of that duty a second time. But Fine and Garrison still refused to follow the law.

We know that because six months after they received Walsh's report, I discovered that ONA and LTSG were *still* storing Tokyo's secrets on an unclassified share drive and sharing them with contractors lacking an official "need to know." If Fine and Garrison had done their "spill assessment" and investigation, those files would have all been removed.

Because Walsh's Report of Investigation (ROI) was exculpatory to me and incriminated my accusers, Westgate concealed it from my lawyer, Sean Bigley, and me for as long as possible. Over a year later, Bigley and I got the unredacted ROI.

"I guess we were wrong about Walsh," Bigley said. "She *exonerated* you and *incriminated* Baker, Westgate, Russell and the DoD Inspector General."

• • •

My accusers' response to Walsh's report was toxic. I was now an even bigger insider threat to them.

As I learned from the playbook, if a Deep State operative doesn't get the investigative results he wants the first time, he simply conducts "do-over" investigations until he does. Since almost no one on the receiving end of that has the financial resources to defend himself against a U.S. government investigatory juggernaut, Deep State operatives meet no meaningful resistance as they grind down and destroy whoever dares threaten to expose their incompetence, malfeasance, or criminality.

In my case, WHS Director Westgate and DoD OIG officials Fine and Garrison overruled Walsh's findings and doubled down, starting yet more investigations. Each new investigation gave them the opportunity to fish for new information, which they could then contort into new charges or discard in favor of outright fabrications.

The official evidentiary base shows that none of the four subsequent "do-over" investigations even attempted to find the actual source of the leak of Japanese classified information.[17]

• • •

The day following U.S. National Security Advisor Flynn's resignation on February 13, 2017, I left my home in Chevy Chase and took the southbound metro to downtown Washington, DC. I enjoyed the early morning walk from the Farragut North station to the White House. It was an opportunity to gather my thoughts before entering the pressure cooker that is the U.S. National Security Council. With Flynn no longer at the helm, I wondered what would now happen to our plan to overcome the bureaucratic tyranny that had incapacitated our military's ability to generate net assessment–informed strategies for winning America's wars.

I crossed Lafayette Square, named after the French general who helped George Washington win our War of Independence, freeing America from a different sort of tyranny. Halfway across the square, a familiar voice called out—"Adam!"

Sitting on a park bench was my former colleague Phillip E. Pournelle.

Of the myriad talented officers who had passed through ONA as military advisors during my dozen years working there, Pournelle was one of my favorites. Pournelle had recently retired from the U.S. Navy, and I was happy to see him.

The first words out of his mouth were ominous. "Now that Flynn is gone, who is going to protect you from Baker?" He then handed me his business card, which read "Senior Director Gaming and Analysis, Long Term Strategy Group."

At LTSG, Pournelle had a front row seat to the Work-Baker-Westgate scheme to scapegoat me for the leak of Japan's classified information. But it also meant that he had a professional interest in shifting blame from LTSG onto someone else.

"What do you mean?" I said.

"You realize that Baker is going to keep investigating you until he gets the results he wants—you know that, don't you?"

With that, he rose from the park bench and walked away.

At the time I couldn't tell if he was threatening or warning me. In Washington, as elsewhere, it is rare for adversaries to become allies. But it's common for one ally to abandon another when the latter becomes the subject of an investigation.

CHAPTER 9

WALKING BACK FROM A STRATEGY OF PRIMACY

In a situation with few parallels in history, the agents of an enemy power were in a position to do much more than purloin documents. They were in a position to influence the nation's foreign policy in the interest of the nation's chief enemy... in what must have been the staggering sum of day-to-day decisions.

—WHITTAKER CHAMBERS[1]

U.S. National Security Advisor Michael T. Flynn was fond of the Roman axiom, "He who desires peace should prepare for war." So that the secretary of defense and president would have net assessment–informed strategies to ensure U.S. primacy and uphold the liberal global order, Flynn appointed me his senior director for strategic assessments. But that appointment posed an existential threat to the Obama Doctrine, which James H. Baker and Andrew D. May were commissioned to protect and advance throughout the U.S. national security bureaucracy.

The "greatest challenge for U.S. foreign policy," Baker declared in one of his canned speeches that he shared with ONA staff and delivered in myriad fora, "is deciding whether to double down or to walk back from a strategy of primacy.... Those who would double down on primacy, have no lack of suggestions for how to do so: by intervening more dramatically in Iraq and the Syrian civil war, or more forcefully challenging Chinese or Russian creeping aggression by increasing the defense, diplomacy, and development budgets."[2]

Doubling down or walking back from a strategy of primacy was no theoretical quibble. As the Pentagon's top strategist, Baker knew that primacy is the difference between victory and defeat on the battlefield. The reason for this relates to DoD's classified war plans, which are the Pentagon's core guidance documents. They describe and enumerate all U.S. military forces and equipment directed to any theater of conflict.

Those operational plans inform decisions on recruitment, training, logistics, transportation, budgeting, and virtually all the organizational and managerial functions of the U.S. armed forces. They also include detailed guidance on shaping the competition with one's adversary (Phase O), followed by deterring (Phase I), seizing the initiative (Phase II), and then dominating the enemy on the battlefield so that U.S. forces emerge overwhelmingly victorious (Phase III).

Baker knew that the surest way to cripple DoD's capacity for Phase III dominance was to "walk back from a strategy of primacy." Though not an economist, Baker justified his proposal to do so on the grounds that "primacy is clearly and increasingly costly,"[3] that the U.S. national debt is America's greatest national security threat,[4] and that "advocates for primacy face a lack of domestic consensus."[5]

"MUDDLING THROUGH"

In place of developing a strategy to ensure American preeminence, Baker advised that having no strategy could suffice for the U.S. military. For Baker, "muddling through, defending present commitments, holding to the status quo...this maintenance mindset may be sufficient."[6]

In August 2021, President Biden evacuated U.S. forces from Afghanistan. The scenes were eerily reminiscent of the Vietnam War. In 1975, desperate Vietnamese tried to scale the U.S. embassy fence as the last U.S. Army helicopter from Saigon departed for good. More recently, under President Biden, desperate Afghans clambered into the wheel wells of a C-17 aircraft, clung from its hull, and fell hundreds of feet to their deaths.

Before evacuating Kabul, the U.S. military had more than enough time to destroy the billions of dollars' worth of cutting-edge military equipment it held in the country. Yet Biden decided instead to gift that equipment to the new Taliban government. Biden then explained that America would adopt an "over-the-horizon" strategy for Afghanistan.[7] He might have called it an "out of sight, out of mind" strategy.

Having served half a century in U.S. politics, Biden knew its iron laws, the most important of which is that politicians pay no consequences for ignoring problems invisible to the American public, no matter how grave.

The Obama Doctrine, precisely the opposite of the Reagan Doctrine, ensured that America had come full circle.

Ten years before Biden's evacuation of Afghanistan, Obama had removed U.S. forces from Iraq and declared victory with the words, "We're leaving behind a sovereign, stable, and self-reliant Iraq."[8] What Obama meant by victory was illustrated in a 2019 U.S. Army assessment of the Iraq War, which concluded that an "emboldened and expansionist Iran" had filled the vacuum in Iraq left in America's wake, and that the Islamic Republic of Iran was the "only victor" in that war.[9]

Obama paved the way for Iran's imperial conquest of Iraq by unfreezing and making available to Tehran tens of billions of dollars as part of his "Iran Deal."[10] Similarly, Biden's decision to leave a treasure trove of military equipment to the Afghan Taliban (the same regime that had hosted Osama bin Laden back in 2001, providing him the support and sanctuary he needed to launch the September 11 attacks on America, which precipitated the 2003 Afghanistan War in the first place) left the terrorist organization better equipped than ever to aid and abet future attacks on America.[11]

"LOSING TAIWAN TO CHINA WOULD NOT BE A GREAT INSULT TO U.S. NATIONAL INTERESTS."

Similar to Biden's "over the horizon" strategy for Afghanistan, years earlier Obama had justified his decision to remove U.S. forces from Iraq and pivot to East Asia on the grounds that it was a more important theater of Great Power geopolitics. That made sense. During the Obama administration, strategic challenges arising from U.S.-China competition had surpassed anything Washington had seen in decades. That was due in part to Beijing's care in drawing the right lessons from history.

World War II had provided the Chinese Communist Party (CCP) a searing cautionary tale about what happens to America's adversaries who attack U.S. strengths head on and too soon. "I fear all we have done is to awaken a sleeping giant and fill him with a terrible resolve," is how Japanese Admiral Isoroku Yamamoto allegedly lamented the attack by Imperial Japan against the U.S. Pacific Fleet at Pearl Harbor.[12]

Beijing would not repeat Imperial Japan's mistake by confronting America directly. Instead China, according to Deng Xiaoping's stated strategy, would "hide capabilities, and bide time." That dictum took on a special resonance in the first two decades of the twenty-first century.

As the Soviets had done during America's Vietnam quagmire, the CCP watched happily as American blood and treasure seeped into the bottomless sands of Iraq and Afghanistan. Beijing knew that, without net assessment–informed U.S. national security strategies to point the way to U.S. victory, America would be depleted by these conflicts and eventually go home. Meanwhile, China's strategists worked overtime to expand what they called the PRC's Comprehensive National Power.

But China's strategy was not merely to observe from the sidelines while the U.S. defeated itself in the Middle East. Rather, Beijing worked diligently to penetrate and subvert the U.S. national security, intelligence, and law enforcement bureaucracies from within. This indirect approach centered on generating economic and political inducements for American elites, including some who worked in such agencies, to tilt U.S. policy in Beijing's favor. As Director of National Intelligence John Ratcliffe said on a Fox News interview in 2020,

> There are a lot of people who, for economic reasons, don't want China to be our greatest threat. There are a lot of people who, for political reasons, don't want China to be our greatest threat in America.[13]

The consequences that flowed from that corruption were foreseeable. As historian Walter Russell Mead would describe it, "The 'pivot to Asia,' had such a modest military component that it did more to reinforce than to counter the Chinese belief that the United States was locked in an irreversible process of decline."[14] Although an astute observer of foreign affairs, Mead was an outsider, and not privy to the internal governmental workings of Obama's Orwellian ways. As with President Biden's "over-the-horizon" engagement strategy for Afghanistan, the forty-fourth president's true purpose was to pivot *away from* Asia.

Breaking with the defense policies of the previous three administrations, Obama ceased to conduct Freedom of Navigation Operations (FONOP) through the Taiwan Strait, instead deeming the U.S. Navy's presence in the region "innocent passage" which, under international law, bolstered Beijing's claims to those disputed territorial waters.[15] It fell to Baker to justify that concession. "Losing Taiwan to China would not be a great insult to U.S. national interests," is what Baker had advised Admiral Michael Mullen, Obama's Chairman of the Joint Chiefs of Staff.[16]

With Baker minimizing the import of Beijing's imperial conquests, Xi Jinping doubled down on China's "fourth industrial revolution,"[17] swapped out its "peaceful rise" in favor of a "wolf warrior"[18] strategy, seized and militarized disputed islands in the South China Sea, and shifted China's indigenous ship-building industry to prioritize the construction of amphibious warships and landing craft, obviously in preparation for an invasion of Taiwan.[19] Xi then warned Western powers to steer clear of the Spratly Islands, one of the most strategically important regions of the world.

Seventy percent of global trade value is transported by sea. Sixty percent of that passes through Asia. The Spratly Archipelago is a major shipping route through the South China Sea, which carries one-third of total global shipping. Expelling U.S. forces from the region and establishing military primacy over those sea lines would become a centerpiece of China's twenty-first-century national security strategy.

"CHINA'S MILITARY PLANS REMAIN DECIDEDLY REGIONAL IN NATURE"

Farther afield, Beijing expanded its Eurasia and Indian Ocean "Belt and Road" initiative by thousands of miles, establishing China's first overseas military base in Djibouti on the east coast of Africa in 2016. That did not keep Baker from informing a foreign delegation the following year that "China's military plans remain decidedly regional in nature" because Beijing is "constrained by historic territorial norms." Baker rounded out his lecture to this perplexed foreign audience with the assurances that "China's domestic troubles are legion" and that the PRC is too feeble to "revise the present international order through violent or coercive means."[20]

In the final month of Obama's eight-year presidency, not one U.S. supercarrier could be found traversing the world's seas and oceans. That same month, ONA Associate Director Andrew D. May provided Pentagon analysts an after-action report on his own and Baker's eight years of "muddling through":

> As a military we have no real conception of what a proper "pivot to Asia" should look like.... We do not know what sort of alliance structure we want, what geography is really most important, or what contingencies we should be thinking about. Consequently we have only the dimmest of ideas about the sort of strategy we should develop, or the character of the force posture we should pursue...we have no good ideas about the sorts of initiatives or institutions we should be fostering, or how those should be administered.

May delivered that assessment on the afternoon of June 10, 2016. By then, he had been in the Senior Executive Service for more than half a decade. It had been his job as ONA's research director to develop "what a proper 'pivot to Asia' should look like." But he had not done that, because doing so could potentially help America compete against China, and that violated the Obama Doctrine. In Baker's words, "We...prefer competent and relatively stable potential adversaries."[21]

For his service in faithfully implementing that policy, on February 28, 2017, Baker promoted May from SES-1 to SES-2—the civilian rough equivalent to a three-star general.

"THERE IS NO WAY THAT WE WILL BE ABLE TO DELIVER MATURE NET ASSESSMENTS ANYTIME SOON"

On his 2009 "Apology Tour," Obama argued, if obliquely, that the United States was an imperialist power that deserved to have its wings clipped so as to achieve a global balance of power with America's adversaries. ONA, as the Pentagon's top strategy office, played a critical role in consummating that mission.

On May 23, 2016, May reported to Baker: "There is no way that we will be able to deliver mature net assessments anytime soon."[22] In December 2018, my lawyer, Sean Bigley, asked James H. Baker "when was the last time ONA did complete a net assessment?" Baker responded under oath "2007 perhaps."[23] For over a decade, including the four years Baker had by then led the office, ONA had completed no net assessments to inform Pentagon leadership of the future security threats to the United States.[24]

Legally, that meant that Baker and May were violating ONA's one and only statutory requirement: to produce at least one net assessment each year.[25] Practically, that meant that the U.S. military was strategically blind. It also meant that Baker's strategic counsel to DoD leadership that there was no significant threat from China was not based on any professional or analytical assessment derived from evidence and reason. Rather, it was deduced from an ideological agenda.

Soon after arriving to take the helm of ONA in 2015, Baker met with me to discuss the continuation of my work for Marshall. After I briefed him on my formal performance plan—"to professionalize the crafting and execution of U.S. national security strategy from within the Office of the Secretary of Defense"—Baker responded, "So, you are recommending that the Department put more effort into 'shaping' the future of Central Asia's security environment?"

"Yes, sir, precisely."

"But isn't 'shaping' other countries 'imperialist'?"

"Sir, 'shaping' is the essence of strategy. If we're not shaping the behavior of other countries, we're not doing our job," I replied, somewhat indelicately.

That meeting clarified everything for me. Not only did Baker not believe in the core mission of the very office he was entrusted to lead. He deemed ONA's purpose anathema.

•   •   •

In 2016, the uniformed military services set up their own net assessment office in the Joint Staff (J8) to fill the void surreptitiously carved out by May and Baker.[26] Admiral Philip Davidson, the U.S. Indo-Pacific Command Combatant Commander, was the beneficiary of J8's analytical work on China, which had reached conclusions radically different from those of ONA under May's and Baker's leadership. According to Davidson, Beijing's headlong push into artificial intelligence, biotech, 5G communications networks, and quantum computing meant that

> China has modernized its military more than any other nation on the planet through the course of this century.... the military balance in the Indo-Pacific is becoming more unfavorable for the United States and our allies. And with this imbalance, we are accumulating risk that may embolden China to act unilaterally...before our forces might be able to deliver an effective response.[27]

On February 5, 2020, Baker attempted to mislead Congress into thinking that he and May had done their jobs. On that day he wrote Republican senator Charles Grassley of Iowa that they had produced "two large-scale net assessment products since 2016."[28] Joshua Flynn-Brown, Grassley's top investigator, picked up on Baker's ruse immediately: anything could be deemed a "net assessment product" because there was no definition of what that was.

"ONA: A CASE IN WASTE, FRAUD AND ABUSE"

Caught red-handed shirking his statutory duty between 2015 and 2018, Baker moved to eliminate that duty retroactively. On April 14, 2020, Baker got Deputy Secretary of Defense David Norquist to remove the word "shall" from a new directive on ONA's responsibility to produce net assessments.[29] Now, he argued, he could go about spending ONA's $10–20 million U.S. taxpayer–funded research budget however he saw fit.

Two months after Baker's scheme to re-write his job description came to the attention of Congress, Senator Grassley wrote to Baker:

> [Y]our February 5, 2020, response appears to show that you have not performed the legally required annual "Net Assessment"—the purpose for which ONA exists.[30]

Visibly upset by Baker's and May's willful pattern of weaseling out of their one and only statutory duty, on July 2, 2020, Grassley delivered a U.S. Senate floor speech in which he said,

> This swamp needs to be drained.... It's pretty clear the Office of Net Assessment lacks leadership and discipline, and it's also pretty clear it has wasted tens of millions of dollars over the years. Congress must take a stand.[31]

That speech was unequivocal about Baker's and May's stewardship of the Pentagon's highest-level strategy office. So too was Grassley's third Senate floor speech excoriating ONA, February 7, 2022.[32]

The failure was deliberate. Incapacitating ONA's net assessment function ensured that the Pentagon would have no option but to adopt Baker's policy of "muddling through." In 2020, a DoD investigation confirmed that ONA—having been led by Baker for half a decade—had not produced a single net assessment, its only statutory duty, in *fifteen years*.[33] Yet in 2021, between Senator Grassley's second speech, entitled "ONA: A Case in Waste, Fraud and Abuse," and his third speech, entitled "The Office of Net Assessment is a Failure," Baker received a "Presidential Rank Award for Meritorious Service."[34] Think about what that says about the integrity of DoD commendations, promotions, and awards. Then ask yourself: Who was the recipient of Baker's meritorious service?

CHAPTER 10

THE "FIND A JUSTIFICATION TO FIRE HIM" SORT OF INVESTIGATION

Someone must have been telling lies about Josef K., for without having done anything wrong he was arrested one fine morning.
—FRANZ KAFKA, *THE TRIAL*[1]

All U.S. government investigations are supposed to be independent and objective. To be valid, they must lack even the appearance of impropriety. That legal doctrine is designed to maintain the integrity of federal investigations. Yet, as I learned the hard way, Deep State operatives thumb their noses at that standard, violating it and other U.S. laws with impunity.

In January 2017, Baker directed U.S. Coast Guard Commander Anthony L. Russell to conduct a second "investigation" of me. Russell was still an official leak suspect for the Walsh investigation, which was ongoing at that time. He was also ONA's security lead and action officer for the Task Force on Enhancing the Japan-U.S. Alliance. In those capacities, Russell had misled Tokyo by telling the government of Japan that the suspected Chinese spy was actually a "U.S. Representative"—that is, a fully vetted individual with the required security clearances. This assurance led Tokyo to share classified information with that person.

Appointing leak suspect Russell to lead this second "investigation" of that very same leak generated a radical conflict of interest.

Yet this was the whole point: Baker used it as a stick to control Russell, pounding him for his gross negligence in allowing the leak to occur in the first place. The only way that Russell could avoid an official reprimand, which would stain his permanent military record, was to follow Baker's directives.

In the real world, one would expect incompetence to result in demotion, not in promotion. But in the Deep State, everything is upside down. Less than a week after punishing Russell for his gross negligence, Baker promoted him to the position of Chief of Staff, Office of Net Assessment.

"SUSPECT NUMBER ONE"

Russell testified under oath to administrative law judge LeRoy Foreman that in addition to being in charge of the Task Force and ONA security, he was also "suspect number one" for the leak. He then said that after Japan's complaint about the leak, Baker's and Russell's top priority was not stopping or investigating the leak, but "salvaging the Task Force" so they wouldn't further embarrass Deputy Secretary of Defense Robert O. Work.

To appease the government of Japan, they told Tokyo that they had investigated the source of the leak and fixed the problem. That was false. They were abusing DoD's investigative authority to cover up the fact that they themselves were either grossly negligent or criminally liable for potentially sharing Japanese classified information with Beijing, Tokyo's most formidable strategic adversary.

Russell also testified under oath that he and Baker had blamed the leak on an American so that a foreign intelligence officer could "save face" over the leak, noting that Japanese culture expected such sensitivity in the conduct of diplomacy: "And I would liken it to more of, 'we [Japanese] need to see some [progress in catching the leaker]'.... I do not claim to be an expert on Asian culture, but

I know enough to understand the concept of face and being able to regain reputation."[2]

Russell admitted he was at fault, but he said that he needed to obey Baker or suffer the consequences. As U.S. law prohibits parties from investigating misconduct that they are themselves suspected of, Baker and Russell interposed a cutout—a trusted middleman who would do their bidding. That role fell to Baker's Military Adviser, Lieutenant Colonel Brian T. Bruggeman (USMC).

Baker then placed Russell, who was now ONA Chief of Staff, in charge of managing Bruggeman. But such an investigation, controlled by the suspected guilty parties and led by someone with whom they had prior personal and professional relations, and over whom they had command influence, was inherently riddled with conflict and could not be considered independent or objective.

• • •

Lieutenant Colonel Brian T. Bruggeman called me at the White House on February 20, 2017.

"Why is Baker investigating me?"

"I can't tell you over the phone," Bruggeman said.

"Why can't you tell me?"

"I need to ask you some questions in person."

By that time, I had known Bruggeman for several years. We had worked in the same office suite and had socialized together both in and out of the Pentagon. Half a dozen times or so, after a long week, we joined ONA's other military assistants and civilian staff for a drink. Over a beer at an Irish pub on Pentagon Row we swapped stories about our kids. He was particularly proud of his son's Little League baseball team.

"Brian, you can't investigate me on behalf of Baker. You and I are both his subordinates. And we've worked together for years, in the same office. That's a second conflict of interest. Is this about the leak of Japanese classified information?"

"That, and other things," he said.

"Baker himself is a leak suspect. That's a third conflict of interest. Don't you see?"

"I think you're being uncooperative."

"Do you want me to be uncooperative?"

"Why would I want that?" Bruggeman said in an unusually distant voice.

"It would make your life easier."

"Well, you're right, that would make my life easier."

"Because then you could write that in your report for Baker."

Silence.

"Brian, you've got an unbridgeable conflict of interest. You need to recuse yourself."

"I can't do that," he said.

Bruggeman was scheduled to retire from the U.S. Marine Corps in a few months, so any misconduct he committed now wouldn't threaten his career. Deputy Secretary of Defense Robert O. Work had done something similar when he used a soon-to-retire Barbara Westgate to do his dirty business.

"Brian, only criminal investigators attached to the DoD OIG are authorized to conduct leak investigations of classified Foreign Government Information."

"What?"

In my dozen years working in the Office of Net Assessment, I had gotten to know six or seven military advisors to the director from the U.S. Marines. Several became my friends. I liked Bruggeman and felt sorry for him.

From the high pitch of Bruggeman's voice, I could tell that Baker had put his subordinate in a vise, was coercing him into breaking the law, and was pressuring him to defile and betray everything the

U.S. Marine Corps stood for. That included, as Bruggeman and all Marine officers knew well, standing up to transgressing superiors and protecting whistleblowers.

In 1776, a Marine captain aboard the *USS Warren* delivered a petition to the Continental Congress detailing wrongdoing by none other than the Commander of the Continental Navy, Esek Hopkins. On July 30, 1778, the Continental Congress chose right over might. It unanimously rallied to the side of the Marine captain, suspended the commodore from his post, and commended the federal whistleblower:

> It is the duty of all persons in the service of the United States to give the earliest information to Congress or other proper authority of any misconduct, frauds or misdemeanors committed by any officers or persons in the service of these states.[3]

For reasons I still do not fully understand, what Baker did to Bruggeman made me angrier than I felt at any time during my five-year ordeal with "administrative due process."

On February 23, 2017, I wrote to the leadership of WHS and the DoD Office of General Counsel, copying WHS General Counsel John Albanese, a subordinate of DoD's top lawyer Paul Koffsky; Christopher "Kappy" Kapellas, WHS Director of the Human Resources Directorate; WHS Executive Services head Karen Finnegan-Myers; and her direct subordinate Marcia Case. All these officials were members of DoD's Senior Executive Service:

> I fear Jim Baker coerced Brian [Bruggeman] into conducting this administrative investigation where he has an unbridgeable conflict of interest.... while this spurious attack has distracted me from my duties at the NSC, I do not want Brian to get hurt. He is an otherwise fine Officer and family man. Please do what you can to minimize the damage.

I assumed that these senior DoD personnel experts and attorneys would know and care about the illegality and potential criminality of this investigation. A day later, Kapellas responded, saying I should cooperate with Baker's newest rogue investigation.

• • •

Baker knew Bruggeman and I were friends, or may have suspected that the Marine was part of the same tradition as his forbears from the *USS Warren*. To test that possibility, he ordered his subordinate in writing to contact WHS lawyer James Vietti should his "independence or objectivity become impaired, preventing a fair and impartial review." That presented Bruggeman with a clear choice. He could follow the law and refuse to follow Baker's clearly illegal directive, or not.

Sure enough, Baker had judged Bruggeman's character accurately. The Marine joined Baker's and Russell's scheme. But, as I discovered in the playbook, Baker gave him a tight deadline of twenty-nine days to investigate me and complete his report of investigation. Unaware that I had the playbook, Baker told Judge Foreman that Bruggeman's only restriction was to "be objective and take your time."

My lawyer then presented Baker with his very own signed directive ordering Bruggeman to complete his task on that unreasonably tight timeline. Baker flushed and, under the courtroom's overhead lights, glistened brightly with sweat. He then turned on a dime, coming up with a completely different explanation for his investigative haste. The real reason for the rush job, Baker told Foreman, with his eyes darting across the courtroom from side to side, was out of mercy for me:

> The reason in my mind for the haste was, this was a terrible thing that was about to happen. I was about to investigate a member of my—a trusted member of my team and that person would—their

teammates would be asked about, Mr. Lovinger's behavior and what they had observed, and Mr. Lovinger would feel threatened and angry probably.

But that was absurd. Baker was in a hurry to scapegoat me to satisfy the demands of a foreign intelligence officer. If Baker couldn't find an American scapegoat, the spy warned Russell, he would cancel the Task Force:

> Without any significant update (such as arrest, or at least, iden-
> tification of the leak perpetrators), I think no parties on our
> side would like to share any of our analyses and participate in
> the [Task Force]. This project deals with one of our immediate
> threats and this type of leak incident could tip a balance in life
> or death competition with our potential adversaries.... I hope
> your side could show us that this would never happen again as
> quickly as possible.[4]

In the middle of Bruggeman's twenty-nine-day investigation, Baker bribed him by promising to nominate him for the Defense Superior Service Medal. Only a few would ever know how Bruggeman actually earned that medal. As he had done with Russell, Baker besmirched the integrity of a high military honor to buy Bruggeman's silence.

• • •

Soon after Westgate subordinate Kapellas told me to cooperate with the Bruggeman investigation, it became clear to me that I was the target of a much bigger criminal conspiracy than I had previously thought. I needed help, starting with a lawyer. Through a mutual friend, I was introduced to Thomas R. Spencer, an expert in national security law. He immediately agreed to represent me, jumped on a plane to Washington the following day, did everything at his own expense, and refused to take a cent from me.

Spencer was the first of ultimately six lawyers who would represent me pro bono. They include Sean Bigley and his superb team of Lee Schachter and Jeff Billett, who selflessly represented me for over three years; former DoD Inspector General Joseph Schmitz, who served as an expert witness during my DOHA appeal; and Judicial Watch lawyers Paul Orfandes and Michael Bekesha, who successfully sued DoD multiple times in federal court for its violation of FOIA in my case. To me and my family, they will all forever remain heroes.

On March 6, 2017, Spencer and I met Bruggeman at the Pentagon. Gone was the Bruggeman I thought I had known. He had become a gray functionary resigned to doing a dirty job for a corrupt boss.

During that interview, I learned that unlike others in ONA, Bruggeman seemed genuinely unaware of the fact that the LTSG employee Baker and May had used to set up the Task Force on Enhancing the Japan-U.S. Alliance had been investigated repeatedly by the FBI on suspicion of spying for China. Bruggeman also seemed worried by the great lengths Baker and Russell had gone to conceal this fact from the government of Japan.[5]

Three days after that interview, Bruggeman completed his investigation of the leak, just as Walsh had done before him. It was a "do-over" investigation, so the Deep State could get the results it wanted.

After over a year of FOIA litigation by Judicial Watch, I learned that by the time Bruggeman interviewed me, Baker had already delivered Bruggeman's investigative results to the government of Japan. That explained a mystery.

Prior to Bruggeman's interview, my lawyer demanded that it be recorded so that both the accuser and accused had a common agreed-upon record of what was said. But Bruggeman refused to record it. Stranger yet, during the interview he took almost no notes.

"How can a factfinder record facts without taking notes?" Spencer asked rhetorically as we exited the Pentagon turnstile. With his retirement and Defense Superior Service Medal just a few short months away, Bruggeman was just filling out the investigative forms to match what his boss had already told Tokyo the previous month.

The reason that my accusers went to such great lengths to hide the fact that they had reached their investigative conclusions before even starting the investigation was explained by WHS attorney James B. Vietti. The Bruggeman investigation had to be concealed because, in Vietti's words, it was too obviously "a 'go forth and find a justification to fire him' sort of investigation."[6]

But Vietti's worry was all for naught. To make sure I was banished for good, Bruggeman declared me an insider threat and recommended suspension of my security clearance. That was illegal because under DoD regulations a finder of fact is forbidden from making recommendations for punishment. But they were in a hurry, so that law was ignored.

Because the Walsh investigation was entirely exculpatory and incriminated my accusers, they ignored it and relied exclusively on Bruggeman's findings and recommendations. That sufficed to ensure that I would face an unwinnable fight against "administrative due process" lasting half a decade (and counting).

•   •   •

On May 1, 2017, WHS Director Barbara A. Westgate suspended my security clearance on the basis of Bruggeman's recommendation. That evening, White House security officers arrived at my office suite on the third floor of the Eisenhower Executive Office Building. Their pained expressions suggested that I was just the latest

Trump administration hit job in a long line of others that they had seen before. They instructed me politely but firmly to surrender my White House access card and to leave the building immediately.

I had just come from an intra-NSC working group meeting. The national security advisor had recently agreed to channel all NSC strategies through the Strategic Assessments Directorate, the office I was then leading, so as to ensure that each White House strategy was mutually reinforcing.

With my removal from the NSC, that process came to an abrupt end, and it was not resuscitated. Deputy Assistant to the President for Strategy Kevin Harrington helped me pack up my office. We carried my personal belongings through a torrential spring downpour to a waiting taxi on 17th Street and Pennsylvania Avenue, and I gave the driver my home address.

● ● ●

On May 3, 2017, two days after my removal from the White House, Baker rewarded Russell for a job well done, recommending him for a U.S. Coast Guard command on the grounds that he had been a model officer exhibiting the "highest standards of integrity and ethics."

Baker then nominated Russell for a prestigious military medal, which he pinned on his uniform at a majestic ceremony on June 29, 2017, proudly attended by his wife, sons, and extended family.

In his medal citation, there was no mention of Russell's role in managing a task force that had leaked America's most important East Asian ally's "life or death" secrets and threatened its fleet in the Western Pacific. Rather, "as the action officer and primary American representative for a high-level United States/Japan Bilateral Task Force, which had a *significant, positive impact* on a key alliance" [emphasis added], Russell had deftly managed an influential, yet delicate, U.S./Japan bilateral analytic effort that significantly enhanced channels for the candid exchange of views, directly contributing to improved alliance relations. The distinctive accomplishments of Commander Russell reflect great credit upon himself, the United States Coast Guard, and the Office of the Secretary of Defense.

Few would know the truth about any of this, and even fewer would understand that Baker was making Russell bulletproof. If anyone ever questioned Russell's role on the Task Force, he would point to the citation accompanying his award, confident that the U.S. Department of Defense would vouch for its sanctity. By then, Baker was well practiced in rigging DoD promotions and medals to reward misconduct, including what seems like the commission of crimes.

Several months before awarding Russell a military medal, Deputy Secretary of Defense Work nominated Baker for a Presidential Rank Award. As with the citation on Russell's medal, the basis of Baker's award was that he had strengthened U.S. alliances, when in fact the evidentiary record showed that Baker had a long history of intentionally doing just the opposite.

U.S. Coast Guard leadership reviewed Russell's official record, liked what they saw, and promoted him. Captain Russell's next assignment was to his alma mater. As Chief of the Department of Professional Maritime Studies at the U.S. Coast Guard Academy, he would model the qualities of honor and integrity for the Republic's next generation of military leaders. After the academy, Russell rounded out his career in uniform as Chief of Public Affairs for the United States Coast Guard. In October 2022, Russell re-joined the Academy's faculty as Executive Director, Center for Arctic Study and Policy.[7]

CHAPTER 11

A TREASONOUS PATH

Washington insiders have an adage: "The easiest money comes from our enemies." America's adversaries count on the disillusionment of ambitious, self-important government officials who, after leaving office, soon discover that the private sector typically values them much less than they value themselves. Casting about, these former officials discover that foreigners will pay them handsomely for their up-to-date knowledge about U.S. national security, intelligence, or law enforcement bureaucracies. Unsurprisingly, the foreign governments most willing to pay top dollar are America's leading adversaries—notably, Beijing, Moscow, and Tehran.

But the problem for these former officials is that, over time, their "inside information" grows stale. To make up for that deficit, some choose to diversify their services, such as passing off enemy propaganda as opposition research and selling it to political campaigns. From there, it is but a small step for them to accept offers of operational assistance from America's enemies. Obama's CIA director John Brennan explained how this process works to the U.S. House of Representatives Permanent Select Committee on Intelligence (HPSCI) on May 23, 2017:

> Frequently, individuals who go along a treasonous path do not
> even realize they're along that path until it gets to be a bit too

late... [Russian intelligence] try to besmirch and tarnish individuals, [and they develop] blackmail, Kompromat, that they would be able to then leverage for their own purposes.[1]

Should those officials ever return to government, which they often do, they enjoy the patronage of a foreign power's intelligence services, which they can weaponize against their political opponents. As Brennan explained to the HPSCI, these blackmail materials over former U.S. officials are priceless to the enemy:

> Having been involved in many counterintelligence cases in the past, I know what the Russians try to do. They try to suborn individuals, and they try to get individuals, including U.S. persons, to act on their behalf, either wittingly or unwittingly.[2]

• • •

Upon his appointment to the Senior Executive Service, and in his role as ONA's research director, Andrew D. May sponsored Stefan A. Halper and former head of Russian Foreign Intelligence General Vyacheslav Ivanovich Trubnikov to undertake several "studies" for ONA over a period of five years.

Halper and Trubnikov were highly suspect as government contractors, and they are crucial figures to our story. A short discussion of their backgrounds provides some necessary context to their troubling relationship with ONA.

Halper had long been known as the world's most infamous presidential-elections-interference operative. As explained in a July 1983 *New York Times* article, Halper earned that sobriquet in 1980 after he was fingered as the "person in charge" of a "highly secretive" scheme to steal President Jimmy Carter's briefing materials for an important presidential debate, which became a national scandal.[3]

Halper later became an academic, and, despite his early public embarrassments, landed at Cambridge University, where he served as Director of American Studies in the Department of Politics and International Studies.

The FBI had serious questions about Halper's loyalty to the United States. Halper's FBI file flagged his "questionable allegiances"[4] and how proud he was of having "a lot of friends in Russia," including the person he called the "director of KGB...and the FSB": General V. I. Trubnikov.[5]

In the late 1960s, Trubnikov began working for the KGB under cover in India. He ended his official government career as Russian Deputy Foreign Minister, followed by Ambassador to India. But before that, from 1996 to 2000, Trubnikov ran the SVR—Russian Foreign Intelligence—the Kremlin's rough equivalent to the Central Intelligence Agency. Of course, by the time May began disbursing taxpayer dollars to sponsor his operations, Trubnikov was technically no longer in charge of Russian Foreign Intelligence. But as everyone in ONA knew, there are no "former" Russian intelligence officers. Their service to Moscow ends when they do.

As head of the SVR, Trubnikov ran an organization that was, and remains to this day, the sharp tip of Moscow's active measures abroad. It specializes in recruiting and amplifying foreigners willing to promote Putin's agenda. Trubnikov was trained in the art of putting Americans at ease, spoke English fluently, and adopted Western mannerisms. This was convenient for Halper, who didn't speak Russian.

Halper bragged about how "really plugged in" Trubnikov was to Moscow. Of course he was. As Greg Myre writes, spies were a "defining theme" for Vladimir Putin: "Russia may not be an economic giant, but one area where it was still a first-class power was espionage, and Putin would double down on his intelligence services as a means to wield power and influence around the world."[6]

More so than perhaps any other human being on the planet, Putin appreciates the power of a professional spy to internally subvert, divide, and conquer an enemy from within. On the occasion of the fortieth anniversary of his joining the KGB, Putin explained how the protagonist of a Russian spy novel that was popular during his youth had inspired his life's work: "What amazed me most of all was how one man's efforts could achieve what whole armies could not."[7]

On October 7, 2011, Halper and Trubnikov completed a 655-page study for ONA titled "The Afghan End-Game." This was described as "a major survey of Allied end game options in Afghanistan" commissioned by Obama's secretary of defense and sourced to "a series of productive roundtables in Moscow."[8]

As everyone in ONA knew, Russian intelligence deployed only its best and brightest to hunt for opportunities such as this, which permitted Moscow to inject disinformation into the work product of the Pentagon's highest strategy office. Once inside DoD, the SVR could conduct unparalleled acts of sabotage. Because of its impressive record of success, the Kremlin's subversion strategy had changed little since Whittaker Chambers described it in 1952:

> The power to influence policy has always been the ultimate purpose of the Communist Party's infiltration. It was much more dangerous, and, as events have proved, much more difficult to detect, than espionage, which beside it is trivial, though the two go hand in hand.[9]

Several months before Halper and Trubnikov completed "The Afghan End-Game," I provided evidence to the U.S. Department of Defense Office of Inspector General (DoD OIG) that Andrew D. May was "rigging contracts" that favored Halper and Trubnikov. But the newly appointed Deputy Inspector General Marguerite

C. Garrison did nothing to stand in the way of that May-Halper-Trubnikov operation.

•   •   •

Soon after his arrival at Cambridge University in 2001, Stefan A. Halper became a co-convenor of the Cambridge Intelligence Seminar (CIS). Current and former spies led that weekly series of lectures and discussions in the oak-paneled New Combination Room of Corpus Christi College (founded 1352).

In the introduction of his 2011 ONA report on "The Afghan End-Game," Halper makes reference to how CIS was used to host Russia spies: those meetings "demonstrated the further opportunities for further dialogue [on U.S.-Russia cooperation in Afghanistan] as during V. I. Trubnikov's visit in May to the Cambridge Intelligence Seminar."[10]

One of Halper's first patrons was Andrei Cheglakov, a billionaire confidant of Vladimir Putin, whose fortune came from owning companies that design computer spy software for the Russian government. The Russian oligarch agreed to bankroll Halper's CIS meetings, which were presided over by Halper or his CIS co-convenor Christopher Andrew. An expert in Russian spycraft, and the former official historian of MI5, Professor Andrew is the co-author of *The Sword and the Shield: The Mitrokhin Archive and the Secret History of the KGB.*

"Russian intelligence agencies do not hesitate at all to use private companies" to advance Russian "objectives," said John Brennan, describing Moscow's collaboration with businessmen such as Cheglakov, and CIS by extension.[11]

To bolster the academic credentials of that Russian intelligence front, Cheglakov paid Neil Kent, who had been a professor at St. Petersburg State Academic Institute from 2002 to 2012, £50,000 a year to serve as editor-in-chief of CIS's decidedly pro-Moscow *Journal of Intelligence and Terrorism Studies*. Listed in that publication as a CIS co-founder, Kent complained in a July 2014 Russian state television interview that "everyone is attacking and demonizing Russia."[12]

In 2016, Kent blamed the West for Putin's 2014 annexation of Crimea: "The main conclusion of this paper," Kent wrote in his journal's June 2016 inaugural edition, "is that the West's complacency and ignorance were some of the principal causes of the Ukraine crisis."[13] Stalin, also a master of doublespeak, had blamed the West for the Soviet Union's annexation of Eastern Europe following World War II.[14]

Another member of CIS was Sir Richard Billing Dearlove, KCMG, OBE. From 1999 to 2004, Dearlove led MI6 under British Prime Minister Tony Blair. Upon his retirement from Her Majesty's Secret Intelligence Service, Dearlove became Master of Pembroke College, Cambridge (founded 1347).

In mid-2012, Halper welcomed General V. I. Trubnikov back to Cambridge to participate in a conference by giving a lecture on "challenges faced while directing the [Russian] Foreign Intelligence Service" and "the likely course of Russia's relations with Britain and the U.S."[15] That conference's conclusions were then turned into a report entitled "Dynamics of Russian and European Engagement in the Next 10 to 20 Years."

The report recounts how "forces within the Russian elite, mainly from an intelligence background and including senior figures such as Evgeny Savostyanov [senior Russian counterintelligence officer, chief of the Moscow KGB/FSB in the 1990's] and Vyacheslav Trubnikov," seek "closer relations with the United States.... These forces, separate from political power but nationalist and patriotic, think that it would be possible to convince Putin of such a course. Savostyanov and Trubnikov both engaged in frank and open discussions while visiting Cambridge."[16] Of course Putin's top spies wanted "closer relations with the United States." To do their job, spies must be very close to their targets.

That report concluded that the Russian threat was minimal and that a strong Russia was good for America. It recommended investment by Washington in a U.S-Russia partnership against China on the grounds that they had a "joint interest in responding to the challenge posed by China's increasing economic, strategic, and military power. This situation opens up new opportunities for strategic co-operation between the two countries."

On December 16, 2016, the *Financial Times* published an interview with former MI6 head Sir Richard Dearlove in which he admitted what ONA staff had suspected since 2011: The Russian oligarch–funded CIS and its *Journal of Intelligence and Terrorism Studies* were fronts for Russia's Foreign Intelligence Service.

Dearlove then claimed that he, Halper, Andrew, and Kent had all been tricked into providing Putin and his spies "an impeccably credentialed platform to covertly steer debate and opinion on high-level sensitive defence and security topics."[17] CIS work product, in Dearlove's words, was contaminated with "unacceptable Russian influence."[18]

•   •   •

On July 12, 2019, nearly three years after Dearlove's article admitted to what ONA staff had long known, Senator Charles Grassley asked Baker and May why, over half a decade, had they been furnishing "a known Russian intelligence officer" with the opportunity to inject Russian disinformation into Pentagon products commissioned for the Office of the Secretary of Defense?

In 2018, I delivered to the senior senator from Iowa the same evidence I had given DoD OIG in 2011 on May's "rigging" of contracts to set up the Halper-Trubnikov influence operation in DoD.

Grassley immediately grasped what they had done and was appalled. On January 16, 2019, he demanded that the DoD OIG do what they should have done in 2011 and conduct an audit of those contracts. The completed DoD OIG audit confirmed what Senator Grassley and I had long suspected.

Presumably to conceal SVR's hand, the Halper-Trubnikov reports commissioned by ONA and completed for the Office of the Secretary of Defense contained dozens of fabricated sources. The malfeasance would grow increasingly obvious over the next half decade. Between 2011 and 2016, May had awarded Halper and Trubnikov a half dozen contracts. Halper used a sea of fabricated sources in those reports to conceal Moscow's hand in generating that ONA work product.

When confronted with that evidence by Grassley, on July 24, 2019, Baker wrote back to the senator and assured him that he had determined that Halper and Trubnikov had "performed satisfactorily" and that the work product deemed fraudulent by the DoD OIG IG was of "high quality."[19]

On January 22, 2020, Senator Grassley followed up with Baker, asking him whether he and May had used U.S. taxpayer funds to mislead the Office of the Secretary of Defense with "biased and unreliable information" courtesy of Putin's intelligence services.[20] The following month Baker responded yes, he had known about Trubnikov's role all along.[21] After that, presumably on advice of DoD counsel, Baker became nonresponsive to congressional oversight.

On June 18, 2020, Baker's foot-dragging prompted Grassley to complain to Baker:

> I have repeatedly requested all records related to Professor Halper's work for ONA, including travel records, pursuant to the contracts that he had with your office. However, despite these repeated requests, ONA has continually failed to furnish all requested records. It appears that either ONA has refused to comply with

my requests, or that ONA simply does not maintain full records of Halper's work.[22]

By the time Baker wrote to Senator Grassley, ONA had employed Trubnikov on contracts between 2010 and 2016 totaling over $1 million, courtesy of the U.S. taxpayer. Each report was filled with Russian propaganda that Baker and May passed off as Office of the Secretary of Defense work product.

CHAPTER 12

ADOPTING RUSSIA'S FOREIGN POLICY FOR AMERICA'S OWN

The Party told you to reject the evidence of your eyes and ears.
It was their final, most essential command.

—GEORGE ORWELL[1]

It is not difficult to see what attracted Moscow to Halper. Between 1991 and 2004, when Halper published his book *America Alone: The Neo-Conservatives and the Global Order* (Cambridge University Press, 2004), the power differential between America and its adversaries was perhaps greater than at any time in world history. But for Halper, U.S. primacy was not something to be celebrated, but rather abandoned.

How Washington should do that, Halper spelled out in his book. In *America Alone* he argues that U.S. national security strategy should prioritize "consensus diplomacy and balance of power"[2] politics. In other words, America, the world's only superpower, should cede its preeminence and strengthen the relative power of its competitors. Of course, this was precisely what America's adversaries wanted as well.

In the 1993 "Foreign Policy Concept of the Russian Federation," the Kremlin announced its plan to establish a "balance of influence in the world."[3] That would be done by weakening the United States and strengthening Russia.

Seven years later, Putin declared his intent to undermine U.S. global primacy and replace it with a new "multi-polar" world order. To leave no doubt about his intentions, in 2000 Putin signed a "National Security Concept of the Russian Federation" that opposed "the attempt to create a structure of international relations based on the domination of developed Western countries, led by the USA."[4] But Halper was not the only one to adopt Russia's foreign policy objectives for his own.

• • •

Six months after assuming the presidency, Obama visited Moscow on a mission to improve communication between Russia and the United States. On the heels of his July 2009 meeting with Putin, Obama helped consummate Putin's dream for a "balance of influence in the world" by gutting the missile defense system George W. Bush had emplaced in Eastern Europe to deter Russia and protect NATO.[5] As with his Apology Tour that same year, he did so in the name of grievance politics against America, as if he saw himself righting some profound historical wrong.

In 2011, the Obama State Department quietly approved the transfer to Moscow of a U.S. hypersonic cruise missile engine. For Russia, cruise missiles are not defensive weapons, but rather offensive precision-strike munitions that would be used in vast quantities to strike military and civilian targets in Ukraine and threaten America's NATO allies. This secretive transfer of cutting-edge military technology to Moscow was only revealed publicly in an unclassified 2013 U.S. military report.[6]

According to that U.S. European Command report, this was no accident. Balance-of-power considerations justified that transfer of power. It was done in "response to the U.S. Department of Defense's Advanced Hypersonic Weapon, part of the Prompt Global Strike program."[7]

In Russia's 2000 "Foreign Policy Concept and Military Doctrine," Putin had placed Washington on notice of his plan to reconstitute the old Soviet empire's historical sphere of influence. Since the collapse of the USSR, Moscow aimed to maintain a "good-neighbor belt along the perimeter of Russia's border" by sustaining frozen conflicts with adjoining countries.

Putin encouraged Russian-speaking separatist movements in former Soviet satellites to break away and join the motherland.[8] That served two key objectives. First, it precluded those former Soviet satellites from ever joining NATO. That defensive treaty organization has "established borders" as a membership requirement.

Second, when those fragmenting countries attempted to resist their dissolution at the hands of Moscow, Putin used that attempt to ward off national suicide as a pretext to invade. Publicly, as he did with Georgia (2008) and Ukraine (2014, 2022), Putin justified reconstituting the former Soviet empire on the grounds of protecting ethnic Russian populations "trapped" in the near abroad.

By all measures the Obama Doctrine was a smashing success. During the Obama administration, Russia reconquered more of the former Soviet Union than during any previous U.S. presidency. But Putin, who enjoys invoking history to benchmark his performance against his imperial predecessors, was just getting started.

Between 1792 and 1798, naval forces deployed to what is now Syria by Catherine the Great protected the underbelly of her empire. In 2015, having faced minimal U.S. resistance to his earlier conquests, Putin waltzed unopposed into Syria after a withering Russian aerial bombing campaign killed thousands of Syrian civilians. As Putin was building a naval base at the Syrian port of Tartus and an air base at Latakia, the Obama Pentagon was sharing U.S. battlefield intelligence on Syria with the Russian military.[9]

The official justification for that Obama-Putin intelligence partnership was to help the Russian leader defeat ISIS. But, as was widely known in the Pentagon at the time, this was false. Later Obama intimated that Putin didn't really need U.S. intelligence support, calling ISIS the "JV team," meaning it posed no strategic threat.[10] Russia's new bases in the Levant would permit Putin to hold sway over the critical Suez Canal, which Europe relies upon for energy shipments from the Middle East.

TRIANGULATING WITH MOSCOW

By March 26, 2012, Obama had spent his first term in office ceding U.S. power to Russia, and now it was his turn to ask something of Putin in return. On that day, Obama was caught on a hot mic asking then–Russian President Medvedev to convey an important message to his de facto boss, Putin. Promising that "after my election I'll have more flexibility" to reward Putin for his assistance, Obama told Medvedev that, in the interim, "on all these issues, but particularly missile defense...it's important for [Putin] to give me space."[11]

That same day, Republican presidential candidate Mitt Romney, Obama's political rival, announced that "Russia [is], without question, our number one geopolitical foe. They—they fight every cause for the world's worst actors."[12] The following day, Putin had Medvedev endorse Obama for president. "It is very reminiscent of Hollywood," said Medvedev in reference to Romney. The Russian president then declared that Republicans should "check their watches from time to time: It is 2012, not the mid-1970s."[13]

By then, Obama had aided and abetted Putin's imperial expansion into Syria, which Syrian president Bashar al-Assad used to buttress his shaky regime. With that Russian security umbrella protecting him from the outside world, Assad had free reign to butcher his people. The London-trained-medical-doctor-turned-Syrian-dictator's weapon of choice was deadly sarin gas. In August 2012, Obama drew a "red line in the sand":

We have been very clear to the Assad regime, but also to other players on the ground, that a red line for us is we start seeing a whole bunch of chemical weapons moving around or being utilized. That would change my calculus. That would change my equation.[14]

Two months later, on October 22, 2012, the president put up an impassioned defense of the Russian leader. In a presidential debate, Obama recycled Medvedev's March 26, 2012, language to pillory his Republican candidate Mitt Romney for calling an imperial, expansionist, nuclear-armed Russia America's primary adversary:

When you were asked, what's the biggest geopolitical threat facing America, you said 'Russia.' Not Al-Qaeda; you said Russia. And the 1980s are now calling to ask for their foreign policy back, because the Cold War's been over for twenty years.[15]

I encourage you to watch footage of that performance.[16] It may be the rawest passion Obama ever projected in his entire eight-year presidency. It visibly stunned Romney and must have warmed the cockles of Putin's heart.

Obama had publicly repeated Moscow's official talking points near verbatim. Through a Russian cultural lens, Obama's parroting of President Medvedev's ridicule of Romney demonstrated to Putin that the president of the United States was closer to Putin on the issues that mattered than he was to his Republican opponent. That act, broadcast on international television to millions of viewers, demonstrated to Putin that Obama was on his side.

In December 2012, a month after Moscow gave the incumbent U.S. president the "flexibility" he needed to win re-election to the highest office of the land, Obama reciprocated the favor by paving the way for Russia to receive Most Favored Nation trading status.

That key gateway to the lucrative World Trade Organization permitted Putin and his inner circle to grow astoundingly rich.

Of course, Obama is no naïf. Triangulating with Putin to beat Romney was a high-wire act, perhaps the most audacious in U.S. history. Although he was safe with Putin, Obama knew that many people inside the U.S. national security bureaucracy understood what he had just done.

On November 21, 2012, as one of his first official acts following his 2012 re-election victory, Obama implemented his National Insider Threat Policy. Officially, his administration would aggressively wield that policy to go after "insiders who misuse their access and endanger our national security."[17] DoD's Robert O. Work, James H. Baker, Barbara A. Westgate, Paul S. Koffsky, Glenn A. Fine, and Marguerite C. Garrison each met the definition of an "insider threat" to U.S. national security many times over. But that policy's real purpose was to destroy any federal whistleblower coming forth with what he knew about the true purpose of the Obama Doctrine.

•   •   •

On August 20, 2012, Obama drew his "red line" on Syria. After that, he appears to have asked Putin to get Bashar al-Assad to give him "space" and hold off a year so he could win re-election to the White House. Assad did so, and Obama won re-election handily.

On August 21, 2013, exactly one year and a day after Obama's "red line" speech, in the Damascus suburb of Ghouta, Syrian forces murdered more than 1,400 civilians with sarin gas.[18] Putin had delivered for Obama. But now it was Obama's turn.

Like many authoritarian dictators, Putin finds pleasure in torture, and the opportunity to torment Obama, by forcing the American president to publicly abandon every humanitarian principle he claimed to stand for was an opportunity that Putin would not squander.

Just as Obama had done with the suppression of Iran's freedom movement in 2009, all Obama had to do to fulfill his side of the bargain was spectate and do nothing from the sidelines. Then, with a free hand, Assad set about displacing more than ten million[19] Syrian civilians from their homes and murdering more than 400,000 of his countrymen.[20]

In contrast to 2009, however, once Obama's silence became deafening, he did not promise to "bear witness" to the slaughter of innocents. Instead, he dispatched his UN Ambassador and human rights crusader Samatha Power to explain his position on what was by then called the "Syrian genocide."[21]

> Well, Syria is a very complex picture. There are thousands of armed groups. The question again of what military intervention would achieve, where you would do it, and how you would do it in a way where the terrorists wouldn't be the ones to take advantage of it—this has been extremely challenging. But the idea that we have not been doing, quote, anything in Syria seems absurd. We've done everything short of waging war against the Assad regime and we are, I should note, having significant success against ISIL on the ground.[22]

The consequences of Obama's parroting of Russian talking points about Romney, and of his other pro-Putin acts and omissions, reverberated globally. As just one example, a friend visiting Japan, which has a mutual defense treaty with the U.S., told me that the first thing then–Prime Minister Shinzo Abe asked him during their meeting in Tokyo was: "What happened to the Syria red line? Was it drawn with erasable ink?"

"OUR GOAL IS TO HELP STRENGTHEN RUSSIA"

All indicators suggest that Hillary Clinton, in the lead-up to the 2016 presidential election, expected that Putin would give her the same deal the Russian leader had struck with Obama in March 2012. In exchange for U.S. military and economic concessions designed to build Russian power directly and erode U.S. primacy, the Russian leader had gladly given Obama the space and "flexibility" he needed to win re-election.

Having witnessed that transaction from the inside, Clinton can be forgiven for thinking that Putin would give her that same special treatment. Nevertheless, Clinton is not the type of politician to leave anything to chance.

Back in 2010, she began to lay the groundwork for her last run for the presidency. She pulled out all the stops. That year, to show Putin that she was on his side, she announced on Russian TV that

> I mean, we want very much to have a strong Russia....
> One of the fears that I hear from Russia is that somehow the United States wants Russia to be weak. That could not be farther from the truth. Our goal is to help strengthen Russia.[23]

To ensure her meaning was not lost on Putin, Clinton deemed Russia a U.S. "ally." That word has special meaning. An "alliance" is the strongest bond of cooperation under international law. Not even friendly democracies like Taiwan or India are U.S. treaty allies. Nevertheless, in 2012, just six days after the Obama-Putin deal of "space" for "flexibility," Clinton made it clear that she would continue Obama's erosion of U.S. power should she win the White House in 2016. "Russia has been an ally," Clinton said publicly. "They're in the P-5+1 talks with us, they have worked with us in Afghanistan and have been very helpful in the Northern Distribution Network and in other ways."[24]

But for Russian leaders, words are cheap. What matters is money and military power. The alacrity with which she embraced leading Obama's "Russia reset" demonstrated that Clinton was eager to craft deals for Russians and Americans alike.

In 2009 U.S. Secretary of State Hillary Clinton granted Rusnano, the Russian State Investment Fund, access to U.S. capital for the purpose of investing in U.S. technology companies.[25] This continued despite Clinton having received a State Department cable warning her that there were "dual use and export control concerns" related to those Rusnano investments.[26] The U.S. State Department, under Clinton's leadership, also approved a Russian-controlled firm purchasing Uranium One, a company that controlled 20 percent of all uranium deposits in the United States.[27] Former mining financier and Clinton Foundation Board member Frank Giustra made the deal.

After brokering the sale of Uranium One, Giustra orchestrated a $145 million transfer of donations from Uranium One shareholders to the Clinton Foundation.[28] As FBI Assistant Director Andrew McCabe later discovered after investigating that transaction, extortion and bribery had taken place.[29] But the Clintons were enriched in other ways as well.

Russian oligarchs benefitting from the "Russia reset" made generous donations to the Clinton Foundation,[30] and ex-president Bill Clinton received $500,000 for an after-dinner "speech," courtesy of Renaissance Capital, a Russian government–controlled bank that had profited from the sale of Uranium One.[31] For Putin, gathering proof of Clinton's graft was the most important part of that deal. It furnished the Russian leader with invaluable blackmail material over any Clinton seeking high office in the future.

While it may appear strange to the American sensibility, by granting Putin blackmail material on her and her family, Hillary

Clinton was sending Putin a message. Just as with the deals Obama had made with Putin to help him win re-election, Clinton showed the Russian leader that he could trust her, that she was on his side.

A 2022 *Washington Post* article suggested that Obama's and Clinton's way of doing business pleased Putin. In that piece, the *Post* summarized a U.S. intelligence assessment that found that soon after Putin helped Obama win re-election to the White House, a secret long-term strategy was hatched in the bowels of the Kremlin.

Between 2014 and 2022, Moscow had spent $300 million on operations that compromised foreign political parties and candidates for political office, and it "planned to spend hundreds of millions of dollars more as part of its covert campaign to weaken democratic systems and promote global political forces seen aligned with Kremlin interests."[32]

Finally, Clinton declared on the campaign trail that she would consider ceding nuclear weapons primacy to Russia: "The last thing we need are sophisticated cruise missiles that are nuclear-armed." Clinton spoke those words, which soon leaked, during a "private" 2016 Democratic Party fundraiser with elite donors. Clinton, who possesses the rare qualities of both a skilled politician and policy wonk, knew full well the strategic implications of that concession to Russia.[33]

On April 21, 2000, Putin signed a "Military Doctrine of the Russian Federation" that lowered the threshold for Russia's use of its nuclear arsenal in the event of war. In 2014, as he was annexing Crimea from Ukraine, Putin issued a decree calling for the full modernization of Russia's nuclear capabilities within a decade.

Beginning that year, and for every remaining year of the Obama administration, the U.S. State Department accused Putin of violating the Intermediate-Range Nuclear Forces Treaty, which banned an entire class of nuclear and conventional "intermediate-range" missiles. In 2015, a year before the fundraiser in which Clinton intimated that, if elected president, she would cede nuclear primacy to

Russia, Putin declared that Russia's technological breakthroughs in nuclear weapons and anti-satellite capabilities would render NATO's missile defense system "useless."

Decades before, President Reagan had said that his Strategic Defense Initiative would do something similar to Soviet weapons systems. But unlike Reagan, who used the presidential bully pulpit to engage in a national conversation with the American people on the topic of the U.S. national interest and his vision for America, Obama and Clinton chose a different field of fight.

After Obama's 2009 Apology Tour failed to win over converts to the wisdom of the Obama Doctrine, he and Hillary Clinton gave up on any attempt to change the hearts and minds of ordinary Americans. Instead, from the back alleyways and shadows of the federal bureaucracy, they would change laws, the allocation of resources, and the way systems operate to mislead their fellow citizens and advance their political and ideological agenda, whatever the cost.[34]

On April 24, 2019, almost three years after losing her final attempt at the White House, the hurt and venom Clinton felt toward Putin for reneging on their deal was palpable. On that day, in a *Washington Post* op-ed, she admitted that she had known of Putin's true intentions for America all along:

> I am also a former senator and secretary of state who served during much of Vladimir Putin's ascent, sat across the table from him and knows firsthand that he seeks to weaken our country.[35]

What her article didn't mention was that she had only soured on Putin because he had not helped her enough to win the presidency. Her op-ed also seemed designed to rewrite history. It conveniently omitted the fact that she had previously advocated for "a strong Russia," viewed Moscow as an "ally," helped to strengthen the Russian military through commissions and omissions with regard to

America's strategic arsenal, and made economic policy adjustments to enrich Putin and his cronies—all in full knowledge of the national security risks these actions posed to the U.S. and its NATO allies.

CHAPTER 13

THE NET ASSESSMENT DOSSIER

In April 2016, Clinton consummated what would become the signature Russia deal of the 2016 presidential election. That month her campaign and the Democratic National Committee commissioned what came to be called the "Steele Dossier."[1] Named for its author, Christopher Steele, the dossier, and the processes that led to its creation and later use, gave Putin invaluable blackmail material on Clinton. The Steele Dossier was the latest in a long line of schemes generated by American elites and wielded by the Kremlin to, in the words of Russian Chief of the General Staff General Valery V. Gerasimov, unleash "a web of chaos…and civil war" to destroy America from within.[2]

CIA Director John Brennan's handwritten notes from an August 3, 2016, meeting with Obama, Vice President Biden, Comey, and other national security team members recount Clinton's role in creating the dossier. Brennan was in possession of a Russian intelligence intercept evidencing the

> alleged approval by Hillary Clinton on July 26, 2016, of a proposal from one of her foreign policy advisers to vilify Donald Trump

by stirring up a scandal claiming interference by the Russian security service.[3]

A follow-on report from the Office of the Director of National Intelligence (DNI), confirmed the veracity of that intercept:

In late July 2016, U.S. intelligence agencies obtained insight into Russian intelligence analysis alleging that U.S. Presidential candidate Hillary Clinton had approved a campaign plan to stir up a scandal against U.S. Presidential candidate Donald Trump by tying him to Putin and the Russians' hacking of the Democratic National Committee.[4]

Two months later, on September 7, 2016, U.S. intelligence officials referred what Clinton had done to FBI Director Comey for potential criminal investigation, describing her smear campaign against the Republican presidential candidate "as a means of distracting the public from her use of a private email server."[5]

That criminal referral, however, was designed to go nowhere. In the end, the FBI looked the other way, as it had done under its previous director, Robert Mueller, when he appointed Andrew McCabe to oversee a bogus investigation of Bill and Hillary Clinton's Uranium One deal.

•   •   •

At the same time as Clinton was being criminally referred to James Comey's FBI for her latest scheme, she was in full projection and deflection mode—accusing Trump of what she herself was doing in an attempt to evade responsibility for her actions. On September 22, 2016, she intimated that she had evidence that Trump was an unwitting agent of Putin, asking in a tweet, "The man who could be your next president may be deeply indebted to another country. Do you trust him to run ours?"[6]

"We've never seen anything like this in American politics," Clinton added. "Every day seems to cast new doubts on what's truly driving Donald Trump's decision-making."[7]

In her telling, "I'm the last thing standing between you [the American people] and the apocalypse."[8]

Less than a month before the 2016 presidential election, Clinton was recorded telling her running mate, Tim Kaine, and his wife, Anne, "I don't say this lightly," but Trump's "agenda is other people's agenda. We're scratching hard, trying to figure it out," Clinton continued, concluding that Trump "is the vehicle, the vessel for all these other people.... This is what scares me...the way that Putin has taken over the political apparatus or is trying to."[9] What she did not say was that she and Obama, not Trump, were responsible for Putin's doing so.

•   •   •

But projection and deflection were not the only techniques Clinton employed to distance herself from her reliance on Moscow and smear Trump. In the lead-up to the 2016 presidential election, she "shortlisted" Robert O. Work, Obama's deputy secretary of defense, for the top Pentagon job in a future Clinton administration. That prize would be his reward for painstakingly creating, with the help of May and later Baker, the institutional architecture for Russia-gate between 2010 and 2016. They did so via six ONA contracts with Halper and Trubnikov.

Those Pentagon contracts were issued in tandem with Clinton's "we want very much to have a strong Russia"[10] charm offensive against Putin. They served to normalize the funding of America's most notorious presidential-elections-interference operative and the former head of Russia's Foreign Intelligence Service with U.S. taxpayer money.

By using Halper and Trubnikov to inject Russian disinformation into Pentagon reports, Work furnished Clinton with an alibi. If Clinton were to face questioning along the lines of "why did you rely on Russian disinformation furnished by Halper and Putin's top spy?" she could respond that "if the U.S. Department of Defense's Office of Net Assessment found those sources reputable, why shouldn't I?"

Yet even while Deputy Secretary of Defense Work provided her that political cover, Clinton took no chances. To maintain plausible deniability, she would attenuate her direct connection to Moscow and her reliance on Russian disinformation. Fortunately for the architects of Russiagate, Washington, DC, is home to a sophisticated industry—composed of law firms, opposition research guns for hire, consultants, and think tanks—devoted to concealment and obfuscation. The Hillary campaign and the Democratic National Committee (DNC) employed them all.

Perkins Coie, the DNC's law firm, dispatched lawyer Michael Sussman to lobby the FBI to investigate Donald Trump on behalf of Hillary Clinton. Perkins Coie also served as a funding passthrough for the DNC to hire Fusion GPS. That political opposition research firm, which counted the Russian government among its clients, had a longstanding relationship with the Clintons.

While Clinton was secretary of state, she had tried to stop the passage of the 2012 Magnitsky Act.[11] That piece of legislation authorized the U.S. president to impose sanctions on individual violators of human rights. Renaissance Capital, a Russian bank that by then had paid half a million dollars for a Bill Clinton speech, was later discovered to have played a key role in a $230 million tax fraud discovered by Sergei Magnitsky, a young Russian lawyer, who blew the whistle.[12]

True to form, Putin made an example of Magnitsky to send a message, torturing him gruesomely before murdering him. Americans of all political stripes were outraged, and the U.S. Congress cobbled together some language for a Magnitsky Act. To derail that legislation, a Russian government–controlled company hired Fusion GPS to spread Russian disinformation about the purportedly benign circumstances leading to Magnitsky's death in a Moscow prison.[13]

• • •

Fusion GPS later hired Christopher Steele to conceal Clinton's use of information provided by Halper and Trubnikov. Steele's background, both operational and ideological, made him a suitable candidate for that job. As an undergraduate at Cambridge University, Steele was known as a "confirmed socialist."[14] After he graduated from Cambridge, MI6 employed Steele for twenty-two years. He worked under diplomatic cover at the British Embassy in Moscow (1990–1993) and ended his government career at MI6 Headquarters as Head of the Russia Station (2004–2009).[15]

Over the summer of 2016, Steele went about legitimizing what would become known as "the Steele Dossier" by propagating it throughout the U.S. government. As Deputy Assistant Secretary of State for Russia Kathleen Kavalec later said, Steele told her that ONA consultant General V. I. Trubnikov was a "still active Russian intelligence officer" and that he was his source for the dossier.[16] Steele was less forthright with Kavalec's State Department colleague who testified, "We were not aware of [Steele's] specific sources but assumed that many of them were close to Putin and were peddling information that was useful to the Kremlin."[17] All of this was old news to officials in the Pentagon's Office of Net Assessment, where Halper had been delivering reports filled with Russian propaganda for over half a decade.

The FBI was Steele's next port of call. As previously noted, Halper informed his FBI handlers that Trubnikov is "really plugged in" and has proven "very helpful... in all kinds of ways. So he's a friend of ours... and I have to say that I've enjoyed his friendship all over the world."[18]

FBI officials Peter Strzok and Lisa Page seemed to agree on the value of those dossier sources. They would use the Steele Dossier to open a counterintelligence investigation on Trump. On July 27, 2016, Page texted Strzok: "Have we opened on him yet?" before sharing the link of an article titled, "Trump & Putin. Yes, It's Really a Thing."[19] Former Assistant Director for the Office of Intelligence at FBI headquarters Kevin Brock disagreed with that premise. According to Brock, Page and Strzok had wittingly or unwittingly overlooked what to him was obvious: that the Steele Dossier had "all the classic earmarks of a Russian information operation run through the Hillary Clinton campaign."[20]

On July 30, 2016, Steele finally handed the dossier over to U.S. Department of Justice lawyer Bruce Ohr at the Mayflower Hotel off Dupont Circle in Washington, DC, telling him, according to Ohr, "that the former head of the Russian foreign intelligence service had said that they had Trump over a barrel."[21] Steele told Ohr his source was a former Russia Foreign Ministry official. Only Trubnikov fit that description.[22]

A DoJ investigation would later conclude that Russian intelligence "'infiltrated a source into the network' of a [REDACTED] who compiled a dossier of information on Trump's activities."[23] In DoJ's assessment, it appeared that this was all "part of a Russian disinformation campaign."[24]

Two months after Steele's meetings with Ohr and Kavalec, ONA Director James H. Baker and WHS Director Barbara A. Westgate sent Halper $282,292. How much of it, if any, went to Trubnikov isn't clear, but everyone in the business knows that senior Russian spies don't work for free.

• • •

Another government report flagged Steele's frequent contacts with representatives of Russian oligarchs, suggesting that they too had contributed to his work product. That made sense, since Putin confidant Andrei Cheglakov was by then also funding Halper and his Cambridge Intelligence Seminar colleagues.[25] As a former MI6 Russia specialist, Steele knew that Russian intelligence routinely employs Russian nationals to propagate disinformation.[26] That did not stop him from employing Russian national Igor Danchenko, who would later testify that he was "responsible for 80 percent of the raw intelligence in the dossier and half of the accompanying analysis."[27]

A DoJ report based on FBI fieldwork found that the Russian Foreign Intelligence Service may have compromised Danchenko and his work product for Steele, and that at least one of Danchenko's sources for the dossier had a Russian intelligence *kurator*, or handler. That made sense.

In 2005, according to an FBI report, Danchenko had made "contact with a Washington, DC–based Russian officer" and they "seemed very familiar with each other."[28] In 2006, the FBI reported that Danchenko "had contact in 2006 with the Russian Embassy and known Russian intelligence officers."

Danchenko also said he was "interested in entering the Russian diplomatic service one day."[29] But Russian intelligence presumably waved Danchenko off from joining the government. He would attract too much scrutiny that way. So, in 2008, Danchenko went to work for Strobe Talbott, Bill Clinton's former deputy secretary of state, at the prestigious Brookings Institution in Washington, DC.

A now-declassified CIA report found that in the 1980s, a decade before Trubnikov became head of SVR, Soviet intelligence had identified Brookings as a target ripe for infiltration.[30] Washington, DC, is one of America's most expensive cities, and low-level think tank staff are paid a pittance. Nevertheless, Danchenko was flush.

He offered to pay his Brookings colleagues cash for classified information.[31] What he planned on doing with that information soon became clear.

According to an FBI report, Danchenko engaged a "Russian Intelligence Officer" to transfer documents to Moscow via the Russian embassy "diplomatic mail pouch" in October 2006.[32] After only a year at Brookings, the FBI designated Danchenko's activities "a threat to national security."[33]

At Brookings, Danchenko worked directly for Charles Dolan Jr. and Fiona Hill, who had introduced the two men. Hill, who later served as a senior director on the U.S. National Security Council and then testified against Trump in his impeachment hearings, would tell Congress the dossier was probably Russian-planted disinformation interspersed with truthful information, "because that's exactly, again, the way that they operate."[34] Putin's objective, Hill continued, was to "divide us against each other, degrade our institutions, and destroy the faith of the American people in our democracy" from within.[35]

"By inserting disinformation in publications, advocating extremist ideas, inciting racist and xenophobic flash mobs," Russian General Igor Dylevsky explained in April 2017, "it is possible to 'heat up' the situation in any country, all the way up to the point of social unrest." Moscow's arsenal of disinformation could "destabilize any society and dismantle any government."[36]

•   •   •

According to filings with the U.S. Department of Justice, Brookings researcher Dolan was himself a paid Russian agent.[37] For nearly a decade, Dolan conducted "global public relations for the Russian government," "attended meetings in the Kremlin," "attended at least three meetings at the Russian Embassy in Washington, DC, and communicated with Russian Embassy staff."[38] When he wasn't working for the Kremlin, Dolan worked for the Clintons. In 1992 and 1996 he was a state chairman for Bill Clinton's presidential campaigns. He then signed on to Hillary Clinton's 2008 and 2016 presidential campaigns.

Dolan assumed that Danchenko "worked for FSB," the successor agency to Russia's KGB, and U.S. law enforcement concurred.[39] An FBI counterintelligence investigation from 2009 to 2011 dug into Danchenko's "documented contacts with suspected Russian intelligence officers."[40] In what seems like a show of moral support for a trusted agent under duress, in the midst of Danchenko's investigation, Russian President Dmitry Medvedev paid a special visit to Brookings to thank think tank staff for their many years of friendship with Russia.[41]

Five years after Medvedev's visit, in September 2015 Clinton also visited Brookings to thank its staff for their support. There are "a lot of long-time friends and colleagues who perch here at Brookings," said the grateful Democratic presidential candidate.[42] In the midst of her presidential campaign, Clinton should have been trying win over centrist or right-leaning voters in key battleground states, so to visit a solidly Democratic think tank in Washington, DC, was unusual—unless, that is, Brookings was providing her invaluable election-year operational assistance.

Later, under oath, Christopher Steele testified that Brookings staff on Moscow's payroll, along with Halper and General Trubnikov, had all sourced Kremlin disinformation for the dossier. This was no low-level or fringe operation. As Fiona Hill would later attest, it went straight to the top. Brookings head Strobe Talbott had given Hill a copy of the dossier the day before it was first released to the public on January 10, 2017, by media outlet Buzzfeed.[43] From there the *New York Times, Washington Post,* CNN, the *New Yorker,* and *Yahoo!News* picked up and ran with the story.

Danchenko mixed facts with fiction in a January 2017 FBI interview, perhaps because he had been trained by Russian intelligence to do so. "Every disinformation message must at least partially correspond to reality or generally accepted views," is how Ladislav Bittman, a former Czech intelligence officer and scholar of Russian propaganda, described that tradecraft.[44] Later Danchenko claimed that much of what he put in the dossier was "word-of-mouth and hearsay" picked up from "friends over beers."[45]

• • •

While a suspected Russian agent at a U.S. think tank merited an FBI counterintelligence investigation, a "known Russian intelligence officer" writing reports for the Office of the Secretary of Defense did not. This was by design. The Obama administration had spent eight years emplacing a formidable cadre of ideological operatives into key offices of the U.S. law enforcement, intelligence, and national security bureaucracies to weaken America and its liberal democratic allies and strengthen America's adversaries.

One such operative was Charles McGonigal, Peter Strzok's boss. As chief of the FBI's New York City counterintelligence department, McGonigal was perfectly positioned to tip off Moscow. James Comey had appointed him to that office a few months after Comey issued a "cease and desist" order to stop investigating the Clinton Foundation, on the basis of some undisclosed counterintelligence concern.[46]

In January 2023 McGonigal was arrested and indicted for taking cash from a Russian oligarch who, according to the DoJ, had "acted or purported to act on behalf of a senior official of the Government of the Russian Federation."[47] McGonigal was not alone. As the DoJ would later suggest, cozy long-running relationships like that between Halper and Trubnikov all but assured "that other individuals—including hostile foreign intelligence services—would learn of and attempt to influence" the contents of the Clinton- and DNC-funded dossier.[48]

Clinton had used "hostile foreign intelligence services" in her scheme to "vilify Donald Trump by stirring up a scandal claiming interference by the Russian security service."[49] As Obama's CIA director John Brennan disclosed to Congress, that had serious consequences: "Russian agencies routinely seek to gather compromising information, or 'kompromat,' to coerce treason from U.S. officials."[50]

In Clinton's case, had she won the presidential election, Putin would have dispatched an envoy to quietly tell her one on one that he knew her little secret. After that, the Russian operative would start making demands, threatening to expose her if she failed to cooperate. It was this concern over what Putin knew about Clinton, not what she was doing to deceive the American people as they went to the polls to choose the next president of the United States, that prompted the Brennan-Obama-Biden-Comey Oval Office meeting on August 3, 2016.[51]

•   •   •

Upon appointment to high office, each of these men had placed their right hands gently on the Bible. Then they had promised hundreds of millions of Americans, as well as their own spouses, children, and close friends assembled before them, that they would protect the Republic against all enemies, foreign and domestic.

Ultimately Obama and his spy chiefs would choose concealment and dissimulation over transparency and truth. Clinton was not elected, so her vulnerability to Russian blackmail was now arguably moot. Obama might have honorably asked Clinton about whether she was lying to the American people and urged her to come clean. But he demurred.

There was a time when it was the "cover-up," not the "crime," that got politicians into hot water. No longer. That quaint adage is from another era. When the truth did finally emerge about what Clinton and Obama had done, the Democratic Party, mainstream media, and the rest of the Establishment shrugged, forgave all, and moved on. To this day, Obama and Clinton remain wealthy and powerful pillars of America's ruling class.

Three days after Brennan's Oval Office briefing on Putin's possession of *kompromat* on Clinton, Obama unleashed a multi-part strategy. The objective was to mislead the American people and preemptively discredit anyone who uncovered Clinton's fabrication of the Trump-Russia collusion narrative. Step one was to open two of what would ultimately become a dozen or so Russiagate-related investigations.[52]

• • •

On July 31, 2016, Comey opened Crossfire Hurricane against Trump and his campaign. The U.S. Department of Justice has issued contradictory statements on the predicate used to launch that counterintelligence investigation. On one hand, DoJ has denied that the Steele Dossier played a role in launching that investigation.[53] But it has also conceded that Crossfire Hurricane was a "full investigation," and that does not get launched when there is no legitimate predicate evidencing wrongdoing, as the DoJ later determined:

> [T]he record reflects, as of early 2017, the FBI still did not possess any intelligence showing that anyone associated with the Trump campaign was in contact with Russian intelligence officers during the campaign.[54]

That inconsistency is reconciled by Comey's reliance on inputs from Stefan A. Halper, who by August 11, 2016, was working for the FBI director.[55] A 2015 letter from ONA's Andrew D. May to Comey suggests that May had introduced Halper to Comey. In that letter, May asked Comey for his assistance in helping ONA contractors perform *domestic* operations. That was unusual for several reasons.

For one, May is a career civil servant, and considerably junior to the FBI director. Stranger yet, May's job is to lead the research effort of the Pentagon's highest-level strategy office. His is a non-operational role, focused on long-term international competition—not the FBI's purview of domestic law enforcement matters.

Comey's hiring of Halper seemed to have nothing to do with national security or law enforcement. His very own FBI security office had suspended Halper's Confidential Human Source status on the grounds of his "mercurial" temperament, "aggressiveness toward [his FBI] handling agents," and untrustworthiness.[56] None of that, nor Halper's earlier arrest in Virginia for possessing crack cocaine, stood in the way of Comey's selecting Halper as the right man to "investigate" purported Trump-Russia collusion.[57]

In addition to questions about a lawful predicate for Crossfire Hurricane, and about Halper's judgment and trustworthiness, there was another legal hurdle Comey had to deal with. Halper had played a central role in generating the Steele Dossier, which Comey conceded to Congress was "salacious and unverified."[58]

Halper was also the intermediary between Christopher Steele's team, on the one hand, and General Trubnikov and his comrades in Russia's Intelligence Service, on the other. As an experienced lawyer, Comey knew that prevented Halper from investigating the matter on the grounds of an unbridgeable conflict of interest. A U.S. Senate investigation would later conclude:

> [B]eginning early on and continuing throughout the FBI's Russia investigation, FBI officials learned critical information streams that flowed to the dossier were likely tainted with Russian Intel-

ligence disinformation. Despite later intelligence reports that key elements of the FBI's evidence were the result of Russian infiltration to undermine U.S. foreign relations, the FBI still pushed forward with its probe.[59]

Finally, there was the problem of political motive. Comey was "investigating" Trump and his campaign for precisely what he, by then, knew Clinton's team was guilty of. Within days of the launch of Crossfire Hurricane, CIA Director Brennan had informed Comey that Clinton and the DNC had paid for the Steele Dossier to generate the Trump-Russian collusion narrative. In hindsight, like the other dozen or so investigations against Trump and his campaign, Crossfire Hurricane seemed designed to wield the awesome powers of U.S. spy agencies to project and deflect.

Not everyone in the FBI approved of Comey's weaponization of the federal investigative process. In testimony before Congress, Kevin Brock, former FBI assistant director for intelligence and principal deputy of the National Counterterrorism Center (NCTC), characterized Crossfire Hurricane as "unconscionable and a direct abuse of FBI authorities."[60]

The U.S. Department of Justice Office of the Inspector General agreed with that assessment. On May 12, 2023, the DoJ OIG conceded that "materials...[relied on by the FBI to launch Crossfire Hurricane] were part of a political effort to smear a political opponent [Trump] and to use the resources of the federal government's law enforcement and intelligence agencies in support of a political objective."[61]

Suggesting that Comey knew he had abused his authority, a DoJ investigation later indicated that Comey had committed multiple felonies. That included leaking information to the press about an ongoing investigation and willfully storing classified information at his home.[62] Of course, Comey was never held to account.

CHAPTER 14

RUSSIAN DISINFORMATION BECOMES A U.S. INTELLIGENCE PRODUCT

*The means of defense against foreign danger have been
always the instruments of tyranny at home.*

—James Madison[1]

Soon after Comey launched his counterintelligence investigation against the Trump campaign, Brennan stepped up to do his bit. In August 2016, the CIA director presented a series of deliberately misleading briefings to select lawmakers in the "Gang of Eight," senior members of the Senate and House intelligence committees. By then, Brennan was an expert at deceiving Congress and subverting its Constitutional oversight function.

In March 2014, CIA Director Brennan had denied under oath that the CIA had spied on Congress. "Nothing could be further from the truth," he said. "We wouldn't do that. That's just beyond the scope of reason in terms of what we'd do."[2] That same month a CIA internal investigation found that Agency operatives had hacked the computers of the U.S. Senate Select Committee on Intelligence. Senator Grassley concluded a month later that those actions "raised serious policy concerns as well as potential Constitutional separation-of-powers issues that must be discussed publicly."[3]

After one of Brennan's August 2016 "Gang of Eight" meetings, then–Senate Minority Leader Harry Reid demanded that FBI Director Comey launch a "full examination" of Trump-Russia collusion, which Comey did. Reid publicly reported on Comey's findings on October 30, 2016, nine days before the presidential election: "It has become clear that you possess explosive information about close ties and coordination between Donald Trump, his top advisors and the Russian government."[4] Had Reid transposed "Hillary Clinton" for "Donald Trump," he would have been barking up the right tree.

Obama seems to have participated directly in that deception of Congress and the American public. Between meetings with the "Gang of Eight" in August 2016, Brennan put on a show designed to generate a buzz in the West Wing. By special courier from CIA Headquarters in Langley, Virginia, he sent to Obama a CIA-generated intelligence product summarizing the Steele Dossier.[5] To heighten its visibility, Brennan extravagantly marked it "Eyes Only,"[6] meaning it was too sensitive for inclusion in the CIA's Presidential Daily Briefing.

Obama appears to have played along with Brennan for the purpose of generating plausible deniability. Both men took exaggerated security precautions to obscure their reliance on a dossier paid for by Clinton and the DNC and sourced to Russian intelligence. Since Obama himself was in on this part of the charade, four other precautions were taken.

The first was to have Susan Rice, Avril Haines, and Denis McDonough also read Brennan's report. This move seems to have backfired to some extent. As she had done before, Rice refused to be used to advance the schemes of her boss. A declassified congressional transcript from September 2017 suggests that Rice knew the dossier was Russian disinformation or, at the very least, bogus. In that testimony Rice said she had seen no evidence that Trump had colluded, conspired, or coordinated, with Russia.[7]

Another precaution was for Obama to distance himself from knowingly propagating a Russian disinformation campaign by giving Putin a symbolic slap on the wrist. He did that by expelling thirty-five Russian diplomats, closing two Russian compounds in the U.S., and imposing non-substantive economic sanctions.

The third precaution was for Brennan to phone Alexander Bortnikov, director of Russia's FSB, Russia's internal intelligence agency, and warn him against interfering in the U.S. presidential election.[8] The call was bizarre on its face. Russian elections interference in the U.S. wasn't run by the FSB, which is Russia's rough equivalent to the FBI, but by the SVR, General Trubnikov's old outfit.

Both Brennan and Bortnikov knew this perfectly well. But for Brennan that was beside the point. Bortnikov played right along with the scheme. By not pointing out that Brennan had called the wrong agency, Bortnikov was doing Brennan a favor—generating a "chit" Bortnikov could "cash in" with Brennan or Obama at some later date. For example, Bortnikov could use his "chit" to have them lobby a future secretary of defense to keep May and Baker at the helm of ONA. That was not strategically insignificant.

Thanks to May and Baker, Trubnikov's half-decade collaboration with Halper had provided Putin an invaluable insider's view of Russiagate. Specifically, Halper's and Trubnikov's roles in generating the Steele Dossier kept Putin fully apprised of Clinton's activities, which the Russian leader could use to blackmail her should she win the presidency. Even more valuable was the contracting vehicle in the heart of the Pentagon through which Trubnikov accessed details of ONA's research agenda and gleaned precious insights into the Pentagon's long-term strategy. That was a massive intelligence and strategic coup for Moscow.

On November 1, 2016, Comey fired Christopher Steele as an FBI source after he was deemed "completely untrustworthy" by his FBI handler.[9] Nevertheless, a few months later, the forty-fourth president of the United States directed his spy chiefs to turn the Russian disinformation–filled Steele Dossier into the U.S. government's January 2017 Intelligence Community Assessment (ICA), Annex A.[10]

That Russian propaganda could be transformed into an official U.S. intelligence product was one thing. But for a president and his top aides to conspire in doing so, and to conceal from the American people what they knew about the Clinton-commissioned dossier as they went to vote for the next president of the United States, elevates the notion of "insider threat" to new heights.

Brennan testified to Congress under oath that the dossier was "not in any way used as the basis for the [ICA]"[11] and that he had no idea that the Clinton campaign and the DNC had funded it. That is precisely the opposite of what he told Obama on August 3, 2016.

Similarly, then–Director of National Intelligence James Clapper testified that "some of the substantive content [of the dossier] we were able to corroborate in our Intelligence Community Assessment."[12] Later, because he knew Russian disinformation was fruit from a poisonous tree and corroborated nothing, Clapper conceded that "we couldn't corroborate the sourcing" for the ICA.[13]

•   •   •

To insert the Steele Dossier into the ICA required turning normal governmental processes on their heads. Standard operating procedure was for all seventeen U.S. intelligence agencies to collaborate in producing the ICA. But that much oversight would make it difficult if not impossible to corrupt the ICA's content. Clapper testified to the Senate on May 8, 2017, that the ICA was a closely held inside job, prepared by "two dozen or so analysts—hand-picked, seasoned experts from each of the contributing agencies."[14] That was false.

Unusually, the Defense Intelligence Agency and the State Department's Bureau of Intelligence and Research were excluded from the

ICA process, while FBI was included.[15] Given that key bureaus from the intelligence community were excepted, the report was not an actual "intelligence community assessment."

Peter Strzok was James Comey's representative to the ICA fusion team. On July 21, 2016, he had texted Lisa Page, the FBI lawyer with whom he was having an affair: "Trump is a disaster. I have no idea how destabilizing his Presidency would be."[16]

For Strzok, there was no such thing as a conflict of interest. Inside FBI headquarters, it was known that Strzok not only refused to recuse himself from issues touching on the Clintons, he actively sought them out. Strzok led the FBI investigation of Clinton's use of her personal email system to transmit classified material.

Strzok and Page came up with a special communications system. "So look," Strzok said to Page, "we text on that phone when we talk about Hillary because it can't be traced."[17] Later, Strzok determined that "we know foreign actors obtained access to some of her [Clinton's] emails (including at least one Secret one) via compromises of the private email accounts."[18] What followed was foreseeable.

Strzok doctored the final FBI report to whitewash what Clinton had done. Before Strzok tampered with it, that report had called Clinton's actions "grossly negligent."[19] But because that legal term of art could trigger criminal prosecution, Strzok deleted it. In its place he wrote "extremely careless," which carries no set legal consequence.[20]

In December 2018, U.S. District Court Judge Royce C. Lamberth described Clinton's actions in regard to her email usage as "one of the gravest modern offenses to government transparency."[21] Had he known then of her role in fomenting the Trump-Russia conspiracy theory, Judge Lamberth might have termed it the "second gravest modern offense."

•   •   •

Brennan, Comey, and Clapper[22] wrote in the January 2017 ICA, titled *Russian Activities and Intentions in Recent Elections*, that

> Putin and the Russian government aspired to help President-elect Trump's election chances when possible by discrediting Secretary Clinton.... We assess Moscow will apply lessons learned from its Putin-ordered campaign aimed at the U.S. election to future influence efforts worldwide.[23]

Even junior intelligence analysts knew that to claim to know what Putin "aspired" to do was an analytical red flag. It might have passed the laugh test with Senator Reid or President Obama, but not with an experienced intelligence officer like Admiral Mike Rogers, the head of the National Security Agency (NSA).

After reading the ICA, Admiral Rogers did what any non-corrupt spy chief would do. He had his staff comb NSA intercepts for indicators of collusion between the Trump campaign and Russians. They did, found insufficient evidence, and admitted they "had no insights into Steele's source network."[24]

Another giveaway to Rogers that something was amiss was Brennan's behavior under questioning. Rogers asked the CIA Director for the ICA's sourcing. "FBI and DOJ OIG investigations discovered that Steele's sources were sometimes several steps removed from the information they provided." That is how a U.S. Senate Select Committee on Intelligence report describes how "cut outs" Halper and Danchenko passed on information for the dossier from General Trubnikov and his colleagues in Russian intelligence.[25] But instead of disclosing that, Brennan refused to answer Rogers's sourcing questions.[26]

Ultimately, the process of generating the 2017 ICA report was corrupted. Typically, if an intelligence agency like the NSA discovers a significant irregularity (such as an assertion for which there is no evidence), that agency lodges a protest in what is called an Annex for Dissent. But there was no such annex to the ICA.[27] Rogers ultimately withheld the NSA's "high confidence" imprimatur from the report's determination that Putin had aspired to help Trump and hurt Clinton in their respective campaigns.[28]

By cutting out the other thirteen intelligence agencies, Brennan, Comey, and Clapper were able to strong-arm the ICA through the system to completion. A U.S. House Permanent Select Committee on Intelligence (HPSCI) investigation would later find that there were "significant intelligence tradecraft failings" in the preparation the ICA, and that the "Intelligence Community Assessment Judgments on Putin's strategic intentions [that is, his favoring Trump over Clinton] did not employ proper analytic tradecraft."[29]

Ultimately, the primary purpose of the 2017 ICA was to serve as cover for Obama and his spy chiefs. Once the ICA was published, they could point to it and say, *Look, U.S. intelligence agencies found these sources to be worthy of an official intelligence product, so they must be credible.*

The whole process was conducted with a ferocity suggesting that reputations and livelihoods depended on it. That fear may not have been unfounded.

CHAPTER 15

AN EXISTENTIAL THREAT TO THE DEEP STATE

Obama and his spy chiefs knew that within weeks of Trump's inauguration, U.S. National Security Advisor Flynn would methodically peel back the layers of the deception on the American people. They knew Flynn would discover how Obama and his spy chiefs had conspired to mislead the American people about that scheme as they headed to the polls to cast their vote.

What's more, Flynn, perhaps better than anyone, knew that those actions made Clinton, Obama, Biden, Brennan, Comey, and Clapper all vulnerable to various forms of Russian blackmail. As one of the new president's most trusted advisors, Flynn would have the power and authority to hold these figures to account.

After Trump hired Flynn against their wishes, Obama and his spy chiefs went on the offensive. To dig up whatever dirt they could find, between November 30, 2016, and January 17, 2017, about forty *different* senior officials[1] in the Obama administration would make unmasking requests of Flynn's identity from classified intercepts.[2] That singular focus on one person only happens when the order comes straight from the top.

Among Obama's spy chiefs, Comey seemed most threatened by Flynn. This led him to advise the president to "not pass sensitive information related to Russia to Flynn" that made up the 2017 Intelligence Community Assessment on Russia.[3] Yet Comey's suggestion came off as overly desperate. Withholding information on one of America's greatest geopolitical rivals from an incoming national security advisor would immediately raise red flags. It could be interpreted as an admission of guilt in any subsequent proceedings.

While Brennan and Comey continued to try their best to finesse Flynn, Obama directed them to brief the phony ICA to the Presidential Transition Team. Flynn immediately spotted the ICA as a fraud. The incoming national security advisor demanded to know the identities of the sources for Annex A, which contained the Steele Dossier. Brennan, Comey, and Clapper rebuffed Flynn's eminently reasonable request. For them that was the bureaucratic equivalent of a "kill or be killed" moment.

•   •   •

Presidential transitions are always chaotic, but the transition to the incoming Trump administration, with its abundance of outsiders unfamiliar with Washington's byzantine ways, was particularly so. That opened a window of opportunity for Obama and his spy chiefs. After eight years in office, they had the organizational advantage. Like a pack of hyenas hunting a solitary lion, they would ambush Flynn and then overwhelm him when he tried to fight back. He didn't stand a chance. But first they had to find the right hook that would allow them to weaponize their federal powers. As I and countless other Deep State targets learned first hand, that begins with generating falsehoods.

On January 4, 2017, FBI investigators reported to Comey that after an in-depth investigation of Flynn, they had found "no derogatory information." Nor were there any leads to possibilities for further investigation.[4] That meant the Flynn investigation, a subset of the Crossfire Hurricane investigation called Crossfire Razor, should have been closed. But it wasn't.

Without a legal predicate or even a credible explanation of any kind, Comey ordered that the Flynn investigation be kept open. "7th Floor involved," the ubiquitous Peter Strzok texted Lisa Page, in reference to the FBI headquarters leadership suite overlooking Pennsylvania Avenue. Relaying Comey's orders, Strzok directed his FBI subordinates, "Don't close RAZOR."[5]

Comey could justify keeping Crossfire Razor open because by then he was receiving a stream of information from ONA operative Stefan Halper.[6] Comey had hired Halper to investigate Flynn in parallel with Crossfire Hurricane. The two "investigations" were intertwined from the start.

"Svetlana Lokhova, supposedly this is Flynn's girlfriend. This is the reason that they open up an investigation on General Flynn," is how House Intelligence Committee Ranking Member Devin Nunes described the predicate Halper furnished Comey and which the FBI chief then used to launch and keep open Crossfire Razor.[7] That was in reference to a February 28, 2014, dinner hosted in DIA Director Flynn's honor by Christopher Andrew and Sir Richard Dearlove in the Master's dining room of Pembroke College, Cambridge.

By then Halper had established a lucrative practice of educating U.S. military personnel stationed at the nearby Royal Air Force base at Molesworth. The purpose of the dinner was to convince Flynn to fund the Cambridge Intelligence Seminar, which by then was a front for Russian intelligence.

Svetlana Lokhova was born in Russia, but she left the country to study history at Cambridge, where she earned undergraduate and postgraduate degrees. In Halper's telling, Flynn and Lokhova had left that dinner and spent the night together. That accusation was absurd on its face.

DIA had investigated Lokhova, who was by then a British citizen, and signed off on her attendance at the dinner. Furthermore, as Comey knew all too well, DIA directors traveling abroad are provided a robust security detail, which watches their every move and guards them while they sleep. For Flynn to have slept with a Russian without setting off major alarm bells was not possible.

Perhaps most absurd of all, the alleged amorous rendezvous had taken place nearly three years before. Since that time, Flynn's Top Secret/SCI security clearance had been reinvestigated and renewed. Had he slept with a Russian, that would have been prominently noted in his security file, investigated, adjudicated, and likely resulted in his removal from federal service. But none of that had happened. With the U.S. taxpayer footing the bill for his services, Halper made up that story to fulfill Comey's agenda.

Comey had nothing on Flynn. That was the purpose of Halper's fictive work product. For Comey, the fact that Halper was a "cut-out" for Russian intelligence was irrelevant. By abusing the FBI's investigative authorities, Comey got the dirt he needed to get Flynn removed as U.S. national security advisor.

•   •   •

In *America Alone*, Halper cloaked his worldview in professions of high principle, bemoaning the "encroachment on civil liberties, domestic polarization, and reduced security" that he saw as byproducts of the Bush administration's "War on Terror." Halper did not divulge his own efforts to undermine U.S. national security, aggravate "domestic polarization," and subvert presidential elections.

Problematic for Comey was that Halper had no firsthand knowledge of the events described in his memo: Halper had not even attended the Pembroke College dinner. To mitigate the threat of the DoJ or Congress investigating Comey for relying on hearsay from a serial liar, the FBI director took his moves out of the Deep State playbook. This meant setting traps for Lokhova in England, and for Flynn in his West Wing office.

Comey's fingerprints were all over the setup. So, too, were those of FBI officials Peter Strzok and Lisa Page. FBI technicians were directed to equip Halper with a "wire." "You get all our oconus lures approved?)," Page texted Strzok in December 2015.[8] "Oconus" is shorthand for "outside the continental United States"—Page was referring to spying operations authorized by the Foreign Intelligence Surveillance Court (FISC).

As Lokhova recounted to me over a lunch meeting in 2020 in Washington, DC, Professor Christopher Andrew had phoned her on January 12, 2017, and invited her to dine with Halper and Andrew at Halper's home. By then Andrew had mentored the talented young émigré from Russia for two decades. He was like a father to her.

Halper had tasked Andrew to lure Lokhova into an in-person meeting and then turn the conversation to whether she had slept with Flynn. "What Halper staged is a textbook 'black op' to dirty up the reputation of a political opponent," Lokhova would recount later. "He needed an innocuous social event to place Flynn in a room with a woman who was ethnically Russian. I was unlucky to be picked."[9]

Halper's aim seems to have been to smear Flynn via Lokhova by selectively reporting misleading bits and pieces of his recorded conversation with her to the FBI, taking statements out of context and doctoring the evidence to create the illusion of a romantic or otherwise embarrassing encounter. As FISC presiding judge Rosemary Collyer would later find, FBI officials were routinely either grossly negligent or intentionally weaponizing federal process:

> The frequency with which representations made by F.B.I. personnel turned out to be unsupported or contradicted by information

in their possession, and with which they withheld information detrimental to their case, calls into question whether information contained in...F.B.I. applications is reliable.[10]

Andrew had not told Lokhova that Halper would be sporting an FBI "wire" for the occasion. Yet sensing that Andrew was up to no good, she declined the invitation to Halper's home, leaving Andrew "outraged." The meeting never took place. Without the Halper-Lokhova contact, they would need to finesse the next phase of their scheme.

On February 19, 2017, Andrew maligned Lokhova in the *Sunday Times* as a Russian spy who had seduced Flynn.[11] Addressing that article, a former Soviet dissident told me that more journalistic integrity could be found in *Pravda*, the former USSR's official newspaper, than in the *Times*.

Unlike Halper, Andrew had attended the Pembroke College dinner. From an evidentiary standpoint, that meant he had critical firsthand knowledge of the event. But while his article grossly mischaracterized what had transpired, it served its purpose, setting off a political firestorm on both sides of the Atlantic. While those flaps soon passed, the personal consequences of that article were devastating for Lokhova.

When I met her in 2020, she was clearly still haunted by her mentor's betrayal. After Andrew publicly smeared her as a Russian agent, Lokhova received death threats and her academic career went into a tailspin. She fled England for America with her husband and infant daughter. As Lokhova sat before me revisiting that sordid scheme in her mind's eye, she paused. Looking up from my note-taking, I could see she was fighting back tears. Christopher Andrew maintained his position in British society as Cambridge University Emeritus Professor of Modern and Contemporary History.

CHAPTER 16

THE KILL SHOT

Although Obama forced Flynn to step down from leading the Defense Intelligence Agency in 2014, the president otherwise left Flynn's professional reputation intact. By January 5, 2017, Obama had decided he would prevent Flynn from ever returning to high office. On that day, the president assembled his senior staff in the Oval Office to discuss how they could malign Flynn by tying him to Russia.

To do that, they would mischaracterize a phone call that had taken place on the heels of the 2016 election between Russian Ambassador Sergey Kislyak and the incoming national security advisor. On that call, Kislyak relayed some threats from Putin to President-Elect Trump. Flynn responded by warning Kislyak not to act recklessly or harm U.S. interests.

In September 2017, Obama's former national security advisor Susan Rice testified before Congress that there was no evidence of any improper relations between Flynn and Moscow.[1] She also expressed surprise that Obama knew so much about that routine phone call. Such weedy operational matters typically fell outside a president's awareness and scope of concern.

Obama was now well down the path of deceiving the American people. Long before the election, Brennan had told him that the Trump-Russia collusion narrative had been fabricated by Hillary

Clinton. To elevate and sanitize that deception, Obama got the Steele Dossier inserted into his 2017 Intelligence Community Assessment.

As Sally Yates, Obama's deputy attorney general, wrote in a memorandum for the file, Obama "specified that he did not want any additional information on the matter,"[2] so that he could claim plausible deniability and absolve himself of all responsibility to correct what he could later characterize as an error arising from insufficient information, or a mistake made largely by others, not him. It also distracted observers from the dirty trick he was about to play on Flynn.[3]

The mere existence of the Flynn-Kislyak call accomplished much of the Obama team's political purpose. Vice President Biden suggested that they could argue Flynn had violated the Logan Act, a law which dates to 1799 and forbids private citizens from conducting U.S. foreign relations. Charging the senior foreign policy advisor to a newly elected president of the United States with violating that possibly unconstitutional statute from a bygone era that had never been used to prosecute anyone was absurd on its face. But to Team Obama, the ends justified the means.

By early January 2017, with just a few days of the Obama administration remaining, Director of National Intelligence James Clapper was in the final stages of pulling off the "kill shot" he would use to take out Flynn. A meticulous planner, he double-checked what he thought he knew and on January 7, 2017, ordered, for a second time, the unmasking of the NSA intercept of the Flynn-Kislyak call. It all checked out. Then he outsourced his perfidy to the media. On January 12, 2017, *Washington Post* columnist David Ignatius published the Flynn-Kislyak transcript, parroting Biden's dubious legal theory that Flynn had violated the Logan Act.[4] The mainstream media had a field day.

One hundred and forty-three pages of records obtained under the Freedom of Information Act by the government watchdog group

Judicial Watch suggest that Clapper used ONA's James H. Baker and Deputy Secretary of Defense Robert O. Work to communicate with Ignatius. A *Washington Examiner* investigation reinforced that conclusion, reporting that Work was briefed on the Flynn-Kislyak NSA intercept and passed on that Top Secret/SCI transcript to Baker, who leaked it to Ignatius.[5] This was also the general view within ONA.

Baker has written of having "a long history with David" Ignatius, his "friend," to whom Baker spoke with regularly. In fact long-time staff found Baker's frenzied meetings with Ignatius during the lead-up to the 2016 presidential election disconcerting. Why would the head of an office charged with conducting long-term strategy meet so often with a journalist? To Andrew W. Marshall, Baker's tight-lipped predecessor, disclosing internal ONA products to a reporter known for publishing the nation's most closely guarded classified information was unthinkable.

What is more, the entire ONA office is a sensitive compartmented information facility (SCIF) with work conducted at the Top Secret/SCI level. Everyone at ONA knew that Ignatius had neither the required security clearances nor a "need to know." From extensive government briefings, ONA staff also knew that many news reporters make extra money from foreign interests in exchange for skewed reporting. It was a threat about which frequent reminders were routinely issued. "Team," Baker himself warned ONA staff on May 28, 2015, "as I have mentioned before, I believe our office presents a consistently interesting and lucrative target for adversary intelligence."

But Baker wasn't concerned so much about the threat to U.S. national security as about covering his own tracks and not getting caught. "David, please," Baker warned Ignatius in an email later released to the public under FOIA, "as always, our discussions are completely off the record." Ignatius responded, "Understood. Thanks for talking with me."

• • •

Baker's commitment to Obama's "Russia reset" continued long after Obama left the White House. In July 2017, after eight years of Putin's imperial conquests under Obama, Baker once again delivered one of his canned speeches to a perplexed foreign delegation. In that address, Baker minimized the threat posed to America by our strategic adversaries and echoed Russia's propagandistic description of itself as a good neighbor:

> Russia and Iran also do not possess the means, and are unlikely to ever possess the means, to permanently change the borders of their neighbors, or to dominate them economically.... There are many retarding factors to aggressive revisionism, including the attitude of most states, the value most elites place on the given ruleset, norms around non-aggression....[6]

Baker concluded his doublespeak-filled address by assuring his audience, preposterously, that "open Russian military adventurism is unlikely if NATO maintains even a semblance of alliance, given the risks for Putin."[7]

Like Baker, David Ignatius supported the idea of a Middle East balance of power comprising America, Israel, and Saudi Arabia on one hand, and Russia and Iran on the other. Ignatius deemed Obama's "Iran Deal" a "great strategic opportunity" that would create a "new regional framework that accommodates the security needs of Iranians, Saudis, Israelis, Russians and Americans."[8] As with Obama and Baker, the reporter's concern for Russia's regional security "needs" suggested an accommodationist sensitivity to Putin's imperial aspirations far beyond Russia's borders.

But what Work, Baker, and Ignatius seemed to fear most was the threat Flynn posed to their operation. Flynn and his closest advisors had long planned on jettisoning the Obama Doctrine, which ensured Iran's acquisition of nuclear weapons. Phase one of their plan was for the U.S. to broker a warm peace between Israel and its Sunni neighbors. Years later that became known as the "Abraham Accords." Phase two was for the U.S. to help the Iranian people free themselves from their tyrannical rulers. Yet while Flynn's policies threatened Obama's foreign policy legacy, it was nothing compared to the existential threat he posed to the Deep State itself.

During the 2016 presidential campaign, Flynn made clear his commitment to reforming and dismantling the Deep State–military contractor nexus. As he saw it, that nexus ensured that America would continue to lose its wars. Obama had removed him as Defense Intelligence Agency director, but as Trump's national security advisor he could finally root out that corruption. This posed an existential threat to the Deep State.

·   ·   ·

While DNI James Clapper boasted how he would use the Ignatius article on the Flynn-Kislyak call as his "kill shot," FBI Director Comey seemed unconvinced of its efficacy to remove the newly installed national security advisor.

To finish Flynn off for good, Comey did "something I probably wouldn't have done or wouldn't have gotten away with in a more organized administration.... And I thought, it's early enough. Let's just send a couple of guys over"[9] to entrap Flynn in a process foul, like getting him to say something that contradicted something he had said previously, which Comey knew he could then characterize as a lie.

One of Comey's "guys" was senior FBI official Peter Strzok. By then Strzok was well-acquainted with Flynn, as he had previously collaborated with Stefan A. Halper and Lisa Page to fabricate the story about Flynn and Cambridge academic Svetlana Lokhova. Strzok also led the FBI "task force" component of the fusion team that used Russian disinformation to fabricate Obama's 2017 Intelligence Community Assessment, which Flynn immediately spotted as fatally flawed.

Strzok interviewed Flynn on January 24, 2017. He then doctored the results of that interview to suggest Flynn had lied to him. Joseph Pientka, the FBI agent who accompanied Strzok in his interview of the national security advisor in his West Wing office, said Flynn had not lied to them.

So Strzok, who had final editorial control over the FBI report (called a "302"), simply re-wrote Pientka's conclusion to say the opposite. By then, that was Strzok's specialty. As we saw in chapter 15, he had doctored an FBI report to downgrade Clinton's actions from "grossly negligent" to "extremely careless."

On March 2, 2017, in an appearance before the House Permanent Select Committee on Intelligence, James Comey would reveal that Strzok had committed a crime. Contrary to Strzok's claims, the FBI Director told Congress that there was no evidence that Flynn had lied to the FBI. The U.S. Department of Justice concurred, and dismissed the case against Flynn for lying on the grounds that

> [t]he Government is not persuaded that the January 24, 2017, interview was conducted with a legitimate investigative basis and therefore does not believe Mr. Flynn's statements were material.... Moreover, we [sic] not believe that the Government can prove either the relevant false statements or their materiality.[10]

But by then it was too late. The damage to Flynn's career and personal reputation was devastating. Flynn was forced to resign from the Trump administration over his non-lie to the FBI and his innocuous call with Kislyak.

Getting rid of Flynn was mission critical for the Deep State because he had stumbled upon its secret plan. The thirty-three-year military veteran and top DoD intelligence officer immediately spotted Russian disinformation in the contents of the 2017 Intelligence Community Assessment (ICA). Was the Obama administration collaborating with Moscow to smear the new president of the United States? Refusing to disclose the ICA's sources was the tell. But after Flynn was dismissed from the White House, leaving his reputation in tatters, no one would listen to what he knew.

With Flynn out of the way, the ICA was released to the public. The path was now cleared for the Deep State to use it as the justification for its partisan guerilla war against the Trump administration, which would ultimately last years on end.

In May 2017, the ICA served as the predicate to appoint Robert Mueller as special counsel to investigate the Trump-Russia collusion claim. Mueller, who had himself hired Stefan A. Halper as an FBI Confidential Human Sources (CHS), took on this task despite the fact that by August 2016, Obama, Putin, Russia's Foreign Intelligence Service, and myriad officials in the CIA, FBI, DNI, and the Executive Office of the President all knew that Hillary Clinton had fabricated that allegation for partisan political purposes.

After an investigation lasting three long years, Mueller's team of forty FBI agents produced a 448-page document concluding that Russian officials "appeared not to have preexisting contacts and struggled to connect with senior officials around the President-Elect." Nor could the Mueller Investigation "establish that members of the Trump Campaign conspired or coordinated with the Russian government to interfere in the 2016 election." On November 18, 2021, CNN summed up the results in this way:

> Two special counsel investigations, multiple congressional inquiries, civil lawsuits in the U.S. and the United Kingdom, and an

internal Justice Department review have now fully unspooled the behind-the-scenes role that some Democrats played in this saga. They paid for the research, funneled information to Steele's sources, and then urged the FBI to investigate Trump's connections to Russia.[11]

In a July 2018 CNN interview, James Clapper described Obama's role in generating the Mueller investigation:

> If it weren't for President Obama, we might not have done the Intelligence Community Assessment that we did that set up a whole sequence of events which are still unfolding today, notably Special Counsel Mueller's investigation. President Obama is responsible for that. It was he who tasked us to do that Intelligence Community Assessment in the first place.[12]

In direct costs alone, the Mueller charade's burden on the taxpayer was $40 million. His report made no mention of Stefan Halper, nor did it mention Fusion GPS, the firm that had hired Christopher Steele.

The worthlessness of the investigation was put on display during a congressional hearing after its release. Mueller claimed amnesia or ignorance on 245 separate occasions in that hearing. On one such occasion, he denied any knowledge of the Steele Dossier, as if he had forgotten that the Steele Dossier, after being jammed into Obama's 2017 Intelligence Community Assessment, was the predicate for his special counsel investigation in the first place. Perhaps it was just too embarrassing to remember.

But the indirect costs of the Mueller "investigation" were orders of magnitude larger than the direct costs. Hundreds, if not thousands, of executive and legislative branch officials spent millions of hours on a ridiculous exercise, time they could otherwise have used to perform duties of genuine importance to the Republic.

The interminable Mueller saga also gave Hillary Clinton and her friends in the press an ongoing opportunity to mislead the public. She wrote an op-ed arguing that "[o]ur election was corrupted" and a "crime was committed against all Americans," but left out that it was she who had committed that crime.[13] In April 2019 she forecast authoritatively, if ironically, that "the Russians will interfere again in 2020."[14]

Clinton may have been signaling to Moscow what the Mueller report would conclude, though it didn't matter to them. The Kremlin's top priority was to ensure the success of the Obama Doctrine. It did that by empowering Deep State loyalists and their political allies.

· · ·

Russian spies aren't supposed to boast about their successes, but the opportunity to gloat over what Putin had effortlessly accomplished thanks to Deputy Secretary of Defense Robert O. Work, ONA Director James H. Baker, and Andrew D. May must have been irresistible to General V. I. Trubnikov.

On June 28, 2016, the normally staid Russian intelligence officer chose America's National Public Radio (NPR) to boast of his five-year effort to infiltrate and subvert America from within. "Today, to get any kind of secret paper, with the top-secret info, that's nothing," the former head of Russia's Foreign Intelligence Service boasted to his NPR interviewer. "It is essential to penetrate into the brains of those who are leading the countries."[15]

The following spring, for the final stage set of his long, illustrious, career, Putin's top spy chose the ornate Art Nouveau lobby of Moscow's grand Metropol Hotel. Moscow had helped Clinton orchestrate Russiagate from the beginning. Thus, as soon as it began, Trubnikov knew how it would end. Crossfire Hurricane, followed by the Mueller Investigation, would bitterly divide America for years.

The Americans had walked into Putin's trap. To celebrate his success, the normally dour Trubnikov permitted himself to have some fun with his National Public Radio interviewer.

"To be frank, I never expected that American society would be so deeply split. I never expected this. I considered this society more solid," said Trubnikov.

"You mentioned a split in American society and how surprising you find it. The fear in the United States is that Russia has also identified these divisions and is working to worsen them, to spread confusion, to make American democracy look bad. Is that true, do you think?" asked NPR's Mary Kelly.

"What for? In what sense Russia—what Russia gets from split American society?"

"If you weaken your adversary, that can work to your advantage."

"It is absolutely incorrect. It reminds me of very old anecdote about two neighbors. One neighbor has two cows, and his neighbor has only one cow. So the neighbor who has one cow does not think in terms to have another one, but that one cow of neighbor would die. This is perverted logic which exists, unfortunately. But be absolutely sure today's Russia, at least the bulk of politicians here, do not think in such terms."

"You don't believe that a weakened America is to Russia's advantage?"

"To have a weak partner does not mean that you become stronger."

"Former Russian spymaster Vyacheslav Trubnikov. Although ask any CIA guy, they'll tell you there's no former KGB,"[16] is how Kelly concluded her interview.

Trubnikov died peacefully on April 18, 2022. Five months later, the *Washington Post* reported that Moscow's orchestration of "Russiagate" had proven so breathtakingly successful that it would replicate that model to advance its interests across the globe: "Moscow planned to spend hundreds of millions of dollars [as] part of its covert campaign to weaken democratic systems and promote global political forces seen as aligned with Kremlin interests."[17]

CHAPTER 17

DEVIL'S ISLAND

Woe to those who say of the evil that it is good and of the good that
it is evil; who present the darkness as light, light as darkness;
who present bitterness as sweet and sweet as bitter.

—Isaiah 5: 20[1]

In college I studied the dystopian literature of Franz Kafka (1883–1924). In Kafka's *The Trial*, the protagonist, Josef K, a bank employee, is charged with an unspecified crime and finds himself subjected to a dark and bewildering legal ordeal. Like the reader, he expects he will receive some modicum of legal due process. At the very least, he assumes that facts will matter in deciding his case. But the clerks and functionaries he meets are astounded by such naiveté.

Everything about governmental process, we learn, is maddeningly upside down. Josef K has been accused of something, but the specific charges are occluded from view, and they seem to change from page to page. Justice delayed is not only justice denied; it is official policy. By the time he realizes that madmen control his destiny, it is too late.

As an undergraduate, and even more so as a law student, I never imagined that senior U.S. officials could, with impunity, put into place the kind of tyrannical system experienced by the fictional Josef K.

On May 1, 2017, Washington Headquarters Services Director Barbara A. Westgate suspended my security clearance and ended my job at the White House. She then summoned me to the Pentagon the following day. One of her clerks ushered me into her grand office. Bedecked with flags and military artwork, it reflected her power and authority over the careers of 125,000 DoD officials.

Seated at a long conference table, Westgate had her back to me and was talking to someone in a stern and authoritative tone. She then turned and saw me.

"Oh, Mr. Lovinger," she said, dropping her voice an octave. She beckoned me to sit next to her.

WHS General Counsel John Albanese was seated at the opposite end of the table. He introduced himself sheepishly as "just the lawyer." Two months earlier I had complained to him about the conflicts of interest and illegalities of the "investigations" of me, the seriousness of the corrupt circumstances around the leak, and the horrible damage that Baker, May, and Russell had knowingly done to U.S.-Japanese relations.

Locking eyes with me and speaking in a soft, lethargic voice, Westgate said, "I have concerns regarding your judgment, trustworthiness, and reliability while carrying out your official duties, specifically relating to your personal conduct, misuse of Information Technology systems, outside activities, and your improper handling and safeguarding of protected information."

"Those are all vague categories of allegations. Can you please tell me specifically what I did wrong?"

Albanese examined his fingernails. Westgate returned my gaze and grew flushed. I couldn't tell if she was becoming angry or excited. After that, like a cat pawing at a half-dead mouse, Westgate taunted me with intimations of what she knew but would not reveal.

"I'm trapped and just have to take it, right?" I asked Westgate.

Her response to me was an exaggerated smirk.

Looking at Albanese plaintively she said "Oof, my back pain is acting up again." He closed his eyes and nodded, indicating he had some non-official duty to attend to.

While I didn't know it at the time, Walsh's investigative findings had implicated Westgate directly in potential criminal misconduct and placed the WHS Director on official notice of her duty to turn the entire matter over to the DoD OIG. But Westgate refused to follow the law.

As I exited her office, Westgate explained to me that "as an administrative matter" I really had two choices. I could quit the civil service with my official record permanently tainted by falsehoods, or I could continue with "administrative due process." I chose the latter. With that, she and Albanese exchanged knowing glances and faint smiles. I would soon understand what they knew: there was no due process in "administrative due process."

I was shown the door and directed to report to Darren Irvine, who sat just down the hall. Irvine later replaced Westgate as WHS Director. Irvine told me that Westgate had some "very important work" for me. I was to work for her direct subordinate, WHS Executive Services head Karen Finnegan-Myers.

• • •

On paper, it is the WHS Executive Services bureau's job to write the very DoD rules Westgate violated when she bypassed DoD OIG to do her "investigations" into the leak of Japanese classified information. In reality, that office serves to hide what goes on in the Pentagon from the legislative branch. This is done by churning out such vast rivers of paper that congressional staff are deterred from even *trying* to conduct oversight. Corrupt bureaucrats also use that office to generate plausible deniability for themselves and their favored operatives, so that they might escape liability for their willful violations of U.S. law.

ONA's collaboration with WHS Executive Services was a case in point. Baker and May had done no annual net assessments for over a decade. This violated U.S. law. So one day, WHS issued a new directive, removing the word "shall" from the December 23, 2009, regulation expressly requiring ONA to produce net assessments. Problem solved. Don't like the law? Rewrite it.

The process can work in the opposite direction, too—functioning not to shield favored administrators, but to target disfavored U.S. officials. By incessantly amending old directives and releasing new ones, the people in charge can ensure that anyone in DoD could be held in violation of one or more directives at any time.

As Director of WHS Executive Services, Finnegan-Myers also administered the Freedom of Information Act for the Pentagon. Congress enacted that law to ensure more transparency and accountability in the federal government. But in practice, FOIA has served instead as a powerful weapon of concealment. Finnegan-Myers was an expert at this deconstructive reversal, a skill she developed in an earlier role working for Secretary of State Hillary Clinton.

As a FOIA lawyer at State, Finnegan-Myers received an email on December 6, 2012. A government watchdog group, Citizens for Responsibility and Ethics in Washington (CREW), had filed a FOIA request for information on Clinton's use of her private email to conduct official government business. Finnegan-Myers sat on that request for almost half a year, then, on May 10, 2013, her office informed CREW that there were "no responsive records" to that FOIA request. That was false. In January 2016, the U.S. State Department inspector general said that Finnegan-Myers's team's performance fit a pattern of "inaccurate and incomplete [FOIA] responses." U.S. District Court Judge Royce C. Lamberth was more direct:

> [T]he court questions, even now, whether they are acting in good faith. Did Hillary Clinton use her private email as secretary of state to thwart this lofty goal [Obama's announced standard for transparency]? Was the State Department's attempt to settle this FOIA case in 2014 an effort to avoid searching—and disclosing

the existence of—Clinton's missing emails? And has State ever adequately searched for records in this case? At best, State's attempt to pass-off its deficient search as legally adequate during settlement negotiations was negligence born out of incompetence. At worst, career employees in the State and Justice Departments colluded to scuttle public scrutiny of Clinton, skirt FOIA, and hoodwink this Court.[2]

Usually "negligence born out of incompetence," gets a person fired. Yet doggedly subverting FOIA to conceal the Clinton email scandal, a criminal act, earned Finnegan-Myers a promotion to lead the WHS Executive Services directorate and serve on the prestigious congressionally mandated FOIA Advisory Committee.

Just as Deputy Secretary of Defense Robert Work had appointed a U.S. Air Force maintenance officer to lead ONA, Finnegan-Myers had been installed to not only *not* do her job, but to actively subvert, at significant taxpayer expense, the purpose of the very office she had been appointed to lead.

By the time Westgate entrusted her subordinate with waging "administrative due process" against me, a federal judge had found Finnegan-Myers to have excessively redacted 143 pages of emails sent between Bob Work, Baker, and David Ignatius. Those emails were sent just prior to the January 12, 2017, Ignatius column insinuating that, by taking a call from Russian Ambassador Kislyak, Flynn had violated the Logan Act. Finnegan-Myers then concealed Jennifer Walsh's investigative report, which incriminated her boss, Barbara Westgate.[3] That gave Westgate the time she needed to generate false-hoods about me, suspend my clearance, and force me out of the government before the truth could catch up.

CHAPTER 18

DISCOVERING THE DEEP STATE PLAYBOOK

The principle of despotic government is subject to a continual corruption, because it is, even in its nature, corrupt. Other governments are destroyed by particular accidents, which do violence to the principles of each constitution.

—MONTESQUIEU[1]

In mid-September 2017, I found the Deep State playbook. It detailed the inner workings of "administrative due process." Another piece by Franz Kafka, his short story "In the Penal Colony," tells of the commandant of a prison who rules supreme as judge, jury, and executioner, all in one. This crushing omnipotence allows him to grind inmates down, exhaust them, and finally eliminate them, slowly and painfully.

These are also the tactics, techniques, and procedures (TTPs) of administrative due process. In my case, ten TTPs (out of dozens of available options) were used:

1 Always use conflicted subordinates.
2 Target an "insider threat."
3 Launch an investigation against him.
4 Suspend his security clearance.
5 Put him in limbo for months or years on end.
6 Launch further investigations to search for any usable speck of dirt.

7 Fabricate more tortured arguments and/or lies.

8 Expel him from U.S. government service.

9 Leak defamatory information to the press to destroy his professional reputation.

10 Ensure he can never return to government service again with what he now knows about Deep State TPPs and the malignant individuals who wield them.

A few days before discovering the Deep State playbook, I popped into the library of Adas Israel synagogue, in upper Northwest Washington, DC, to pick up my daughter from Hebrew school. Having arrived a bit early, I passed the time by perusing a shelf of newly arrived books. *The Affair: The Case of Alfred Dreyfus* by Jean-Denis Bredin caught my eye.

A contemporary of Kafka, the artillery officer Alfred Dreyfus enjoyed an exemplary career until he found himself in the crosshairs of a corrupt cabal, having been spuriously accused of passing military secrets to Germany. Two figures, Chief of the French Army's General Staff General Boisdeffre and Major-General Gonse, ensured there was no proper investigation for Dreyfus, giving their subordinates a free hand to isolate, contain, and destroy him. The story felt eerily familiar.

They fabricated a story, accused the Jewish Dreyfus of harboring "divided loyalties," and scapegoated him for the crimes of a fellow officer. To ensure maximum degradation of the man and his reputation, the French military leadership orchestrated an elaborate, public display of phony due process by military tribunal.

Dreyfus was paraded through the majestic grounds of the military school of Paris to Morland Court where, before an assembled crowd of hundreds of jeering spectators, his superior officers ripped his insignia from his uniform and broke his sword. Dreyfus was then exiled to a tropical penal colony on the menacingly named

"Devil's Island" off the coast of French Guiana and left to rot in solitary confinement, shackled in irons. A solid wall was erected to block any view of the ocean from his shoreside hut.

The specious excuse that he might attempt to escape incarceration was used to keep him locked up in these conditions. Deprived of medical treatment, he contracted myriad tropical diseases and developed bedsores from lying in his own waste. His tormentors intercepted and confiscated his wife's letters. This torture had a purpose—to provoke Dreyfus to insubordination, so that he could be accused of conduct unbecoming an officer , which would retroactively justify his punishment.

•   •   •

Compared to the physical and psychological torture inflicted on Dreyfus, my experience fighting administrative due process was a walk in the park. After Westgate expelled me from the NSC, she dispatched me to a bleak DoD facility in Northern Virginia called the Mark Center.

Before that time, my DoD performance record was officially designated "Exemplary"—the highest possible rating. Now, I was assigned to a non-descript office suite containing hundreds of empty desks and given my very own morale officer.

Edward Burbol, a soft-spoken former U.S. Air Force officer, warned his staff that I was an "insider threat" and they should treat me as such. While I was sitting with him in his office one day, he seemed to relax. In that unguarded moment, he let slip that he was following Westgate's instructions to make me do clerical work, far below my pay grade, as a form of punishment. Realizing he had said too much, he wrote to me by email "please don't misinterpret what I said about your detail and Ms. Westgate."

Newly enlightened about what Westgate was up to, I notified her that according to her own staff, the job she had designed for me constituted fraud, waste, and abuse. U.S. taxpayers were still paying my salary and deserved value for their money. Since Westgate was indifferent to that, I took it upon myself to find a job teaching military strategy to U.S. officers at the National Defense University that did not require a security clearance. But she refused to allow it:

Mr. Lovinger: On May 2, 2017, I directed you, orally and in writing, to report to Darren Irvine, who would serve as your first-line supervisor and assign you duties that do not require access to classified information or occupancy of a national security position.... Your insistence that, once you do report for duty, Mr. Irvine will assign you "clerical work" that is a "waste and abuse . . ." is simply incorrect. Mr. Irvine has meaningful work to assign you, work that is important to the Department of Defense.... You are to report to Mr. Irvine, who is copied above. Please raise any further concerns you have through your chain of command, including Mr. Irvine as your first-line supervisor.

Undeterred, I secured a second offer from the Marine Corps University to teach strategic studies. That, too, was denied. At the time I couldn't fully believe what is now apparent to me, that the entire system of administrative due process is its own form of punishment, from which no justice can be obtained. My security clearance had been suspended based on known falsehoods—they all knew that. All they were doing now was searching for something, anything, they could use to retroactively justify that punishment. That is why Westgate kept me in her latter-day penal colony, under a bureaucratic microscope.

· · ·

The U.S. Supreme Court has ruled that the U.S. Constitution grants Americans the right to receive "notice and an opportunity to be heard…at a meaningful time and in a meaningful manner."[2] The Court holds that due process is violated if a practice or rule "offends some principle of justice so rooted in the traditions and conscience of our people as to be ranked as fundamental."[3] Deep State operatives violate such laws with impunity.

Executive Order 12968 required Westgate to abide by due process in suspending my security clearance. Then it required her to give me my security file, which would contain the evidence she had relied on and detail "the reason(s) for the suspension" of my clearance. Westgate, in short, was required to cite my specific violations, so that I could adequately defend myself. But on the day of my security clearance's suspension, she had only alleged vague "concerns regarding your judgment, trustworthiness, and reliability while carrying out your official duties, specifically relating to your personal conduct, misuse of Information Technology systems, outside activities and your improper handling of and safeguarding of protected information." As I told Westgate in person, I had no clue what this specifically referred to.

Westgate sent a second, more specific memo about me to her subordinates, WHS Consolidated Adjudication Facility (CAF) Director Edward "Ned" Fish and his general counsel, James "Jim" Clark. She had no proof to support her allegations, so it fell to Fish and Clark to find or fabricate the evidence. Arguably, this was an example of "blatant command influence" that undermined their independence and objectivity, tainting their work on my case, as former DoD Inspector General Joseph Schmitz later testified.

I asked that Westgate comply with EO 12968, which required that I receive my "security file" within thirty days. Baker then asked the Office of Personnel Management (OPM), which conducts six-year periodic reviews of the conduct of security clearance holders, to review my security clearance two years early. He did so as soon as he knew I was getting detailed to the NSC. This meant that I wouldn't get to see my security file, and the supposed evidence against me, until OPM completed its background check. I seemed to be treading over a series of trapdoors, where every request I made led to further retaliations, dissimulations, and delays.

A childhood friend from Oregon put me in touch with Democratic senator Ron Wyden. His staff made inquiries and in October 2017 characterized Westgate's actions as violating my due-process rights. The OPM scheme, designed to prevent me from accessing information on my case for as long as possible, was aborted. That put WHS CAF Director Ned Fish in the hot seat. To get out of it, he resorted to the "lie, leak, and investigate" playbook gambit.

CHAPTER 19

LIE

Westgate had not made Fish's life easy. She was herself guilty of abusing the federal investigative process after conspiring with Baker, May, and Work. Fish's job was to clean things up retroactively. He would do so through a tactic known as "accretion-dissimulation," the process of slowly normalizing an absurd or unbelievable tale.

This tactic was widely used during the Obama administration. Take the Steele Dossier. Having been placed into Obama's 2017 Intelligence Community Assessment, the ridiculous claims of the dossier, obviously infused with Kremlin misinformation, were normalized and rendered believable by their insertion into an official U.S. government intelligence product.

Former DoD Inspector General Joseph Schmitz immediately spotted what Westgate and Fish were doing and was appalled. He would testify on my behalf that each investigative scheme Westgate relied on to suspend my clearance was neither a "real investigation [n]or even a real preliminary inquiry."

For official purposes, Ned Fish magically transformed Bruggeman's fake investigation into "a national security investigation, as that term is used in the Adjudicative Guidelines, because it sought to uncover the source of the information security leak." Fish, and everyone else who touched my case, knew that was false. No professional criminal investigation had been done, and the leak had never been investigated. Bruggeman himself was conflicted. Legally, that meant that even if his investigative product had been sound, it was immaterial.

• • •

Westgate's memo to her subordinates was packed with about a dozen false charges, by my count. I had not mishandled classified information. That allegation, in what became known as the "Airliner Matter," has done more damage to my career as a U.S. national security professional than any other. To make it more believable, it was mixed with a nugget of truth. It's true that on September 15, 2016, I reviewed a document, prepared by a Duke University professor and later published online, while on official travel.[1]

Baker had given me that document shortly before we left on the trip. To minimize compromising America's secrets, U.S. national security protocols have clear rules for marking classified documents. But as Baker later testified under oath, the document he gave me was not properly marked.

Austin Maxwell, a U.S. Navy commander sitting next to me on a commercial plane, saw me reading it and reported to Baker through his commanding officer at the U.S. Pacific Fleet in Hawaii that he believed the document was classified. As a naval officer, Maxwell knew that if he saw classified information in public, his duty was to immediately secure those secrets. But he didn't do that. He said nothing to me. The thought has crossed my mind that the whole thing was a set-up.

I would later learn from government evidence that Baker develops blackmail files on pretty much everyone he works with, presumably in order to influence them into doing his bidding. That might help explain how he rose so rapidly to become the Pentagon's top strategist, and how he has stayed in that position for nearly a decade while ignoring his one and only statutory duty.

Russell investigated the Airliner Matter and concluded categorically that there had been no compromise of classified information. With that, Russell closed the Airliner Matter, telling my lawyer, Sean Bigley, under oath that there had been no further investigation.

"[In] your contemporaneous inquiry report at the time [you] indicated that the document was marked Draft and Classification Pending. Is that correct?" Bigley asked Russell.

"That's correct."

"Okay. So just to be clear, you did not send this document to an original classification authority for an official determination as to whether the document was classified?"

"I did not," Russell said.

"Okay. And I'm assuming nobody...was brought in to review the document and determine if it was classified?"

"They were not."

Russell finalized his "preliminary inquiry" report on the Airliner Matter on October 18, 2016, and delivered it to Baker that day. The day before, I had informed Baker of the danger of sharing Japanese classified information with the suspected Chinese spy. His response to my whistleblower disclosure materialized four days later.

On October 21, Baker issued me a formal reprimand that stated the exact opposite of what Russell had determined in his "preliminary inquiry" report three days before. Overruling his security officer, Baker stated that I had "failed to safeguard classified information" on that commercial flight. But Baker was just getting warmed up.

Later I would learn from the playbook that "Big Lies" are used against those with spotless records. Small lies won't work against these individuals, as fabricated minor infractions might generate only a wrist slap and a warning. Big Lies are used to turn Dr. Jekyll into Mr. Hyde. When people say the Big Lie sounds preposterous, the response is, "Oh, if you only knew Lovinger, you'd understand." Few in the U.S. national security bureaucracy want to admit to being blind to insider threats, so they stay silent.

"If you tell a lie big enough and keep repeating it, people will eventually come to believe it." This adage, apocryphally attributed to Joseph Goebbels, Hitler's propaganda minister, describes a process that psychologists now call the "illusory truth effect." "That's how our brains work," explains Yale medical Professor F. Perry Wilson. "It's well documented that if you hear the same statement again and again, you're more likely to believe it's true.[2]

To broaden and amplify his lie, Baker, with Russell and Westgate, informed the NSC that I had "mishandled highly classified information and sought to conceal that fact." That charge, like so many others, I discovered in the playbook. Later, during my administrative trial, my lawyer asked Baker to testify under oath whether he had written the following memorandum to Michael Flynn, the incoming U.S. national security advisor:

MEMORANDUM FOR LT GEN (Ret) FLYNN
13 January 2017
SUBJECT: Detailing of Adam Lovinger to the NSC

Last night, Mr. [Redacted] called me to convey your wish to detail Adam to your NSC staff. He asked that I take no action which would prevent Adam from carrying out his duties as a detailee. I was caught unaware by the fact that Adam had been offered and accepted a position with you. I would not have recommended Adam for a position of such responsibility. There are two distinct inquiries ongoing into Adam's alleged misconduct. If found substantiated by a preponderance of evidence, the alleged misconduct is serious. These inquiries should finish NLT the end of February, and if substantiated, open the door for disciplinary action. He also has been recently reprimanded for *mishandling highly classified materials*, and for denying or obfuscating that fact. In light of these inquiries, I was prepared on Friday to place Adam on administrative leave and suspend his security clearance. Post my conversation with [Redacted], and in accordance with your wishes, I will instead ask Adam to prepare for his detail in a location apart from our team. Given our prior working relationship and friendship, and having worked with the NSC in different capacities for nearly a decade, I could not in good conscience fail to notify you, personally, of my concerns. I would ask that you keep these concerns private, as I do not wish to damage his reputation unnecessarily with other members of his new team. You have my commitment to support your efforts in coming months. I believe strongly in the mission and criticality of the work of the National Security staff.[3]

When, at the DOHA hearing on the revocation of my security clearance, Baker was shown the memo, which I had found in the playbook, he visibly bit his lip and clenched his fists. Then, after a long pause, he admitted that he had authored and disseminated the memo.

Baker's lie that I had mishandled classified information was repeated by LTC Brian T. Bruggeman in his investigative report, omitting Russell's contrary finding. Westgate then repeated it in her secret memo to Ned Fish on May 1, 2017, saying that I had "violated security policy and regulations" and adducing as an "example" (suggesting it was just one violation among others) that I "possessed and viewed information marked and classified at the TS/SCI-level on a commercial aircraft."

Westgate, Fish's boss, had just suspended my security clearance and removed me from the U.S. National Security Council on the basis of fabricated charges. But instead of alerting the proper authorities that a felony had occurred, Fish moved the goal posts.

When caught lying, Deep State operatives are taught to backtrack. At that point they narrow the scope of their false accusations to only those details that are most nebulous and obstruse. Fish did just that. Recharacterizing my actions, he claimed I had "mishandled sensitive information." In DoD, "sensitive information" is not a term of art. It's subjective. Anything can be called "sensitive."

CHAPTER 20

LEAK

History shows that the most successful tyrants are keen manipulators of human psychology. After months of unlawfully keeping me in the dark about "the reason(s) for the suspension" of my security clearance, Westgate and Fish knew I would be anxious to learn what I had been accused of. They used that anxiety to test the strength of their made-up allegations, before committing to them in my upcoming administrative trial. The first step of this process was leaking those allegations to the press.

Like all defamation, these false allegations hurt my reputation, leading to professional marginalization. Indeed, shortly after Westgate's charges against me were reported in the press, most of my colleagues, allies, and sponsors either dropped me like a load of bricks or just faded away, never to be heard from again.

On May 4, 2017, just three days after Westgate suspended my clearance and got me expelled from the White House, defense reporter Bill Gertz wrote his first of several articles on my case in the Washington Free Beacon:

[T]he clearance dispute appears to involve a bureaucratic turf battle, as well as a larger, behind-the-scenes effort by anti-Trump officials in the national security bureaucracy to neutralize key Trump aides. Lovinger is senior director for strategic assessments at the NSC. In that position, he has proposed shifting the Office of Net Assessment from the Pentagon to the White House, where it was located when established during the Nixon administration. Lovinger wrote a memo to current National Security Adviser H. R. McMaster on the need for a net assessment capability within the NSC.[1]

Titled "Pentagon Pulls Security Clearance of Trump White House Aide," Gertz's article was 100 percent accurate, especially about the turf battle between the Pentagon's ONA and the White House's NSC. Gertz's May 2017 article was also sympathetic to my plight. Gertz had gone out of his way to gather and print quotes from national security luminaries who had sung my praises. But then, four months later, the reporter did an about-face. On September 13, 2017, Gertz published Westgate's charges in a *Washington Times* article that included a subsection on my case titled "Clearance of NSC Aide to be Revoked."[2]

The night before his article went to press, Gertz called my lawyer, Sean Bigley, and identified Fish as the leaker of those charges against me. Upon hearing what the charges were, Bigley told Gertz they were all lies and that we had official U.S. government evidence to prove it. Gertz then told Bigley that if Bigley sent evidence to refute Westgate's charges, Gertz wouldn't even consider it for the purposes of his article.

One of the accusations Gertz published on September 13, 2017, was that I had taken an unauthorized trip to Israel. Like most of the charges against me, it had an element of truth but was mostly not true. I had, in fact, gone to Israel with my family to celebrate my son's bar mitzvah the month before I had started work at the NSC—but that trip was authorized. My lawyer offered Gertz my official travel documentation for that family holiday, signed by both a DoD security officer and the U.S. national security advisor himself. That level of authorization far exceeded even the most strenuous requirements for foreign travel to any country, much less to one of America's closest allies.

As I discovered in the playbook, the ominous-sounding "unauthorized trip to Israel" charge was Anthony Russell's idea. By then he had accused me of harboring "divided loyalties,"[3] and of being "actively engaged in a 'campaign' to undermine" my chain of command. Soon after Gertz published that charge, it was picked up by online commentators who deemed me a "Jewish spy."

Russell's slur, which Fish and Clark turned into an official charge against me, prompted my former Penn professor Dr. Zell Kravinsky to write this to Judge Foreman:

> As far as...the Allegation...of "divided loyalties," I feel compelled to perhaps too baldly point out, before opining on Mr. Lovinger's character...that it's occasionally employed as a coded and scattergun derogation of American Jews who have disconcertingly (in the eyes of the envious) risen in U.S. Government service.

Gertz's niche was reporting leaks from within the Pentagon, which made it imperative that he kept those sources happy. When issues arose that threatened key Deep State interests, as in my case, he simply couldn't afford to tell the truth. As he explained to a mutual acquaintance, "I am not a well-paid writer at the *Atlantic*. I live article to article." If he refused to do his sources' bidding, they would stop leaking insider information, his sources would dry up, and he "would be finished."

Fish's motives were equally straightforward. The ambitious bureaucrat had made his career by delivering results, even if it meant committing potential felonies, such as leaking my Privacy

Act–protected information to a reporter. For Fish, that was not without purpose. It was a calculated risk, which he used to compel me to disgorge my strongest evidence to him. That gave Fish the best evidence he could get to adjust the charges against me before needing to commit to them for the duration of my lengthy "administrative due process." Fish had used Gertz to turn up the heat on me by having the reporter write that the suspension of my clearance would become a permanent revocation, regardless of anything I might have to say.[4]

The leak of my Privacy Act–protected information to Gertz was a criminal violation. Once that leak became public, one would have hoped that DoD leadership would step in and demand accountability. But that didn't happen. That omission tacitly endorsed senior leader misconduct, which helps normalize criminality, ensuring that it is repeated again and again.

• • •

My lawyer, Sean Bigley, and I pled our case to senior DoD lawyers. But that was like talking to a brick wall. We asked WHS General Counsel John Albanese to conduct an investigation into Fish's leak of my Privacy Act–protected information. In explaining his refusal to lift a finger, Albanese repeated that he was "just the lawyer," following orders from above. Disgusted by his Nuremberg excuse, Bigley refused to give up.

If DoD lawyers refused to obey the law, Bigley would do his own investigation. He filed a FOIA search on all of Fish's emails to Gertz. Seventy-six pages of Fish's email were responsive. The bureau Fish led has its own dedicated FOIA office. All but confirming what Gertz had said about Fish being the leaker, Fish bypassed his own FOIA office and personally blacked out *every single word* of his own responsive emails. He sent us seventy-six entirely black pages. Fish was thumbing his nose at U.S. law.

Judicial Watch sued DoD on my behalf a second time in U.S. District Court for violating FOIA. Lawyers from the U.S. Department of Justice represented Fish in that suit at taxpayer expense. The federal judge ruled that Fish had violated a federal statute. But since the ruling carried no consequences, Fish and his co-conspirators were free to continue to violate the law with impunity, and they did.

During those judicial proceedings, a DoD lawyer named Mark Herrington informed the court that all evidence of Fish's leak to Gertz was missing from DoD computer systems. The files had been destroyed. Even the backup files had mysteriously vanished. How was that possible? Around the same time Fish's emails went missing, DoJ announced that texts sent between FBI paramours Peter Strzok and Lisa Page had mysteriously vanished too. But the DoJ Office of the Inspector General, under pressure from Congress and the White House, was able to recover those texts in less than twenty-four hours.

Bigley again demanded an investigation into the destruction of U.S. government evidence. But like all our attempts to hold Deep State operatives accountable, this was denied. The entire matter was swept under the rug. To this day, DoD has not investigated that crime.

Senior government officials used to have a sense of honor and shame. No longer, it seems to me. Soon after subverting those federal processes, Fish was promoted to the leadership of the Defense Counterintelligence and Security Agency, where he remains as of this writing.

CHAPTER 21

INVESTIGATE

When I became a government official, I took an oath to uphold the Basic Obligation of Public Service, which required me to report illegal acts to the proper authorities. On September 13, 2017—the same day Fish and Gertz smeared me in the press—my lawyer reported to Glenn Fine and Marguerite Garrison at the DoD Office of Inspector General that Baker, May, and Russell were committing a crime. They were storing on ONA's *unclassified* computer systems the same Japanese *classified* information that had been leaked to Gertz and published on November 23, 2016. This serious leak was still ongoing, ten months later.

Fine and Garrison learned of the leak more than six months prior to the Walsh Report of Investigation. That report placed them on notice for a second time that a leak spill assessment and investigation were necessary. Those senior DoD OIG officials had a choice to make.

Either they could follow the law and do their job, or they could continue the cover-up. They chose the latter. The very entity entrusted by the U.S. Congress to protect whistleblowers, the U.S. Department of Defense Office of Inspector General, turned that purpose on its head. Administrative law judge Foreman followed suit.

He said that my discovery of that crime, and my reporting it to the DoD OIG, violated the ONA-WHS attorney-client privilege. The absurdity of this prompted my lawyer to gently remind Judge Foreman that the law was unambiguous. Conflict-of-laws doctrine places reporting criminal misconduct before upholding the sanctity of attorney-client confidentiality. But Westgate and her colleagues could rest assured that their membership in the Deep State meant they were above the law.

They chose to focus on how I had discovered that DoD OIG's Fine and Garrison had not performed their duty to investigate the leak of Japanese classified information. Fish's theory was that I had somehow tricked an information technology (IT) "help desk" technician into giving me access to that incriminating file. My lawyer asked for evidence of that charge.

Fish's evidence was a work order receipt for a "hardware issue" that read "central access card not working." But the incriminating files placed on my computer were neither hardware nor related to my "central access card," a plastic badge that I wore around my neck on a string. What was that about, and why did the Director of WHS know about that work order? Edward Burbol provided an answer.

Westgate subordinate Burbol had let slip that Westgate had directed her staff into provoking me into doing something they could use as evidence of misconduct to retroactively justify their weaponized investigations. But that seems to have backfired.

One of their games was to lock me out of my office in the Mark Center and disable my phone and computer. In the course of repeatedly cutting off and re-establishing my computer access, it seems that a technician must have changed my computer settings and given me access not just to the Deep State playbook but also the file on ONA's unclassified share drive with the Japanese classified information on it. Or maybe their intent was to give me access to those files, and then to charge me with having access to those files?

Whatever the case, the absurdity of Westgate's and Fish's schemes suggested they were getting desperate.

They had zero evidence for their allegations and charges against me. Westgate had intentionally defied Walsh's recommendation, issued on behalf of the deputy secretary of defense, to do a proper leak investigation. If word of this ever got out, Westgate could face jail time. The seriousness of the situation only made her turn up the heat on me.

Westgate would charge me with criminality. That required teaming up with Fine and Garrison, senior DoD OIG officials, who readily jumped on the bandwagon. After all, it was their dereliction of duty that had resulted in the continued failure to investigate and stop the ongoing leak of Japanese classified material. All told, these officials targeted me with three progressively more invasive criminal investigations.

The first was a Naval Criminal Investigative Service (NCIS) counterintelligence (CI) and counterterrorism (CT) investigation. A Westgate lackey named Chris Forshey alleged that "foreign contacts" that I had voluntarily reported for over a decade, and that DoD had previously deemed innocuous, had suddenly made me a potential enemy agent or terrorist.

At the direct behest of the U.S. secretary of defense, I had conducted collaborative net assessments with U.S. allies and strategic partners. After Westgate suspended my security clearance, I had a few loose ends to tie up from those duties. One was to deliver a lecture to several dozen German and U.S. naval officers at the U.S. National Defense University.

Forshey claimed that my lecture was unauthorized and launched his NCIS counterintelligence and counterterrorism investigation against me in turn. That was deranged. The U.S. National Defense University, which stretches along the Anacostia River in Washington, DC, is a federal facility. DoD does background checks on all its foreign visitors. The chance of a terrorist German naval officer slipping through that screening process to meet with me was slim. And Westgate had authorized my delivery of that lecture—at 3:32 p.m. on May 26, 2017, to be precise. But Forshey was just getting started.

DoD had also authorized my teaching at Georgetown University since 2014, and that authorization continued through my exile at the Mark Center. DoD policy did not require me to report my meetings with students, but by then it was clear to me that Westgate and her minions were desperate to nail me for something, anything.

For that reason, out of an abundance of caution, I had exceeded my reporting requirements and reported to Forshey that during office hours, I had met one of my graduate students from Thailand. I reported that meeting to Forshey, but I failed to foresee that he would turn my excessive transparency and caution against me.

For his third predicate to launch his counterintelligence/counterterrorism investigation against me, Forshey fixed on a holiday I took with my family to Costa Rica to visit my wife's relatives. As Forshey could see from my Joint Personnel Adjudication System, for my entire career at DoD, starting in 2004, Jessica and I had been married. And each year we packed up our three kids and visited her family in Costa Rica:

"Subject disclosed foreign travel for pleasure and contact with foreign nations."

"Subject maintains contact four times yearly via phone and while on vacation in CR."

"Contact with foreign nations was infrequent and does not create a risk for foreign influence or exploitation."

"Foreign contacts have no hostile interest toward the U.S. and subject feels no pressure or duress. He cannot be blackmailed or coerced due to his contacts."

All of a sudden, however, Forshey deemed my Costa Rican in-laws a threat to national security. A September 29, 2021, DoD Office of Inspector General report showed that all of Forshey's alleged concerns about my "foreign contacts" were bogus.

Those three data points had been generated *after* Westgate had launched her NCIS counterintelligence and counterterrorism investigation. Westgate had launched the NCIS investigation *before* Forshey learned about any of those three "foreign contacts"; the so-called issue was only brought up *after* the NCIS investigation found that I had done nothing wrong. There was no "predicate." But by then, "administrative due process" had run its course. Obviously, my accusers were accustomed to getting away with preposterous actions.

I later learned from Judicial Watch's FOIA lawsuits on my behalf that Fish and DoD OIG had gotten updates from NCIS officials during the course of that investigation. Over email, Fish had lobbied NCIS investigators to conceal those communications, and their exculpatory findings, from Judge Foreman.[1]

• • •

For their second criminal investigation, acting DoD Inspector General Glenn Fine sent a couple of guys over to try and catch me making a "process foul," just as FBI Director Comey had "sent a couple of guys over" to ambush National Security Advisor Flynn. Those officials from DoD OIG's Defense Criminal Investigative Service (DCIS) asked to meet at my home on May 11, 2018.

My wife welcomed them with coffee, and my twelve-year-old daughter made them cookies before setting off for school that morning. While sitting at our kitchen table they expressed concern that Fine and Garrison were using DCIS to cover up their own illegal acts, specifically, regarding their failure to conduct a "spill assessment" and investigation of the Japan leak.

Years later I learned from a FOIA release that those two DCIS investigators were not what they seemed. They had been dispatched on a mission not to investigate Fine's and Garrison's alleged criminal misconduct, nor the leak of Tokyo's secrets, but to play "good cop" in order to lure me into divulging all the evidence I had of Fine's and Garrison's malfeasance. After I gave them everything I had on that, they took a last swig of coffee, thanked me for my time, and left.

The third criminal investigation Westgate and Fine triggered against me was undertaken by their colleagues over at the FBI. That was a Criminal & Subversive Seat of Government (SSoG) investigation. My performance record had somehow gone from describing my work as "Exemplary," with not one violation of any kind during the entirety of my fourteen-year DoD career, to presenting me as an "insider threat," even a potential domestic terrorist threat.

Years later I learned from a FOIA release that the FBI investigators appeared perplexed and even annoyed that a Criminal & Subversive Seat of Government investigation had been used to target me.

CHAPTER 22

THE DEEP STATE'S JUSTICE MACHINE

In November 2017, WHS CAF Director Fish provided me a "statement of reasons" for Westgate's suspension of my security clearance, citing evidence in my "security file" for all his charges. In violation of U.S. law, he refused to turn that file over to me. That presented me with a choice. I could either not respond and lose all legal standing to challenge those accusations or respond without the benefit of knowing about the evidence they were using against me. My lawyer, Sean Bigley, objected to that perversion of due process. Westgate had suspended my security clearance, then refused to comply with EO 12968, which required her to hand over my security file, on the grounds that it contained classified information.

WHS General Counsel James Clark apparently didn't get the memo on Westgate's latest fabrication. He revealed to my lawyer in writing that there was nothing classified in my security file. Caught red-handed, they shrugged and carried on. Their plan was to force me to make a FOIA request to Finnegan-Myers to see my security file, which would come so late that the deadline for our response to Fish's "statement of reasons" would have long passed. Sure enough, it took fourteen months and two lawsuits in federal court filed pro bono by Judicial Watch to see what should have been handed over within thirty days.

Eight months into that ordeal, Finnegan-Myers released my security file with 90 percent of it redacted, rendering it indecipherable. We had been down this path before—recall that Fish personally redacted *every single word* of his seventy-six pages of emails regarding the leak of my Privacy Act–protected information to Bill Gertz.

After our second lawsuit, Bigley and I discovered what was so sensitive about my security file: irrelevant newspaper articles. To delay release, Finnegan-Myers had packed my security file with hundreds of pages of newspaper articles that she bogusly claimed were exempt from release under FOIA. That prompted Bigley to demand that my case be transferred to a non-conflicted U.S. Government agency such as DOJ, DHS, or even HHS. Typically, government bureaucrats jump at the opportunity to relieve their work burden. But WHS lawyers James "Jim" Clark and John Albanese refused Bigley's offer. The last thing they wanted was to have another agency review what they had done.

• • •

Baker, Westgate, Fish, and their subordinates fought so hard to conceal my security file, not because of those innocuous newspaper articles, but because it painted a devastating picture of their own misconduct. Of the five "investigative actions" taken against me, four cleared me and incriminated them. Baker, Westgate, and Fish tried to hide these investigations from me (a crime), destroyed government evidence (another crime), and doctored the record (yet another crime).

A few months later, WHS Director Barbara A. Westgate was preparing for her second retirement. She sent an email to all DoD employees thanking them for their service, then reminded everyone about their duty to follow the Federal Employee Antidiscrimination and Retaliation (No FEAR) Act, which protects federal whistleblowers reporting on misconduct.

At the end of her farewell address, Westgate was asked in an interview posted online to describe herself in three words. Her response was "ethical, driven, and fair." That was perverse. By then my lawyer Sean Bigley had caught her in numerous egregious lies. After placing that evidence in the official record, Bigley requested that DoD refer Westgate to the U.S. Department of Justice for criminal prosecution. Of course, DoD refused to do any such thing.

THE APPEAL THAT WAS NO APPEAL

After Fish revoked my security clearance, my next stop on the administrative due process train was to appeal the revocation before the presiding administrative law judge, LeRoy Foreman, at the Defense Office of Hearings and Appeals. Foreman, then seventy-eight years old, had worked at DOHA for four decades. Before that he had been a U.S. military officer. He had lived the mistakes of the Vietnam War when America went to war with no net assessment–informed strategies. I used my opening remarks to explain why ONA had been set up in 1973—to ensure that another Vietnam would never happen. As it was not fulfilling its duties, I was obliged to report that fact to the proper authorities.

I launched into this, fortified by my belief that I had a secret weapon: the Deep State playbook. I could force them to admit authorship of all sorts of incriminating memos. But, as I discovered with growing dread over the course of my week-long trial, none of that mattered. Judge Foreman had no interest in recognizing the significance of any evidence that crossed his boss's foregone conclusions.

In my *appeal* of my security clearance revocation, Foreman permitted my accusers to spring new charges on me—ones I had never seen before. My 765-page security file swelled by another 300 pages on the eve of my trial.

My expert witness, former DoD Inspector General Joseph Schmitz, was the author of *The Inspector General Handbook: Fraud, Waste and Abuse and Other Constitutional "Enemies, Foreign and Domestic"* (2013). He told Foreman that nothing about my case was legal.

But like LTC Brian T. Bruggeman, who had taken no notes during our interview, Foreman seemed uninterested in anything anyone had to say in his court room. He would go through the motions and then rule as Westgate and her co-conspirators had decreed. Why he did that soon became clear to Bigley and me. Deputy Secretary of Defense Work, Westgate, and Baker had ensured that DoD acting General Counsel Paul Koffsky, the boss of Foreman's boss (DOHA Director Peregrine D. Russell-Hunter), was responsible for providing legal counsel on the two illegal investigations used to suspend my security clearance. That was their "insurance policy."

AN INHERENT CONFLICT OF INTEREST

Over the course of five days in December 2018, Baker and Russell paraded their years of malpractice: not producing net assessments; lining the pockets of political allies like Newmyer-Deal and LTSG; handing out fat contracts to pro-Russia Stefan A. Halper; failing to obtain security clearances for LTSG operators; permitting a suspected Chinese agent to paw through Japanese classified information; allowing Putin's former top spy, General V. I. Trubnikov, to inject Kremlin disinformation into ONA reports for half a decade; and doctoring official records to reprimand me for mishandling classified information, when Baker admitted under oath to knowing that the only inquiry into the matter had cleared me of that allegation.

On the stand, Baker accused his staff of manipulating him. He "testified that he signed [a] document, even though his questions [about it]...had not been answered" because his staff had peer-pressured him. On other issues he bobbed and weaved with half-truths, responded to questioning by trying to change the subject, and contradicted his own and Russell's testimony. He claimed not to have read the Walsh and Bruggeman investigative reports, but then, when presented with evidence that he had, was forced to recant.

Baker admitted to telling the U.S. National Security Council that I had "mishandled highly classified information and sought to conceal that fact." But then Baker and Russell both conceded that there was no evidence that I had mishandled any classified information. None whatsoever.

Baker, Russell, and Judge Foreman were all on the same side, a situation that the Framers of the U.S. Constitution, which prescribes a vital separation of powers, would have found intolerable. As my DOHA "appeal" came to a close, my lawyer asked the judge to refer Westgate, Baker, and Russell to the U.S. Department of Justice for criminal prosecution.

The Deep State's scheme was unraveling. To correct that, and send the right message to Judge Foreman, smack dab in the middle of my DOHA "appeal" Deputy Secretary of Defense Robert O. Work and the *New York Times* stepped in to do their bit.

•   •   •

On December 18, 2018, the *New York Times* published a piece authored by Adam Goldman and Julian Barnes that contradicted Baker's and Russell's testimony, under oath, that I had not mishandled classified information. The primary source was Bob Work. "It is quite surprising to me," Work was quoted as saying, "that someone would think this is some sort of deep state." Everyone at ONA, he said, was "fiercely apolitical," and the *Times* reporters cited his assertion that "there is no evidence Mr. Lovinger's clearance was revoked for political reasons."[1] This was Work sending a message to Foreman, one he could not ignore.

I'm not important enough to merit a *New York Times* hit piece sourced to Deputy Secretary of Defense Robert O. Work. But what I *knew* was. I was being discredited in the *Times* because of what I knew about Work employing Stefan A. Halper and General V. I. Trubnikov and their colleagues in Russia's Foreign Intelligence Service on ONA/WHS contracts from 2011 to 2016.

Work expected to land the top job in the Pentagon if Clinton won the presidency. To curry favor, he built for her the institutional infrastructure for Russiagate and normalized Putin's top spy as an important source for the Steele Dossier. That was used to launch Crossfire Hurricane, the counterintelligence investigation into alleged Trump-Russia collusion, and its sub-investigation, Crossfire Razor, which was designed to take out Mike Flynn.

May and Baker allowed Trubnikov to insert Russian disinformation into reports for the Office of the Secretary of Defense. Since 2011, I had been alerting my leadership, and later whistleblowing to higher authorities, about that problem. At first their response was to ignore that threat to national security. Later they changed tack to whistleblower retaliation.

As long as I remained Work's and Baker's subordinate, they could control me. When I was tapped to join the NSC, they lost that control. At the White House, Flynn asked me to do two things. First, I should produce net assessments, which he knew ONA was no longer doing. Second, Flynn asked me to assist his efforts in eliminating the threat posed to America by the Leviathan administrative state.

This meant exposing Work's role in misleading the American people on behalf of Moscow. The consequences of Work's actions have been profound. As Trubnikov stated to NPR, Moscow employed

Russiagate to "deeply split" American society. Our government has lost its reputation for integrity and credibility in ways that will be difficult to recover.

•   •   •

After his hit piece on me ran in the *Times* I reached out to Julian Barnes. A mutual acquaintance had put us in touch. They had gone to Harvard together and the acquaintance thought that Barnes was ethical and that if I showed him the DoD report that exonerated me from the charge of mishandling classified information, he'd have the *Times* correct the record.

When Adolph Ochs bought the *New York Times* in 1896, he had promised to "give the news impartially, without fear or favor."[2] But those days are long gone. When I confronted the *Times* reporter with the facts, he refused to correct his error, as Bill Gertz had done before him. As my experience with both these reporters reinforces, they and their editors and publishers alike prioritize doing the bidding of Deep State operatives, in exchange for getting inside scoops, over printing the truth. This self-defeating bargain ensures that the cancer of "journalism for rent" and its inevitable progeny, "fake news," will continue to erode the integrity of a once-honorable profession.

CHAPTER 23

WHO WATCHES THE WATCHERS?

The only morality they recognize is what will further their cause,
meaning they reserve unto themselves the right
to commit any crime, to lie, to cheat.

—RONALD REAGAN[1]

A t some point in our nation's 250-year history, the U.S. Congress seems to have lost track of the wisdom undergirding the U.S. constitutional order. Specifically, our legislative branch seems to have forgotten that it is impossible for the executive branch to "check and balance" itself.

The creation of inspectors general has been a minor attempt to deal with the structural conflicts of interests created by the administrative state. But as I and countless other whistleblowers have experienced first hand, permitting executive branch agencies to investigate themselves simply does not work. The leaders of so-called "internal watchdog" offices too often see their jobs first and foremost as covering up for the agencies that pay their salaries and pensions.

In 2011, I reported Andrew D. May's rigging of contracts to Deputy Inspector General for Administrative Investigations Marguerite C. Garrison. Over the course of half a decade, those contracts were employed to build the institutional infrastructure for what became known as "Russiagate." But Garrison refused to investigate those disclosures.

Seven years later, Senator Grassley did what Garrison should have done in 2011. In October 2018, I reported to Grassley what I had previously reported to the DoD OIG. He found my disclosure compelling and demanded that DoD OIG perform an audit of those contracts. Acting DoD Inspector General Glenn A. Fine[2] and Garrison promised to act but then became non-responsive. This prompted Grassley to write that their audit was just "getting kicked around the OIG bureaucracy instead of being subjected to aggressive, hard hitting oversight."

Then Fine and Garrison assured the senator from Iowa that there was nothing to see. They arrived at that determination on the Halper/Trubnikov contracts without even looking at the evidence. "How did OIG make judgements about contracts without ever looking at them?" an incredulous Grassley asked Fine in a letter dated January 16, 2019.

Several months after Grassley reminded Fine of his duty to conduct a proper audit of ONA's contracts, I sat down for lunch with a former DoD OIG investigator. As we were exiting a Persian restaurant in Alexandria, Virginia, he asked, "What do you know about Steven Luke?"

"Who?"

"The DoD OIG whistleblower. And who is overseeing your case? Margie Garrison and Glenn Fine?"

"That's right."

"Garrison and Fine were on his case, too."

"Okay. What are you saying?"

We were in the parking lot, and it started to rain.

"Never mind. Forget about it." We parted ways.

·   ·   ·

If DoD OIG had done its job back when I had first reported on those rigged contracts in 2011, Russiagate might never have happened. The Republic might have been spared what some are calling America's most divisive episode since the Civil War. Yet I was only beginning to learn just how inspectors general, perhaps more than any other officials, work to cover up senior leader misconduct and to retaliate against federal whistleblowers.

In 2015, the year before Obama appointed Fine to the top job at the DoD OIG, a government watchdog group called the Project on Government Oversight published a paper titled "Toxic Culture toward Whistleblowers." That report determined that the

> DoD IG's systemic weaknesses and apparent cultural aversion to whistleblowers create a substantial barrier to DoD IG effectively performing its duties to protect whistleblowers, prevent abusive misspending of taxpayer dollars, and support the war fighter.[3]

Starting in late 2017, internal DoD OIG whistleblowers began sharing with me information on what Fine and Garrison were up to. I learned that my protected disclosures had deepened a schism between DoD OIG leadership and the organization's rank and file. Grassley had spoken of this schism from the floor of the U.S. Senate on April 6, 2016:

> What I hear is disturbing. This [DoD OIG] report is allegedly being doctored, causing a bitter internal dispute. On one side are the investigators. They appear to be guided by the evidence. On the other side is top management. They appear eager to... arbitrarily dismiss the evidence.[4]

One internal document that those DoD OIG whistleblowers gave me showed that Fine and Garrison were well aware that Baker had retaliated against me for alerting him to the fact that ONA officials were sharing classified information with an alleged Chinese spy. Immediately after that, Baker targeted my security clearance and tried repeatedly to impede my detail to the White House based entirely on known falsehoods.

These internal DoD OIG whistleblowers also told me that Fine had instructed his staff to launch only a "phony" Whistleblower Retaliation Investigation into my case. To oversee it, he put Garrison in charge—yet my history of reporting crimes to Garrison, and of her ignoring them only for them to become national scandals years later, meant that she had a conflict that precluded her from touching my case. Instead of recusing herself, as she was duty bound to do, she did what I have repeatedly found all corrupt bureaucrats do. She took over the investigation and aggressively scapegoated the whistleblower in order to shift blame away from herself.

THE U.S. OFFICE OF SPECIAL COUNSEL

But Deep State predations are not relegated to DoD OIG alone. In 1979, in the wake of the Watergate scandal, the U.S. Congress created the U.S. Office of Special Counsel (OSC). Its purpose is to serve as a whistleblower advocate against administrative lawlessness. But, like all federal "watchers," the OSC was an early example of "institutional capture."

In my case, after learning from internal DoD OIG whistleblowers that Fine and Garrison were weaponizing the Whistleblower Retaliation Investigation process against me, I reached out to the OSC. Under U.S. law, the OSC was required to render a "finding" on my disclosure of DoD whistleblower retaliation within 45 days. Instead, OSC spent 379 days pretending to investigate the actions of Work, Baker, and Westgate. Then OSC leadership spent an additional 510 days sitting on my case, only to shut it down without ever making their statutorily mandated legal "determination." An internal DoD OIG whistleblower, who knew how OSC corrupted federal processes, had warned me this would happen.

He told me that, in general, the cases that are dragged out the longest are the ones with the most damning evidence against the Deep State. This, he explained, is because OSC and DoD OIG leadership believe that their job is to cover up corruption in the senior ranks. And as a professional investigator himself, he spoke from experience when he said that the surest way to do that is to taint the evidentiary base by sitting on it interminably.

For professional investigative purposes, he explained, a stale evidentiary base, no matter its content, is simply unusable. These stonewalling strategies explain why so many DoD OIG "investigations" neither "substantiate nor non-substantiate" whistleblower retaliation. To spike an embarrassing case, all DoD OIG management has to do is to endlessly drag out the process, which it does with impunity.

"IT HAS BEEN DETERMINED TO BE A HOMICIDE"

In the film *The Godfather*, a fish is delivered by one gangster to another as a warning. Another type of warning was issued on January 8, 2019. On that day, Steven Luke, a long-time DoD OIG investigator of senior leader misconduct, and direct report to Marguerite Garrison, took the elevator down from his office to the lobby of the Mark Center building in Northern Virginia. He then crossed a narrow bridge linking that building to a dimly lit parking garage, for the last time. Luke never made it out of the parking garage alive. He was found dead, in the trunk of his car.

In 2013, Luke had informed Senator Grassley that Marguerite Garrison was tampering with DoD OIG investigations to reach her predetermined conclusions. At least once a year between 2016 and 2019, Luke disclosed to Grassley via the "whistleblower safe channel" that Garrison and her boss, acting DoD Inspector General Glenn A. Fine, were rigging or had "doctored" investigations. This subversion of the federal investigative process prompted Luke to write to colleagues "I take no joy in doing this. I like my co-workers. However, our ISO [Investigations of Senior Officials] process is broken and no one here is willing or able to change it."[5] That indicted Garrison, who had by then led that office for eight years.

As Amy Mackinnon reported in a long 2020 article for *Foreign Policy*, in the days leading up to Luke's death, he told his superiors that he had arranged to meet with members of Grassley's office on February 4, 2019.[6]

Mackinnon further reported that on January 7, Fine "wrote to Luke and offered to meet with him to talk through his concerns. Luke replied the next day to say he would be happy to meet that morning.... Later that day, when Luke failed to return home at the usual time, his wife raised the alarm. His body was found later that evening."[7]

Luke's death was reported by Mackinnon as a "suicide."[8] This outcome is not uncommon for those who face the legal labyrinth that is administrative due process, often having been unjustly charged with crimes they didn't commit. If Luke had indeed killed himself, that would have triggered a provision in the Dr. Chris Kirkpatrick Whistleblower Protection Act, the 2017 law named after a whistleblower who killed himself after succumbing to post-traumatic stress, anxiety, and severe depression.

According to that statute, following the suspected suicide by a federal whistleblower, there must be an immediate report to the U.S. Office of Special Counsel and a thorough investigation. But it appears that never happened. In lieu of alerting the proper federal authorities, it seems that acting DoD Inspector General Fine turned the investigation over to the City of Alexandria, Virginia. The results of that investigation were released pursuant to a FOIA request on April 11, 2022.

An email sent from the City Attorney's Office that accompanied the FOIA release of documents was the first indicator that something was not quite right.[9] The email specified that records provided by the Office of the City Attorney of Alexandria were "part of a criminal investigative file relating to a criminal investigation." Luke had died on the property of a federal facility. If there was to be a criminal investigation, it should have been conducted by federal criminal investigators, not the City of Alexandria.

Much of the FOIA file on the investigation was redacted: "Records being entirely withheld total approximately 68 pages." But the results were not suppressed. Page seven of the city attorney's file read: "RE: APD# 19-002531 Date: Tuesday, January 15, 2019, 1:25:00 p.m.

"It has been determined to be a homicide."[10]

A careful examination of the Alexandria Police Department (APD) FOIA file revealed a familiar pattern. In my case, Jennifer C. Walsh had investigated me and ended up incriminating my accusers. So Westgate, Baker, and Russell had Bruggeman conduct a "do over" investigation to get the results they wanted.

In Luke's case, the APD investigated Luke's death and determined that the whistleblower was murdered. But that investigative determination was covered up. In a series of emails sent over the course of January 30 and 31, 2019, DoD OIG and APD agreed to conduct a do-over investigation. But this time they agreed to consider only suicide as the "manner of death," ruling out the other four possibilities—natural, accident, homicide, or undetermined.

Even though APD was conducting that investigation, DoD OIG Associate General Counsel Michael J. Buxton insisted that DoD OIG had final release authority under FOIA of any APD work product: "Before releasing any documents, we want to confirm with you that these communications...would not be released to any outside parties."[11] The following day, Buxton reminded APD that "with respect to any FOIA requests....these documents are all marked For Official Use Only, and cannot be released without our authorization."[12]

The murder of a senior DoD OIG investigator reporting on the criminal misconduct of Fine and Garrison via the farcical "whistleblower safe channel" to Congress should have immediately triggered an FBI investigation. But that never happened. For the Deep State, that omission makes sense. A proper investigation into Luke's murder would have defeated the purpose of killing him in the manner it was done.

Like the fish in *The Godfather*, the whole point of murdering a senior DoD OIG investigator on the premises and stuffing his corpse crudely into the trunk of his car was to send a message. The audience for that message was Luke's fellow DoD OIG investigators of senior leader misconduct. They were to stay away from even thinking about holding Deep State operatives to account for their crimes. To make sure they got the point, the murderer and that individual's coconspirators were never held to account.

Several days after Mackinnon published her piece in *Foreign Policy*, I called the former DoD OIG official I had lunched with at the Persian restaurant. When I mentioned Luke, he hung up. He then texted me "OPSEC." That's DoD language for "operational security." He then asked to meet in person, and we did later that day.

"So, you thought I should know about Steven Luke," I began.

"No, no, that's not what I said."

"That's exactly what you said."

"But then I changed my mind. I told you to forget it."

"You said we were both whistleblowers and up against Margie Garrison and Glenn Fine. Did Luke have a reason to kill himself?" I asked.

"None. He suffered from depression, but it didn't get in the way of his work. He was on a mission, had the bit between his teeth. No one kills himself at the starting gate. That makes no sense. And it makes even less sense to kill yourself inside the trunk of your car at work. That's ridiculous," he said.

So why was the case completely dropped? That's precisely what needs to be investigated. Based on my knowledge about how Deep State operatives work, my hypothesis is that once the Alexandria Police Department determined that Luke was the victim of homicide, the DoD OIG's Glenn Fine or Marguerite Garrison could have scared local law enforcement away.

Perhaps they told the local officials that the circumstances surrounding Luke's death were highly classified, that he was the victim of a counterintelligence hit by a foreign power, or they simply had no "need to know." That is just an educated guess, but what other likely explanation could there be? The burden is now on Congress and the U.S. Department of Justice to ensure there is a proper criminal investigation into how Steven Luke died.

•   •   •

A year after Luke's body was found stuffed into the trunk of his car, Fine left DoD OIG and landed at the Brookings Institution. That prestigious think tank had served as Russiagate ground zero, or something close to it, and had boasted on its payroll Russian agents like Charles Dolan Jr. and Igor Danchenko.

Upon Fine's departure from government service, Senator Grassley said "The next inspector general needs to aggressively root out fraud, waste, abuse and mismanagement and make hard-hitting recommendations for corrective action." The senator had said almost the same thing when Fine first arrived at DoD OIG in January 2016: "Mr. Glenn Fine needs to grab the bull by the horns.... He needs to call the top officials involved on the carpet. This would include Mrs. Garrison."[13] That too was ignored.

In bidding good riddance to Fine, Grassley also suggested that DoD OIG's senior management team needed to be fired. Without a clean sweep, he argued, "bad outcomes" would persist as they had for years. Of course not only did that not happen, but just the opposite occurred.

In 2021, the Biden administration bestowed prestigious Presidential Rank Awards on both Marguerite Garrison and James Baker. Russell and Bruggeman had also by then received prestigious military medals for doing the opposite of what their commendation narratives said they had done.

212 | **THE INSIDER THREAT**

"At stake is nothing less than liberty under law," is how Columbia Law Professor Philip Hamburger describes what to expect if America fails to rein in the administrative state.[14] One wonders: How many more corpses of DoD whistleblowers need to be found before the U.S. Congress and Supreme Court recognize that it is simply impossible for the Deep State, a criminal, even murderous, enterprise infiltrated by Moscow and Beijing, to hold itself to account?

DEEP STATE END GAME

The past was erased, the erasure was forgotten, the lie
became the truth.

—GEORGE ORWELL[1]

The Framers of the U.S. constitutional order knew that human nature was invariable and that men driven by political gain could not be trusted. With nearly 250 years of data to draw upon, it should be clear to all that the U.S. Supreme Court decisions of the last half century that rely on a "presumption of regularity," the presumption that government officials will act according to their duty, are either hopelessly naïve or willfully subversive. What is more, it should be equally clear that deferring to the rulings of the administrative state poses a threat not just to the integrity of U.S. institutions and rule of law, but to the Republic as a whole.

After sitting on my case for 1,133 days, on January 13, 2021, Marguerite Garrison released my Whistleblower Retaliation Investigation (WRI) report to Senator Grassley. Then Garrison told me that if I wanted to see her report on my case (the results of which had already been reported to me in October 2017 by internal DoD OIG whistleblowers), I would need to file a FOIA request. That delaying tactic ensured further degradation of the evidentiary base, which would obstruct any future attempt to challenge her "findings."

The following year, on January 25, 2022, the DoD Office of Inspector General published a separate report titled "Audit of the

Office of Net Assessment's Contract Administration Procedures."
That report painted an illuminating picture of May's and Baker's
contracting practices, which had transformed ONA into a vehicle
for Moscow and Beijing to undermine America and our allies. It
also clearly evidenced that Garrison had been negligent (or worse)
in dismissing my disclosures to her in 2011, which had shown the
threat posed to U.S. national security by employing Halper and
Trubnikov on ONA contracts.

I would ultimately get Garrison's report on September 29, 2021,
1,391 days after it was first initiated and nearly 4 years to the day
after DoD OIG internal whistleblowers had told me that my case
incriminated Fine and Garrison personally. They had repeatedly
refused to investigate the leak of Japanese classified information
that I had reported to them. And they would stop at nothing to
cover that up.

Garrison's report paraded her Orwellian craft. Procedurally,
upon initiating her Whistleblower Retaliation Investigation, she
had promised to conduct an "investigation." But even that was not
done. Rather, she explained on page four, to conduct her four-year
long investigation she had conducted no investigation. She had also
employed the wrong legal standards for her legal analysis.

Substantively, Garrison's work product was so much the opposite of the federal investigative process that it seemed as if she had
swapped out the evidentiary base of my case and its applicable body
of law with something out of a Kafka novel. Her report contained
forty-two material false statements of fact. For instance, she wrote
that Baker had not acted to suspend my security clearance and
had done nothing to prevent me from moving to the NSC. She
asserted that Baker had done everything to help me move to the
NSC "unimpeded."

Garrison's staff had warned me back in 2017 that she would make
that false claim. For that reason, they gave me a document that they

had prepared for Garrison that evidenced just the opposite of what she later wrote in her report. Garrison's staff had also told me that she would gloss over the fact that both the Walsh and Bruggeman "investigations" were illegal. And she did.

Second, Garrison wrote that all of the internal investigations by conflicted insiders had been intended to investigate the source of the leak of Japanese classified information. Yet Baker had admitted under oath that they weren't—they were only intended to investigate me. Baker had also admitted he was both a leak suspect and the architect of both leak "investigations." Garrison found no problem with any of that.

Nor did she report that all of the five investigations, except Bruggeman's—the most conflicted of all, because he was investigating me on behalf of our mutual boss, who himself was an official leak suspect—exonerated me. Nor that the investigations had all been illegitimate from their inception because they were based on no evidence. Nor that evidence had been withheld illegally from me and my lawyer. Nor that the sole purpose of the internal investigations was to harass me into silence, to cover up my accusers' misconduct, and to shift the blame away from them and onto me.

Next, Garrison falsely attested that Jennifer C. Walsh's investigative report only "recommended that an electronic records search be conducted of U.S. government computers, portable devices, and telephones used within the ONA and by ONA personnel associated with the inquiry." It had done no such thing.

Garrison repeated the charge that I had carried classified information on a commercial airliner. She ignored the fact that the only investigative inquiry into that matter had determined that "[t]here was no evidence that classified information was compromised," and that the outcome of my actions "cannot reasonably be expected to, and does not, result in the loss, suspected compromise, or compromise of classified information."[2]

Most egregious of all, Garrison twisted my attorney's September 13, 2017, report to her that Baker, May, and Russell had shared Japanese classified information with a suspected Chinese spy and were still storing that same classified information on ONA's unclassified, shared computer drive. Garrison said that this report was not "related to [Lovinger's] official duties." That, too, was false. As a federal official I was bound by the Basic Obligation of Public Service to duly report criminal misconduct to the proper authorities, which in this case was the DoD OIG.

After reading Garrison's handiwork, Sean Bigley, who had by then represented me *pro bono* for more than three years, apologized to me. He did so not because of anything he had done wrong. Just the opposite. Bigley had vigorously defended me from beginning to end with skill and determination. He apologized because, to do his job, a lawyer needs to work in a baseline environment where the facts and law matter. But because these corrupt officials were free to change the facts and ignore the law with impunity, the most fundamental tools of his profession had been rendered irrelevant. Frustrated by the impossibility of getting justice for his clients against a rogue Deep State, Bigley closed his federal whistleblower law office soon thereafter.

CHAPTER 25

A WARNING FROM HISTORY

The deepest message, the most tragic [lesson from Thucydides for our modern times] is his picture of civilization as a very thin veneer. When you punch a hole in it, what you find underneath is hollow, the precivilized characteristics of the human race, animalistic in the worst way possible.

—DONALD KAGAN, PROFESSOR OF HISTORY, YALE UNIVERSITY[1]

A month before Garrison released her report to me, Kabul fell to the Taliban. Like America's ignominious withdrawal from Vietnam in 1975, our departure from Afghanistan, after twenty years of "muddling through" in that country, was a sad commentary on what passed as U.S. national security strategy.

Four years before, I had emerged from the metro at Farragut Square into the piercing early morning light. It was a bitterly cold day in the early months of my job at the NSC. The normally bustling Lafayette Park just north of the White House was cordoned off and nearly empty. Since I had a White House "blue badge," the Secret Service waved me through.

As I crossed Pennsylvania Avenue I looked up and saw, hanging at Blair House, the official guest residence of heads of state, an enormous blue and white Jewish prayer shawl with a Star of David in the middle. Israel's prime minister was visiting as a guest of the American people. At that moment, I thought of my father's family who, when he was four years old, were brutally rounded up by Nazi collaborators in Beled, Hungary, a town they had called home for over two hundred years. Placed in cattle cars, they were deported to Auschwitz and never heard from again.

In *The Dual State* (1941), Ernst Fraenkel described how the liberal democracies of Europe descended into perpetrators of evil on an industrial scale. A Jew from Cologne, Fraenkel served as a defense attorney in the Berlin Court of Appeals from 1933 to 1938. From that vantage point he witnessed the corruption of Germany's administrative state at the hands of bureaucrats. Within a few short years they had replaced a system of blind justice and due process with a highly efficient two-track system—one track for those like themselves, and another for undesirables.

The "Normative State" was track one. Fraenkel described it as "an administrative body endowed with elaborate powers for safeguarding the legal order as expressed in statutes, decisions of the courts, and activities of the administrative agencies." Track two, the "Prerogative State," was "that governmental system which exercises unlimited arbitrariness...unchecked by any legal guarantees."[2]

The Prerogative State turned a blind eye when administrative operatives systematically stripped Fraenkel's co-religionists of their property, civil rights, and dignity. By the time Germany mobilized its scientific-bureaucratic power to eliminate European Jewry on an industrial scale, the two states had merged into one. The steady corruption of administrative processes had ensured first the triumph, and then the normalization, of barbarism.

•   •   •

Mark Twain is credited with observing, "History may not repeat itself. But it rhymes." I would agree, as I would with Winston Churchill, who declared to the House of Commons in 1948, "Those that fail to learn from history are doomed to repeat it."

Alfred Dreyfus and I were both privileged to live in liberal democracies. We both had spotless careers and believed that our respective militaries were governed by the rule of law. We were confident that as long as we did our duty and followed the rules, the legal system would uncover and punish any systemic abuses of authority. But we were wrong. And while I did not face anything near the same kind of brutality that Dreyfus underwent, his case "rhymed" with mine in ways that may prove instructive to the readers of this book:

1. We were both accused of harboring "divided loyalties,"[3] not because of anything we did, but because of who we are.
2. Without even a scintilla of evidence, we were both accused of treasonous behavior. I was accused of leaking an ally's classified information to a journalist, and Dreyfus was charged with leaking his country's classified information to the German embassy in Paris.
3. We were scapegoated for the crimes of others. Baker, Russell, and LTSG contractors, not I, had egregiously mishandled Japanese classified information, and Westgate was grossly negligent (at best) for contracting on a classified project with not only individuals who lacked security clearances, but also an alleged Chinese spy. Dreyfus was accused of betraying France to Germany, but his accusers knew that it was Major Ferdinand Walsin Esterhazy who had leaked to the Germans. In both our cases, no one cared a whit who actually leaked, or how to prevent future security violations.
4. We were both maligned as "insider threats." Dreyfus posed no security threat but was nevertheless exiled to a penal colony in South America and placed under armed guards. Westgate and Baker knew they were the real "insider threats," but they accused me of being a terrorist subversive to launch their illegal investigations.

5 We were both found innocent by secret investigations that were withheld from us and the public.

6 After concealing exculpatory evidence exonerating us of their charges, our accusers continued to press charges against us based on known falsehoods. They did so in order to deflect blame from themselves.

7 We both languished for years under a cloud of unwarranted suspicion.

8 Our respective governments spent vast sums persecuting us, irrespective of their fiduciary responsibilities to the taxpayer.

9 The "watchdogs" responsible for examining our cases saw immediately that the charges against us were unfounded, but they did nothing about it. Instead, they fabricated new charges to keep up the charade.

10 Both our cases implicated larger issues concerning the strategic fate of our countries. This is where the denouement of the Dreyfus Affair may prove most instructive for the present.

By all measures, France should have had the most formidable army in continental Europe in the late nineteenth century. But the French military's culture of covering up malfeasance, which became engrained and normalized during the Dreyfus Affair, spread an invisible rot. Dreyfus was accused of leaking to Germany, and German intelligence knew that was false. This gave Germany a ringside seat to an invaluable spectacle: its greatest adversary consuming itself in internecine treachery. The lesson is unmistakable. A corrupt military is a weak one—divided, ripe for infiltration, subverted, and ultimately doomed.

Nearly two millennia earlier, the philosopher and poet Cicero made a similar point, which earned him the enmity of the tyrants who would ultimately put an end to the Roman Republic. His masterpiece *De Republica* is still considered the gold standard in describing an ethical state. When Caesar crossed the Rubicon in violation of Rome's law, Cicero saw that the demise of the Republic was at hand. As Stefan Zweig recounts:

> The Senate and the assembled populace listened to [Cicero's] Philippics with astonishment. Many, perhaps, foresaw that this was the last time for centuries when such words could be uttered in the market-place. Soon in this public spot people would only bow silently before the marble statues of the emperors, for instead of the free speech of old, all that would be tolerated in the realm of the Caesars would be the whispering of flatterers and place-hunters. The audience shuddered, with mingled fear and admiration of this old man who, with the courage of despair continued to defend the independence of the disintegrated Republic. But even the fire-brand of his eloquence failed to kindle the rotting stem of the Roman pride. While the lonely idealist was in the Forum advocating self-sacrifice, the unscrupulous masters of the legions were already entering into the most atrocious pact in Roman history.... It was a momentous turn in universal history when the three generals, instead of obeying the Senate and respecting the laws of Rome, united to form a triumvirate and to divide, as easily won spoils of war, a mighty empire which extended over a considerable part of three continents.... One who wishes to found a dictatorship must above all, in order to safeguard his rule, silence the perpetual opponents of tyranny.... Cicero was more dangerous than any others of his stamp, for he had mental energy and a yearning for independence. Mark him down, then, for death.[4]

The rhyme of history is unmistakable. Like Rome before it, France never recovered from the Dreyfus Affair. In World War I, the German High Command exploited the French military's institutional rot to devastating effect.

After Dreyfus's accusers passed from the scene, their place was taken by their bureaucratic offspring, Vichy's Nazi collaborators. Lacking honor themselves, those vain, bigoted men, who wore medals they knew they had not earned, unleashed their own assaults on all that was noble and good. France, once a Great Power, never recovered.

The same corrupt culture that permitted the Dreyfus Affair now infects our U.S. national security, intelligence, and law enforcement bureaucracies. Abraham Lincoln warned in 1858 that "a house divided against itself cannot stand." During World War II and the Cold War, enemy agents leveraged that insight by triangulating with American fellow-travelers to divide and subvert our Republic from within. Ronald Reagan, who spent his early career as an actor in Hollywood, where he witnessed that first hand, provided his own warning from history. "Freedom," Reagan said, recognizing the fragility of democratic society,

> is never more than one generation away from extinction. We didn't pass it on to our children in the bloodstream. The only way they can inherit the freedom we have known is if we fight for it, protect it, defend it and then hand it to them with the well-thought lessons of how they, in their lifetime, must do the same. And if you and I don't do this, then you and I may well spend our sunset years telling our children and our children's children what it once was like in America when men were free.[5]

Reagan's "one day" might be today. In 2021, a Project on Government Oversight poll found that 70 percent of Americans were "very" or "extremely" concerned about corruption in the federal government.[6] A 2022 Pew Research Center poll found that only about 20 percent of Americans trust the federal government, a finding that "is among the lowest trust measures in nearly seven decades of polling."[7]

The surest way to undermine confidence in the U.S. government is to parade before the American people how those who are relied upon to enforce the law are actually the greatest lawbreakers of all. To turbocharge this process, corrupt officials team up with "enemies foreign and domestic" to subvert our governmental institutions. As a trained national security analyst and lawyer, I believe that all the key indicators suggest they have succeeded.

Growing fastest of all is a sense among ordinary Americans that a real "insider threat" infects the U.S. government. According to pollsters from the *Washington Post* and University of Maryland, 34 percent of Americans in 2022 believed that violence against internal enemies within the federal government is sometimes justified.[8] Think about that for a minute. Yet as alarming as that poll may seem, it should also remind us how little Americans have changed over the centuries. What has changed, and is eliciting that sentiment among so many Americans, is the current state of our government.

On July 4, 1776, the Continental Congress tasked a committee comprising Benjamin Franklin, Thomas Jefferson, and John Adams to design the Great Seal of the United States of America. Their proposed seal, which was abandoned after being deemed far too visually complex, had Moses and the Hebrews standing up on high as they watched Pharaoh's army receiving God's wrath below. Those Egyptian soldiers not drowned in the waves of the Red Sea had their hearts pierced by heavenly fire. Perhaps warning future generations of Americans about the imperative to safeguard our democracy from the subversive designs of corrupt officials, the committee's proposed motto for the fledgling United States of America was "Rebellion to Tyrants Is Obedience to God."

"Let other peoples live as slaves. We Romans refuse. If we cannot win freedom, let us die," Cicero bellowed from the rostrum. But Cicero's warning to the people of Rome came too late to make a difference, and Rome's preeminent whistleblower lost his head as a result of speaking truth to power.[9] Rome transformed from a Republic into a dictatorship.

CHAPTER 26

A CALL TO ACTION

When once a republic is corrupted, there is no possibility of remedying
any of the growing evils, but by removing the corruption and
restoring its lost principles: every other correction
is either useless or a new evil.
—MONTESQUIEU[1]

I have taught in three Georgetown University graduate programs since 2014. Many of my students are U.S. military officers earning a master's degree in public policy or foreign service. Most of them are distinguished graduates of our military academies at West Point and Annapolis. They are, hands down, the most idealistic, patriotic, and public service–minded young Americans I have ever encountered. But in the past five years, I have detected a change. The conflict between what they learn in their studies and from the oaths they take as military officers and the reality of what they face in the U.S. government, has troubled some of them deeply.

On one hand, the values and ideals they learn from the military academies and Georgetown instill in them a love of classical liberalism, truth, honor, and reverence for the U.S. Constitution. On the other hand, they have increasingly become aware that the upper ranks of the U.S. national security, intelligence, and law enforcement bureaucracies are all too often the exclusive preserve of lawless and corrupt officials who hold shockingly anti-American world views. While my students, America's sons and daughters, are deployed to war zones overseas, these Deep State operatives advance their dream of a balance of power between America and its allies on one side and Communist China, Putin's Russia, and the Islamic Republic of Iran on the other.

To cut America down to size, the Deep State emplaced saboteurs in the Pentagon's highest strategy office. There, instead of doing their job and completing net assessment–informed national security strategies to win our wars, they advance a plan to "muddle through" for decades on end, guaranteeing our defeat. This has resulted in not only the needless death, maiming, and cognitive trauma of U.S. military forces, but also the insidious destruction of America's most hallowed institution from within.

My students have learned that if they put their education to use and try to fix this horrendous state of affairs, which places the U.S. military and their very lives at risk, they will necessarily become whistleblowers. Yet as a result of that honorable action, they will be labeled "insider threats" by the Deep State, and treated as such.

Once charged, a sophisticated, well-organized cabal of corrupt officials will hound them for years. As they are pushed through an interminable and maddening ordeal called administrative due process, they will discover that nothing they learned about the proper functioning of the U.S. government bears any resemblance to reality. In a process unbeholden to both either facts or the law, their careers will be ruined, at best. Worse, they could find themselves murdered and stuffed into the trunks of their cars.

Foreseeably, for many of these students, discovering the reality and extent of U.S. government corruption can be soul-crushing. As one brilliant young West Point graduate told me, "Professor Lovinger, based on what happened to you, I no longer trust the senior leadership of the Pentagon to have my back when I'm deployed overseas. I'm going to serve my time and get out."

But for others, the existence of the Deep State is a call to action. They are the spiritual progeny of America's Revolutionary generation.

For our Founding Fathers, the preservation of what was good, virtuous, and honorable was of greater importance than life itself. They knew that the only thing necessary for the triumph of evil is for good men to do nothing. In his 1928 novel *The Magic Mountain*, Thomas Mann would echo that idea, writing that "Tolerance becomes a crime when applied to evil."[2] So too would Holocaust survivor and human rights leader Elie Wiesel: "Indifference is what allows evil to be strong, what gives it power."[3]

To my students who see the existence of the Deep State as a treasonous foe unworthy of this land, I have advised as follows.

First, fight on, but never underestimate what you're up against. Of the fifty-six signers of the Declaration of Independence in 1776, many sacrificed their lives and fortunes fighting for the principles they swore to uphold. Nine of the fifty-six died in the ensuing Revolutionary War; five were taken prisoner and tortured; and twelve had their family homes burned to the ground. But for them, it was axiomatic to fight on, because not doing so was a fate worse than defeat. As Alexis de Tocqueville would later articulate, the Founders saw it as the central task of every generation to transmit "the whole moral and intellectual state of a people"[4] to the next generation. Giving up on that sacred duty means thymotic death.

Second, while the Deep State is a formidable cancer, and more insidious and deeply rooted today than at any time in U.S. history, it is not invincible. Rather, it is a hulking Goliath with myriad vulnerabilities that one David (or, better yet, many Davids) can exploit.

Third, look to history for strength. Your mission is noble, and you are part of a glorious tradition. Cicero's death marked the end of the Roman Republic, but his essential message was preserved for posterity: "My one wish is that in dying I shall give back liberty to the Roman people. What greater favor than this could the immortal gods bestow on me?"[5]

Fourth, and relatedly, the job at hand—defeating the subversive designs of corrupt government officials—has been achieved before, and much can be learned from those historical victories. In the wake of President Nixon's resignation, Democratic senator Frank Church spearheaded the congressional effort to rein in Deep State abuses against the American people. "Hiding evil is the trademark of a totalitarian government," Church stated in 1975.

> There is no more pernicious threat to a free society than a secret police which is operating beyond the law.... If these abuses had not been uncovered and had the agencies gone unchecked, we might well have seen a secret police develop in the United States. Once that begins, the Constitution itself is in very real danger.[6]

The senator knew whereof he spoke. No less than "three of the Church Committee's witnesses turned up dead—one shot right before his testimony, one killed by a car bomb, and one found dismembered in a barrel."[7]

Fifth, there is growing momentum in favor of accountability. A growing critical mass of informed citizens understands that the Deep State is not "Trump's crazy talk," as its fellow travelers want Americans to believe, but a real, existential threat to liberal democracy.

Sixth, the Deep State can be picked apart with a targeted, surgical effort. While that cabal as a whole may now be more powerful than all three branches of the federal government combined, its individual members are weak and cowardly gangsters. Indeed, like all authoritarian thugs throughout history, their power is like an empty eggshell: seemingly strong, but with a little force, surprisingly fragile, and vacuous. Their hatred, bitterness, and anger are toxic to the human spirit and everything our Republic stands for. By partaking in their illicit enterprise, they crush their own souls.

Finally, the playbook is no longer a secret. The playbook reveals the Deep State's strategic character and enduring predispositions, and it provides detailed descriptions of its tactics, techniques, and procedures. It also reveals the Deep State's weaknesses, which can be exploited. It does this by showing us which U.S. laws, rules, regulations, and directives can be ignored or corrupted, and which ones cannot.

This reinforces what I experienced in my own case, and what I discovered in my study of others: the Deep State operates in a rote, unimaginative manner, constrained by its own rigid administrative architecture. That is the Deep State's Achilles heel.

I debated with my mentors whether I should write this book and expose the Deep State for what it is. Some said that I should publish what I have learned about this morally inverted universe ruled by corrupt ideologues who think nothing of undermining U.S. interests while zealously advancing those of Russia, China, and Iran.

Others said, no, keep it quiet, play it safe, be like most Deep State victims, bring as little attention to your case as possible. The more attention it gets, the more professionally tainted you'll become in the risk-averse U.S. national security community.

But I can't do that. Too many Americans who chose to serve their nation find their careers, families, reputations, and lives destroyed by the Deep State simply for doing their jobs honestly and with integrity. Exposing the Deep State is a duty I owe to my family, my students, and my country.

EXHIBIT A

On December 1, 2016, ONA director James H. Baker drafted an appointment letter for a "preliminary inquiry" into the leak of Japanese classified information. Baker named himself as a leak suspect and chose (by name) the other leak suspects. But then Baker admitted to the true purpose of the inquiry. This was not to investigate the source of the leak, but only to investigate a certain "DoD employee" (see "PURPOSES AND USES" section), whom he later admitted under oath was me.

MEMORANDUM FOR XXXX XXXX[1]

SUBJECT: Appointment of Investigation Official

You are hereby appointed to conduct an investigation to determine whether improper disclosures were made by personnel in the Office of Net Assessment. An article appearing in the Washington Free Beacon on 23 November 2016 disclosed sensitive information and put at risk ONA's ability to conduct its mission. This information was disclosed with intent to harm the office and our relationship with the Japanese. I would like you to investigate who disclosed this information, based on a preponderance of the evidence. If this finding is indeterminate, I would like your judgment on who most likely had both motive and opportunity to disclose the information.

Please take care to make your investigation as discrete as possible. The fact of an investigation will erode morale and trust within the office. You should begin with limited number of individuals who could have overheard the conversation disclosed in the article, as well as had access to the confidential Japanese materials. That would include Mr. Baker, CDR Tony Russell, Mr. Adam Lovinger, and Ms. Kristin Fitzgerald. Support ONA has received for the effort mentioned in the articles has come from a contractor, LTSG. They have voluntarily agreed to support the investigation. LTSG personnel with access to the materials and the conversation included Steve Rosen, Jackie Deal, and Michael Mort. You will also have access to email, copier and phone records of the ONA personnel. Post these interviews, you should speak to whomever else you feel necessary to reach conclusive findings.

This memorandum authorizes you to interview and/or obtain sworn statements from government personnel, and gather facts related to any potential impropriety described above.

Legal advice and guidance should be obtained from the Office of General Counsel regarding administrative regulatory matters, and other issues that may arise in the course of the investigation. The point of contact for this investigation is myself. The point of contact within the Office of General Counsel is Mr. XXXXX, Deputy General Counsel, at (703) 604-6588.

A written report of findings is due to me as soon as practical. Do not make recommendations for management action; rather, discuss your fact-finding. In the event you encounter any challenges requiring an extension of the original suspense, please contact me immediately. Should your investigation uncover evidence of serious misconduct outside the scope of this inquiry, immediately cease actions and obtain further legal advice.

                                        Steve Hedger
                                        Chief of Staff

cc:
Director, HRD
OGC

Privacy Act Notice

Pursuant to Public Law 93-579 (Privacy Act of 1974), as an individual, supplying information for inclusion in a system of records, you are being informed of the following:

EFFECTS OF NONDISCLOSURE: Military members and civilian employees of the Department of Defense (DoD) and its components and agencies are obligated to cooperate in official inquiries/investigations and may be subjected to administrative action for failing to do so. If you are not a military member or civilian employee of DoD, the disclosure of information by you is voluntary; however, your failure to respond will result in a recommended disposition of the case on the basis of information available.

AUTHORITY: The authority to collect the information requested by this interview is derived from one or more of the following: Title 5, Code of Federal Regulations (CFR), Sections 5.2 and 5.3; title 5, United States Code, Sections 1302, 1303, 1304, 3301, and 3302; Executive Order 11478 as amended; Executive Order 10577; and 29 CFR 1614.

PURPOSES AND USES: The information supplied will be used as part of the record in an inquiry into alleged statements and actions made by a DoD employee. The record will be furnished to designees of agencies and departments of the Federal Government in order to resolve the matter. The record may also be disclosed to any agency of the Federal Government having oversight or review authority with regard to Office of Personnel Management or Department of Defense activities, to the Federal intelligence agencies, or to others as published in the Federal Register.

---------------------------------⊠

1 According to U.S. Government evidence, this draft appointment memorandum was generated by ONA Director James H. Baker on December 1, 2016, at 10:16AM.

EXHIBIT B

The final appointment letter, signed by Deputy Secretary of Defense Robert O. Work's Chief of Staff, Steven Hedger, omits the incriminating "PURPOSES AND USES" section of Baker's draft.

OFFICE OF THE SECRETARY OF DEFENSE

1000 DEFENSE PENTAGON
WASHINGTON, DC 20301-1000

JAN 04 2017

MEMORANDUM FOR JENNIFER C. WALSH

SUBJECT: Request for Preliminary Inquiry and Assessment

This is to request that you conduct an independent preliminary inquiry to determine the reasonable credibility of the allegation described below, followed by a report to me containing a recommendation for appropriate disposition.

On November 23, 2016, an article was published in The Washington Free Beacon (http://freebeacon.com), entitled "Japanese Intelligence Tells Pentagon China Engaged in Multi-Year Takeover Attempt of Senkaku Islands" (attached). The article may be found at URL http://freebeacon.com/national-security/japanese-intelligence-tells-pentagon-china-engaged-multi-year-takeover-attempt-senkaku-islands.

Within the article are discussions concerning official United States Government positions regarding China and Japan. There are specific discussions concerning the Office of the Secretary of Defense, Office of Net Assessment. The allegation has been made that the discussions are of such specificity that the author of the article could not have been aware of the specifics without the assistance of someone with knowledge of the inner workings and deliberations of the Office of Net Assessment. The allegation also suggests that specific information that was discussed at a meeting held between United States and Japanese Officials was disclosed in the article.

You should interview the following persons who may have knowledge concerning this matter: James Baker, Director of the Office of Net Assessment; Commander Tony Russell; and Mr. Adam Lovinger. The following employees of contractor LTSG should also be interviewed: Steve Rosen; Jackie Deal; and Michael Mort. If, during the course of your Inquiry, you determine that other Government and/or contractor personnel should be interviewed, you should also interview such personnel. You may also request access to email and phone records of Office of Net Assessment personnel and contract personnel working on Government computers and using Government telephone equipment. You may also review such documentary evidence as will be of assistance to you in your Inquiry.

Before beginning your Inquiry, you should consult with ▮▮▮▮▮ and ▮▮▮
▮▮▮ of the WHS & PFPA Office of General Counsel for advice and counsel
in this matter. They will serve as your legal advisors during the course of your Inquiry.

I would appreciate your written report and recommendations no later than 30
days from receipt of this Memorandum.

Stephen Hedger
Chief of Staff to the Deputy Secretary of Defense
    and Deputy Chief of Staff to the Secretary of Defense

Attachment:
As stated

NOTES

CHAPTER 1: DISCOVERING THE DEEP STATE

1 "*The Federalist* Number 51, [6 February] 1788," Founders Online, National Archives, https://founders.archives.gov/documents/Madison/01-10-02-0279. Original source: *The Papers of James Madison*, vol. 10, *27 May 1787–3 March 1788*, ed. Robert A. Rutland et al. (Chicago: The University of Chicago Press, 1977), 476–480.

2 Max Fisher, "What Happens When You Fight a 'Deep State' That Doesn't Exist," *New York Times*, March 10, 2017, https://www.nytimes.com/2017/03/10/world/americas/what-happens-when-you-fight-a-deep-state-that-doesnt-exist.html.

3 The Intelligence Community "SES" equivalent is called the "Senior Intelligence Service," or "SIS."

4 See Exhibits A and B for the "before" and "after" versions of this form, which I discovered in the Deep State playbook.

CHAPTER 2: THE OFFICE OF NET ASSESSMENT

1 Fort Washington was completed in 1824 in response to the British burning of the capital city during the War of 1812.

2 Craig Whitlock, "At War with the Truth," *Washington Post*, December 9, 2019, https://www.washingtonpost.com/graphics/2019/investigations/afghanistan-papers/afghanistan-war-confidential-documents.

3 Whitlock, "At War with the Truth."

4 Lucius Annaeus Seneca, quoted in Ugo Bardi, *Before the Collapse: A Guide to the Other Side of Growth* (Switzerland: Springer, 2020), 81.

5 Marvin Zois, "Veiled Prejudice," *New York Times*, August 5, 1990, https://www.nytimes.com/1990/08/05/books/veiled-prejudice.html.

6 Whitlock, "At War with the Truth."

7 Greg Jaffe, "From Hubris to Humiliation: America's Warrior Class Contends with the Abject Failure of its Afghanistan Project," *Washington Post*, August 14, 2021, https://www.washingtonpost.com/national-security/us-hubris-afghanistan-humiliation/2021/08/14/47fb025a-fc67-11eb-9c0e-97e29906a970_story.html.

8 Dan Merica, "ISIS Is Neither Islamic nor a State, Says Hillary Clinton," CNN, October 7, 2014, https://www.cnn.com/2014/10/06/politics/hillary-clinton-isis/index.html.

9   Baktash Ahabi, "Opinion: I Was a Combat Interpreter in Afghanistan, Where Cultural Illiteracy Led to U.S. Failure," *Washington Post*, August 31, 2021, https://www.washingtonpost.com/opinions/2021/08/31/afghanistan-combat-interpreter-baktash-ahadi-us-cultural-illiteracy.

10 *Stabilization: Lessons from the U.S. Experience in Afghanistan*, Special Inspector General for Afghanistan Reconstruction (Arlington, VA, 2018), i.

11 Ahabi, "Opinion: I Was a Combat Interpreter in Afghanistan."

12 Craig Whitlock, "Stranded without a Strategy," *Washington Post*, December 9, 2019, https://www.washingtonpost.com/graphics/2019/investigations/afghanistan-papers/afghanistan-war-strategy.

13 George Orwell, "In Front of Your Nose," in *The Collected Essays, Journalism and Letters of George Orwell* (London: Secker & Warburg, 1968), 124.

14 Bob Crowley, quoted in Whitlock, "Stranded without a Strategy."

15 Whitlock, "Stranded without a Strategy."

16 Craig Whitlock, "Built to Fail: Despite Vows the U.S. Wouldn't Get Mired in 'Nation-Building,' It's Wasted Billions Doing Just That," *Washington Post*, December 9, 2019, https://www.washingtonpost.com/graphics/2019/investigations/afghanistan-papers/afghanistan-war-nation-building.

17 Craig Whitlock, *The Afghanistan Papers: A Secret History of the War* (New York: Simon & Schuster, 2021), xii–xiii.

18 Colbert I. King, "There Must be a Public Accounting for the Afghanistan Failure," *Washington Post*, December 13, 2019, https://www.washingtonpost.com/opinions/there-must-be-a-public-accounting-for-the-afghanistan-failure/2019/12/13/915cfb30-1d32-11ea-b4c1-fd0d91b60d9e_story.html.

19 Ronald Reagan, "Address before a Joint Session of the Congress Reporting on the State of the Union," January 26, 1982, The American Presidency Project, accessed June 22, 2024, https://www.presidency.ucsb.edu/documents/address-before-joint-session-the-congress-reporting-the-state-the-union-2.

20 "Deaths in Wars, Battle Deaths per Million People," Gapminder, accessed June 29, 2024, https://www.gapminder.org/topics/deaths-in-wars.

CHAPTER 3: THE OBAMA DOCTRINE

1   "Book of the Week—M. Tullii Ciceronis, Orationum ...," J. Willard Marriott Library, University of Utah, January 12, 2016, https://blog.lib.utah.edu/book-of-the-week-m-tullii-ciceronis-orationum.

2   Timothy Shenk, "A Lost Manuscript Shows the Fire Obama Couldn't Reveal on the Campaign Trail," guest essay, *New York Times*, October 7, 2022, https://www.nytimes.com/2022/10/07/opinion/obama-lost-book-manuscript.html.

3   "Obama's Interview with Al Arabiya," transcript, Al Arabiya, January 27, 2009, https://english.alarabiya.net/articles/2009/01/27/65096.

4   Barack Obama, "Remarks by the President at Cairo University, 6-04-09" June 4, 2009, The White House, https://obamawhitehouse.archives.gov/the-press-office/remarks-president-Cairo-university-6-04-09.

5 Dennis Ross, "Being There: A Slice of U.S.-Israeli Relations," *American Interest* 2, no. 12 (October 14, 2015), https://www.the-american-interest.com/2015/10/14/being-there-a-slice-of-u-s-israeli-relations.

6 Barack Obama, "Remarks by President Obama at Strasbourg Town Hall," The White House, April 3, 2009, at http://www.whitehouse.gov/the_press_office/Remarks-by-President-Obama-at-Strasbourg-Town-Hall.

7 Barack Obama, "News Conference by President Obama, 4/04/2009," The White House, April 4, 2009, https://obamawhitehouse.archives.gov/the-press-office/news-conference-president-obama-4042009.

8 "Americans again widely agree that the United States should be actively engaged abroad, with 64 percent of Americans saying the United States should play an active role in world affairs, an increase of six percentage points from last year." "2015 Chicago Council Survey," The Chicago Council on Global Affairs, September 15, 2015, https://globalaffairs.org/research/public-opinion-survey/2015-chicago-council-survey. "Americans are not...backing away from their long-held commitment to take an active part in world affairs. They support a strong global military posture and are committed to alliances, international treaties and agreements, humanitarian interventions, and multilateral approaches to many problems. Americans also support many direct U.S. actions to address critical threats to U.S. vital interests." "2010 Chicago Council Survey," The Chicago Council on Global Affairs, September 16, 2010, https://globalaffairs.org/research/public-opinion-survey/2010-chicago-council-survey. See also "2019 Chicago Council Survey," The Chicago Council on Global Affairs, September 16, 2019, https://globalaffairs.org/research/public-opinion-survey/2019-chicago-council-survey.

9 "Gallup Daily: Obama Job Approval," Gallup, accessed June 22, 2024, https://news.gallup.com/poll/113980/gallup-daily-obama-job-approval.aspx. See also "Presidential Job Approval Center," Gallup, accessed August 8, 2024, https://news.gallup.com/interactives/507569/presidential-job-approval-center.aspx.

10 James Kirchick, "Squanderer in Chief," *Los Angeles Times*, April 28, 2009, https://www.latimes.com/archives/la-xpm-2009-apr-28-oe-kirchick28-story.html.

11 "2010 Chicago Council Survey"; "2015 Chicago Council Survey"; "2019 Chicago Council Survey."

12 Thomas Sowell, "Obama's 'Balanced' Approach," Hoover Institution, July 29, 2011, https://www.hoover.org/research/obamas-balanced-approach.

13 Madeleine K. Albright, quoted in "Interview on NBC-TV 'The Today Show' with Matt Lauer," February 19, 1998, U.S. Department of State Archive, accessed June 22, 2024, https://1997-2001.state.gov/statements/1998/980219a.html.

14 S. E. Cupp, "Hillary Clinton's Depressing Defeatism," CNN, August 19, 2015, https://www.cnn.com/2015/08/19/opinions/cupp-hillary-clinton-defeatist-mindset/index.html.

15 Hillary Clinton, *Living History* (New York: Scribner, 2003), 38.

16 "From George Washington to Officers of the Army, 15 March, 1783" (the Newburgh Address), Founders Online, accessed August 9, 2024, https://founders.archives.gov/documents/Washington/99-01-02-10840.

17 John F. Kennedy, "The President and the Press: Address before the American Newspaper Publishers Association," the Waldorf-Astoria Hotel, New York City, April 27, 1961, transcript, John F. Kennedy Presidential Library & Museum, accessed June 22, 2024, https://www.jfklibrary.org/archives/other-resources/john-f-kennedy-speeches/american-newspaper-publishers-association-19610427.

CHAPTER 4: TRANSFORMATION FROM WITHIN

1 When Marshall died in 2019, it was only natural for the *Washington Post* to ask Pillsbury to sum up the long arc of his mentor's storied career and distill its essence: "'He had an uncanny ability to pick out only the most significant questions, then to drill down deeply,' Michael Pillsbury, a colleague of 45 years, said in an interview." Matt Schudel, "Andrew Marshall, Pentagon's Gnomic 'Yoda' of Long-Range Planning, Dies at 97," *Washington Post*, March 27, 2019, https://www.washingtonpost.com/local/obituaries/andrew-marshall-pentagons-gnomic-yoda-of-long-range-planning-dies-at-97/2019/03/27.

2 Draft, Job Opportunity Announcement, OSD-05-8611-EL, Office of the Secretary of Defense.

3 Agency Position No. DDES 2378, Associate Director, Net Assessment, Office of the Secretary of Defense.

4 The chairman of the Joint Chiefs of Staff serves merely in an advisory role to the president and secretary of defense. He is not part of the legally mandated chain of command, cannot transmit battle orders, and cannot countermand or interfere with any such order.

5 James H. Baker, "Application for Vacancy: Director, Net Assessment, Department of Defense, Office of the Secretary of Defense, SES-1292546-RM", 5–6.

6 Baker, "Application for Vacancy."

7 Bill Gertz, "Pentagon's Office of Threat Assessment under Fire from Military, Congress," *Washington Times*, August 24, 2016, https://www.washingtontimes.com/news/2016/aug/24/pentagons-offic-of-threat-assement-under-fire-from.

8 Joe Gould, "New Face to Lead Pentagon Strategy Shop," *Defense News*, May 16, 2015, https://www.defensenews.com/pentagon/2015/05/16/new-face-to-lead-pentagon-strategy-shop.

9 Michael J. Glennon, "Security Breach: Trump's Tussle with the Bureaucratic State," *Harper's Magazine*, June 2017, https://harpers.org/archive/2017/06/security-breach.

10 James Comey, quoted in Michael Goodwin, "Comey's Media Tour Shows Why We're Better Off without Him," *New York Post*, April 28, 2018, https://nypost.com/2018/04/28/comeys-media-tour-shows-why-were-better-off-without-him.

CHAPTER 5: A NUCLEAR IRAN WOULD "MORE FAIRLY REBALANCE AMERICAN INFLUENCE"

1 Jeffrey Goldberg, "The Obama Doctrine," *The Atlantic*, April 2016, https://www.theatlantic.com/magazine/archive/2016/04/the-obama-doctrine/471525.

2 Robert Malley, "The Unwanted Wars: Why the Middle East Is More Combustible than Ever," *Foreign Affairs*, October 2, 2019, https://www.foreignaffairs.com/articles/middle-east/2019-10-02/unwanted-wars.

3 The Joint Comprehensive Plan of Action is not a treaty, but a "deal," signed in July 2015 by China, France, Russia, the United Kingdom, the United States, and Germany. The JCPOA was sold to the public as a way of preventing Iran from developing nuclear weapons.

4 Jeremiah Wright, quoted in "Reverend Wright Transcript," ABC News, April 24, 2008, https://abcnews.go.com/Blotter/story?id=4719157&page=1.

5 Dan Roberts and Ben Jacobs, "Iran Deal: Obama May Have Support He Needs to Avoid Using Veto," *The Guardian*, September 8, 2015, https://www.theguardian.com/us-news/2015/sep/08/senate-democrats-support-iran-nuclear-deal-block-disapproval-resolution.

6 Ali Khamenei, quoted in Carol Morello, "Ayatollah Says Nuclear Deal Will Not Change Iran's Relations with U.S.," *Washington Post*, July 18, 2015, https://www.washingtonpost.com/world/national-security/ayatollah-says-nuclear-deal-will-not-change-irans-relations-with-us/2015/07/18/7470b531-ff12-4913-81e1-21101130fbdd_story.html.

7 Mohammad Javad Zarif, quoted in Adam Kredo, "Iran Nuke Deal Permits Cheating on Arms, Missiles," Washington Free Beacon, July 27, 2015, https://freebeacon.com/national-security/iran-nuke-deal-permits-cheating-on-arms-missiles.

8 Mike Mullen, "Why I Like the Iran Deal (Sort Of)," *Politico*, April 16, 2015, https://www.politico.com/magazine/story/2015/04/iran-deal-mike-mullen-117010/. Emphasis added.

9 James H. Baker, "Rise of Eurasian Revisionist Powers (Iran, Russia, China) and the Implications for the Japan-U.S. Alliance," speech, July 2017.

10 Baker, "Rise of Eurasian Revisionist Powers."

11 Baker articulated this view in an address titled "Global Challenges: What Are the Threats Ahead?" Baker would give this speech to multiple closed-door audiences. Baker had several go-to speeches like this that he used to articulate the Obama Doctrine. Baker stored this one on the ONA share drive, a Pentagon computer drive accessible to everyone in ONA.

12 Director General, IAEA Board of Governors, *Verification and Monitoring in the Islamic Republic of Iran in Light of United National Security Council Resolution 2232 (2015)*, IAEA, November 22, 2022, https://www.iaea.org/sites/default/files/23/03/govinf2022-24.pdf.

13 George Jahn, "UN Said to Let Iran Inspect Its Own Alleged Nuclear Activity Site," Times of Israel, August 19, 2015, https://www.timesofisrael.com/un-to-let-iran-inspect-alleged-nuke-work-site.

14 Imam Sayyid Ali Khamenei (@khamenei_ir), "US president has said he could knock out Iran's military. We welcome no war, nor do we initiate any war, but...," Twitter July 25, 2015, 7:48 a.m., https://x.com/khamenei_ir/status/624909057573408768.

15 Julie Pace and Josh Lederman, "Obama Defends Iran Deal as Only Option to Avert Arms Race," *PBS Newshour*, July 15, 2015, https://www.pbs.org/newshour/politics/iran-deal-obama-sees-validation-diplomatic-gamble.

16 Lee Smith, "The Art of Undoing the Iran Deal," *Weekly Standard*, November 11, 2016, accessed at Hudson Institute, https://www.hudson.org/national-security-defense/the-art-of-undoing-the-iran-deal.

17 Amir Taheri, "Obama and Ahmadinejad," *Forbes*, October 26, 2008, https://www.forbes.com/2008/10/26/obama-iran-ahmadinejad-oped-cx_at_1026taheri.html?sh=76e00148c069.

18 Fariborz Ghadar, "Iran's Nuclear Negotiations and the West," Center for Strategic and International Studies, November 12, 2009, https://www.csis.org/analysis/irans-nuclear-negotiations-and-west.

19 Mohammad Ali Jafari, quoted in Reuel Gerecht and Ray Takeyh, "How Trump Can Help Cripple the Iranian Regime," *Washington Post*, April 7, 2017, https://www.washingtonpost.com/news/global-opinions/wp/2017/04/07/how-trump-can-help-cripple-the-iranian-regime.

20 Ayatollah Ali Khamenei, quoted in Gerecht and Takeyh, "How Trump Can Help Cripple."

21 Adam Kredo, "Iran Nuke Deal Permits Cheating on Arms, Missiles," Washington Free Beacon, July 27, 2015, https://freebeacon.com/national-security/iran-nuke-deal-permits-cheating-on-arms-missiles.

22 This pattern was repeated following the Biden administration's release of $6 billion to Tehran in September 2023. Israel bore the devastating brunt of that cash infusion when Iran-backed Hamas launched a devastating surprise attack on the country the following month.

23 Jay Solomon, "Inside Iran's Influence Operation," Semafor, September 29, 2023, https://www.semafor.com/article/09/25/2023/inside-irans-influence-operation.

24 Solomon, "Inside Iran's Influence Operation."

25 Solomon, "Inside Iran's Influence Operation."

26 Appeal of Adam Lovinger Revocation of Security Clearance, Defense Office of Hearings and Appeals, December 2018, U.S. Department of Defense Case No. WHS-C 18-01018, "Statement of Reasons for Adam S. Lovinger," Response Exhibit CCC.

27 Christopher Layne, "The End of Pax Americana: How Western Decline Became Inevitable," *The Atlantic*, April 26, 2012, https://www.theatlantic.com/international/archive/2012/04/the-end-of-pax-americana-how-western-decline-became-inevitable/256388/.

28 Ronald Reagan, quoted in John Lehman, "'We Win and They Lose': The U.S. Naval Institute Proceedings, 1980–89," *Proceedings*, vol. 141/4/1,346 (April 2015): https://www.usni.org/magazines/proceedings/2015/april/special-we-win-and-they-lose-us-naval-institute-proceedings-1980.

CHAPTER 6: SABOTAGING THE U.S.-JAPAN ALLIANCE

1 Bill Gertz, "Clinton Sought Pentagon, State Department Contracts for Chelsea's Friend," Washington Free Beacon, October 6, 2016, https://freebeacon.com/national-security/clinton-sought-pentagon-state-department-contracts-chelseas-friend.

2 "The point of using LTSG was an example of…institution building." James H. Baker, testimony, Appeal of Adam Lovinger Revocation of Security Clearance, Defense Office of Hearings and Appeals, December 2018, U.S. Department of Defense Case No. WHS-C 18-01018, transcript, vol. 4, 52.

3 "Chelsea Clinton Offers Remarks at Shakespeare Theatre Event," *Women's Wear Daily*, October 19, 2011, https://wwd.com/feature/chelsea-clinton-talks-shakespeare-5312140-782872.

4 Appeal of Adam Lovinger Revocation of Security Clearance, Defense Office of Hearings and Appeals, December 2018, U.S. Department of Defense Case No. WHS-C 18-01018, Exhibit M.

5 *Inquiry Report & Recommendations*, U.S. Department of Defense, March 30, 2017.

6 Adam Lovinger, "Note to File—Corruption in ONA," October 19, 2016, 9:43 p.m.

7 Appeal of Adam Lovinger Revocation of Security Clearance, transcript, vol. 5, 177.

8 Bill Gertz, "Japanese Intelligence Tells Pentagon China Engaged in Multi-Year Takeover Attempt of Senkaku Islands," Washington Free Beacon, November 23, 2016, https://freebeacon.com/national-security/japanese-intelligence-tells-pentagon-china-engaged-multi-year-takeover-attempt-senkaku-islands.

9 Appeal of Adam Lovinger Revocation of Security Clearance, transcript, vol. 5, 47; U.S. Department of Defense, Evidentiary Base for Appeal of Adam Lovinger Revocation of Security Clearance, WHS 18-A-1073-A1, 610, 722, and 725.

10 Lovinger, Appeal of Suspension of Security Clearance, transcript, vol 3, 300.

11 "Whistleblower and Reprisal Investigation Mr. Adam S. Lovinger, Office of Net Assessment, Office of the Secretary of Defense, Pentagon, Arlington, Virginia," CASE 20170914-046986-CASE-02, Inspector General, Department of Defense, January 13, 2021, 13.

12 Appeal of Adam Lovinger Revocation of Security Clearance, transcript, vol. 5, 177.

13 Appeal of Adam Lovinger Revocation of Security Clearance.

14 James H. Baker, "Subj: Trip Report on the Third Meeting of the Task Force for the Enhancement of the Japan/U.S. Relationship," memo, October 2015.

15 Rowan Scarborough, "James H. Baker, Top Pentagon Official, Dismissed U.S. Alliances with Taiwan and Australia," *Washington Times*, January 4, 2021, https://www.washingtontimes.com/news/2021/jan/4/james-h-baker-top-pentagon-official-dismissed-us-a.

16 Baker, "Global Challenges."

CHAPTER 7: TARGETING A PRESIDENTIAL TRANSITION TEAM

1 Michael Pillsbury, *The Hundred Year Marathon: China's Secret Strategy to Replace America as the Global Superpower* (New York: St. Martin's Press, 2016).

2 James H. Baker, "Global Challenges: What Are the Threats Ahead?" (speech).

3 Ash Carter, *Inside the Five-Sided Box* (New York: Dutton, 2019), 53.

4 Those who posed no threat to the Deep State, and those who collaborated with the Deep State to remove other Trump appointees, would be left in place and rewarded.

5 Anthony L. Russell, email to James H. Baker, "Documenting Conversation with Adam Lovinger," January 13, 2017," 2:47 p.m.

6 James B. Vietti, email to Anthony L. Russell, "Re: Investigation Update/Next Steps," January 17, 2017, 10:07 a.m.

7 Kristen Welker, Dafna Linzer, and Ken Dilanian, "Obama Warned Trump against Hiring Mike Flynn, Say Officials," NBC News, May 8, 2017, https://www.nbcnews.com/news/us-news/obama-warned-trump-against-hiring-mike-flynn-say-officials-n756316.

8 Michael T. Flynn, Matt Pottinger, and Paul D. Batchelor, *Fixing Intel: A Blueprint for Making Intelligence Relevant in Afghanistan* (Center for a New American Security, January 2010), accessed online, July 7, 2024, at https://s3.us-east-1.amazonaws.com/files.cnas.org/hero/documents/AfghanIntel_Flynn_Jan2010_code507_voices.pdf.

9 Michael Flynn, "Lt. Gen. Flynn INSA IC Summit Remarks" (speech), Defense Intelligence Agency, September 12, 2013, https://www.dia.mil/Articles/Speeches-and-Testimonies/Article/567074/lt-gen-flynn-insa-ic-summit-remarks.

10 James Kitfield, *Twilight Warriors: The Soldiers, Spies, and Special Agents Who Are Revolutionizing the American Way of War* (New York: Basic Books, 2016), 2.

11 Ken Dilanian, "Trump National Security Adviser Pick Michael Flynn Has Medals—and Baggage," NBC News, November 18, 2016, https://www.nbcnews.com/news/us-news/trump-national-security-adviser-pick-has-medals-baggage-n685681.

12 Bill Priestap, quoted in Adam Goldman and Katie Benner, "Ex-F.B.I. Official Is Said to Undercut Justice Dept. Effort to Drop Flynn Case," *New York Times*, May 13, 2020, https://www.nytimes.com/2020/05/13/us/politics/bill-priestap-michael-flynn.html.

13 Vietti, email to Anthony L. Russell.

CHAPTER 8: "SHOW ME THE MAN, AND I WILL FIND YOU THE CRIME"

1 This quotation has been commonly attributed to Lavrentiy Beria, Joseph Stalin's secret police chief.

2 Nc-410735@cas.go.jp [Japanese intelligence officer], email to Anthony L. Russell, "[Non-DoD Source] RE: Next Engagement," December 4, 2016, 3:37 a.m.

3 On November 23, 2016 (the press article with the leaked Japanese classified information); March 30, 2017 (Jennifer C. Walsh's report urging DoD OIG to investigate the leak); September 13, 2017 (Sean Bigley, attorney, informing DoD OIG that Japanese classified information had been exposed on ONA's declassified share drive); and December 8, 2017 (my response to the "Statement of Reasons" for the suspension of my security clearance).

4. James H. Baker, "Subj: Trip Report on the Third Meeting of the Task Force for the Enhancement of the Japan/U.S. Relationship," memo, October 2015.

5 Adam Lovinger, email to Bill Gertz, "Mr. Gertz: I Am Being Fired from the Civil Service Because of the False Charge That I Leaked Sensitive Information to You," December 12, 2017, 1:22 p.m.

6 Bill Gertz, email to Adam Lovinger, "Re: Mr. Gertz: I Am Being Fired from the Civil Service Because of the False Charge That I Leaked Sensitive Information to You," December 12, 2017, 2:26 p.m.

7 See Exhibit B.

8 See Exhibit A.

9 Nc-410735@cas.go.jp [Japanese intelligence officer], email to Anthony Russell.

10 Appeal of Adam Lovinger Revocation of Security Clearance, Defense Office of Hearings and Appeals, December 2018, U.S. Department of Defense Case No. WHS-C 18-01018, transcript, vol. 5, 202.

11 Appeal of Adam Lovinger Revocation of Security Clearance, transcript, vol. 5, 202.

12 Appeal of Adam Lovinger Revocation of Security Clearance, transcript, vol. 5, 202.

13 Appeal of Adam Lovinger Revocation of Security Clearance.

14 Jennifer C. Walsh, email to Adam Lovinger, "Reply to Email on Inquiry," February 10, 2017, 11:30 a.m.

15 Adam Lovinger, email to Jennifer C. Walsh, "Re: Reply to Email on Inquiry," February 20, 2017, 3:12 p.m.

16 Jennifer C. Walsh, Report on Investigation.

17 Appeal of Adam Lovinger Revocation of Security Clearance.

CHAPTER 9: WALKING BACK FROM A STRATEGY OF PRIMACY

1 Whittaker Chambers, *Witness* (Random House, 1952), 472.

2 James H. Baker, "Global Challenges; What Are the Threats Ahead?" (speech), 6.

3 Baker, "Global Challenges," 6.

4 James H. Baker, "Your Tenure: An Early Retrospective," memo to Chairman of the Joints Chiefs of Staff Admiral Mike Mullen, 2010, 9.

5 Baker, "Global Challenges,"6.

6 Baker, "Global Challenges,"6.

7 Joseph Biden, "Remarks by President Biden on the Drawdown of U.S. Forces in Afghanistan," The White House, July 8, 2021, https://www.whitehouse.gov/briefing-room/speeches-remarks/2021/08/31/remarks-by-president-biden-on-the-end-of-the-war-in-afghanistan.

8 Barack Obama, "Remarks by the President and First Lady on the End of the War in Iraq," The White House, President Barack Obama, December 14, 2011, https://obamawhitehouse.archives.gov/the-press-office/2011/12/14/remarks-president-and-first-lady-end-war-iraq.

9 Jeanne F. Godfroy et al., *US Army in the Iraq War Volume 2 Surge and Withdrawal* (US Army War College Press, 2019), https://press.armywarcollege.edu/monographs/940, 639.

10 Though Trump stopped Obama's practice of transferring huge sums to Tehran, Biden resumed it upon entering the Oval Office. Tom Norton, "Fact Check: Did the US under Obama Give Iran $150 Billion?," *Newsweek*, October 18, 2023, https://www.newsweek.com/us-give-iran-150-billion-barack-obama-jack-posobiec-1835083.

11 Jack Detsch, "The U.S. Left Billions Worth of Weapons in Afghanistan," *Foreign Policy*, April 28, 2022, https://foreignpolicy.com/2022/04/28/the-u-s-left-billions-worth-of-weapons-in-afghanistan.

12 Isoroku Yamamoto, quoted in General Paul V. Hester, "December 7, 1941: The Sleeping Giant Awakens," United States Pacific Air Forces, December 8, 2006, https://www.pacaf.af.mil/News/Commentaries/Display/Article/598205/december-7-1941-the-sleeping-giant-awakens.

13 John Ratcliffe, quoted in Emily Jacobs, "Top Chinese Professor Boasts of Operatives in Top of US 'Core Inner Circle,'" *New York Post*, December 8, 2020, https://nypost.com/2020/12/08/professor-claims-china-has-people-in-americas-core-inner-circle.

14 Walter Russell Mead, *The Arc of a Covenant: The United States, Israel, and the Fate of the Jewish People* (New York: Knopf, 2022), 519.

15 Joseph Bosco, "US FONOPs Actually Conceded Maritime Rights to China," *The Diplomat*, March 8, 2017, https://thediplomat.com/2017/03/us-fonops-actually-conceded-maritime-rights-to-china.

16 Rowan Scarborough, "James H. Baker, Top Pentagon Official, Dismissed U.S. Alliances with Taiwan, Australia," *Washington Times*, January 4, 2021, https://www.washingtontimes.com/news/2021/jan/4/james-h-baker-top-pentagon-official-dismissed-us-a.

17 Rush Doshi, "The United States, China, and the Contest for the Fourth Industrial Revolution" ("Prepared Statement before the U.S. Senate Committee on Commerce, Science, and Transportation, Subcommittee on Security"), July 30, 2020, https://www.commerce.senate.gov/services/files/6880BBA6-2AF0-4A43-8D32-6774E069B53E.

18 The strategy is named after a series of Chinese action films titled *Wolf Warrior*. Ben Westcott and Steven Jiang, "China Is Embracing a New Brand of Foreign Policy. Here's What Wolf Warrior Diplomacy Means," CNN, May 29, 2020, https://www.cnn.com/2020/05/28/asia/china-wolf-warrior-diplomacy-intl-hnk/index.html.

19 *How Is China Modernizing Its Navy?*, China Power Project, Center for Strategic & International Studies, December 17, 2018, updated November 9, 2023, https://chinapower.csis.org/china-naval-modernization.

20 James H. Baker, "Rise of Eurasian Revisionist Powers (Iran, Russia, China) and the Implications for the Japan-U.S. Alliance" (speech), July 2017.

21 Baker, "Rise of Eurasian Revisionist Powers."

22 Andrew D. May, email to James Baker, "ONA Research Program," May 23, 2016.

23 Appeal of Adam Lovinger Revocation of Security Clearance, Defense Office of Hearings and Appeals, December 2018, U.S. Department of Defense Case No. WHS-C 18-01018, transcript, vol. 4, 22.

24 Pentagon Chief of Staff Kash Patel investigated ONA's job performance and determined that ONA had not produced a single net assessment in fifteen years. See Kash Patel, *Government Gangsters* (New York: Post Hill Press, 2023), 176.

25 10 U.S.C. § 113 (i)(1).

26 Bill Gertz, "Pentagon's Office of Threat Assessment under Fire from Military, Congress," *Washington Times*, August 24, 2016, https://www.washingtontimes.com/news/2016/aug/24/pentagons-offic-of-threat-assement-under-fire-from.

27 Kori Schake, Eric Sayers, and Philip S. Davidson, "A Conversation with US Indo-Pacific Command's Adm. Philip Davidson," American Enterprise Institute, March 4, 2021, https://www.aei.org/podcast/a-conversation-with-us-indo-pacific-commands-adm-philip-davidson.

28 James H. Baker to Charles E. Grassley, February 5, 2020, https://www.grassley.senate.gov/imo/media/doc/2020-02-05%20ONA%20to%20CEG%20(Halper%20Follow%20Up).pdf.

29 "Director of Net Assessment," DOD Directive 5111.11, April 14, 2020, https://www.esd.whs.mil/Portals/54/Documents/DD/issuances/dodd/511111p.pdf.

30 Charles Grassley to James H. Baker, June 18, 2020, https://www.grassley.senate.gov/imo/media/doc/2020-06-18%20CEG%20to%20ONA%20(Halper%20Second%20Follow%20Up)1.pdf.

31 Charles Grassley, "A Case in Waste, Fraud and Abuse: The Office of Net Assessment" (speech on the floor of the U.S. Senate), July 2, 2020, https://www.grassley.senate.gov/news/video/watch/grassley-a-case-in-waste-fraud-and-abuse-the-office-of-net-assessment.

32 Charles Grassley, "The Office of Net Assessment is a Failure," (speech on the floor of the U.S. Senate), February 7, 2022, https://www.grassley.senate.gov/news/video/watch/grassley-the-office-of-net-assessment-is-a-failure.

33 Patel, *Government Gangsters*, 176.

34 "2021 Presidential Rank Award Winners," U.S. Office of Personnel Management, accessed June 22, 2024, https://www.opm.gov/policy-data-oversight/senior-executive-service/presidential-rank-awards/2021/presidential-rank-awards-2021.pdf.

CHAPTER 10: THE "FIND A JUSTIFICATION TO FIRE HIM" SORT OF INVESTIGATION

1 Franz Kafka, *The Trial*, trans. Willa and Edwin Muir (London: Vintage Classics), 1.

2 Appeal of Adam Lovinger Revocation of Security Clearance, Defense Office of Hearings and Appeals, December 2018, U.S. Department of Defense Case No. WHS-C 18-01018, transcript, vol. 5, 72.

3 Betsy George, "America's First Whistleblowers," University of South Carolina archives, July 18, 2021, https://sc.edu/about/offices_and_divisions/audit_and_advisory_services/about/news/2021/americas_first_whistleblowers.php.

4 Nc-410735@cas.go.jp [Japanese intelligence officer], email to Anthony L. Russell, "[Non-DoD Source] RE: Next Engagement," December 4, 2016, 3:37 a.m.

5 For example, Bruggeman was unaware that Baker and Russell had informed Tokyo in writing that the uncleared suspected Chinese agent was a U.S. Government official or, as Russell had put it, a "U.S. Representative."

6 James B. Vietti, email to Anthony L. Russell, "Re: Investigation Update/Next Steps," January 17, 2017, 10:07 a.m.

7 "Anthony L. Russell, Captain, USCG (ret.), Executive Director," Center for Arctic Study and Policy, United States Coast Guard Academy, accessed June 22, 2024, https://uscga.edu/academics/osri/casp/trussell.

CHAPTER 11: A TREASONOUS PATH

1 John Brennan, testimony before the U.S. House of Representatives, Permanent Select Committee on Intelligence, May 23, 2017, transcript accessed June 22, 2024, http://www.cnn.com/TRANSCRIPTS/1705/23/ath.01.html.

2 Greg Miller, "CIA Director Alerted FBI to Pattern of Contacts between Russian Officials and Trump Campaign Associates," *Washington Post*, May 23, 2017, https://www.washingtonpost.com/world/national-security/cia-director-warned-russian-security-service-chief-about-interference-in-election/2017/05/23/ebff2a7e-3fbb-11e7-adba-394ee67a7582_story.html.

3 Leslie H. Gelb, "Reagan Aides Describe Operation to Gather Inside Information on Carter," *New York Times*, July 7, 1983, https://www.nytimes.com/1983/07/07/us/reagan-aides-describe-operation-to-gather-inside-data-on-carter.html.

4 *Review of Four FISA Applications and Other Aspects of the FBI's Crossfire Hurricane Investigation*, U.S. Department of Justice, Office of the Inspector General, declassified April 15, 2020, December 2019, 313, https://www.justice.gov/storage/120919-examination.pdf.

5 "Transcript of George Papadopoulos and a Confidential Human Source," Federal Bureau of Investigation, United States Department of Justice, declassified March 13, 2020, 8–9, https://www.judiciary.senate.gov/imo/media/doc/2020-3-13%20FISA%20Senate%20-%20Transcript%20of%20George%20Papadopoulos%20and%20FBI%20Confidential%20Human%20Source%20declassified%20March%2013%202020.pdf.

6 Greg Myre, "The Cold War Roots of Putin's Digital-Age Intelligence Strategy," review of Gordon Corera, *Russians Among Us: Sleeper Cells, Ghost Stories, and the Hunt for Putin's Spies* (New York: William Morrow, 2020), *Washington Post*, April 10, 2020, https://www.washingtonpost.com/outlook/the-cold-war-roots-of-putins-digital-age-intelligence-strategy/2020/04/09/1fd2e922-624a-11ea-b3fc-7841686c5c57_story.html.

7 Steven Lee Myers, *The New Tsar: The Rise and Reign of Vladimir Putin* (New York: Alfred A. Knopf, 2015), 17.

8 Syllabus for the Cambridge Intelligence Seminar, listing Halper as leading an October 7, 2011, discussion on "The Afghan End-Game" report, which he produced "for the Office of Net Assessment."

9 Whittaker Chambers, *Witness* (New York: Random House, 1952), 472.

10 Syllabus for the Cambridge Intelligence Seminar.

11 John Brennan, testimony, May 23, 2017.

12 Neil Kent, "West Projects Russia's Soviet Past onto the Situation in Ukraine," interview with *Russia Today*, July 24, 2014, https://www.rt.com/op-ed/175332-mh17-plane-ukraine-demonizing-russia.

13 Neil Kent and Vsevolod Samokhvalov, "The Ukraine Crisis: a Russian-European Cold War?," *Journal of Intelligence and Terrorism Studies* 1 (June 2016): 1–12, https://access.portico.org/Portico/auView?auId=ark:%2F27927%2Fphx81qz8gdd.

14 Albert Resis, "Spheres of Influence in Soviet Wartime Diplomacy," *Journal of Modern History* 53, no. 3 (September 1981): 417–39.

15 Stefan Halper, quoted in "Cambridge Intelligence Seminar Programme," May 2012.

16 Stefan A. Halper et al., "Dynamics of Russian and European Engagement in the next 10 to 20 Years," occasional paper, Cambridge Intelligence Seminar, 2012.

17 Sam Jones, "Intelligence Experts Accuse Cambridge Forum of Kremlin Links," *Financial Times*, December 16, 2016, https://www.ft.com/content/d43cd586-c396-11e6-9bca-2b93a6856354.

18 Jones, "Intelligence Experts."

19 Charles Grassley, "A Case in Waste, Fraud and Abuse: The Office of Net Assessment" (speech on the floor of the U.S. Senate), July 2, 2020, https://www. grassley.senate.gov/news/video/watch/grassley-a-case-in-waste-fraud-and-abusethe-office-of-net-assessment.

20 Charles Grassley to James Baker, January 22, 2020, https://www.grassley.senate.gov/imo/media/doc/2020-01-22%20CEG%20to%20ONA%20(Halper%20Follow%20Up).pdf.

21 James H. Baker to Charles Grassley, February 5, 2020, https://www.grassley.senate.gov/imo/media/doc/2020-02-05%20ONA%20to%20CEG%20(Halper%20Follow%20Up).pdf.

22 Charles Grassley to James H. Baker, June 18, 2020, https://www.grassley.senate.gov/imo/media/doc/2020-06-18%20CEG%20to%20ONA%20(Halper%20Second%20Follow%20Up)1.pdf.

CHAPTER 12: ADOPTING RUSSIA'S FOREIGN POLICY FOR AMERICA'S OWN

1 George Orwell, *1984* (London: Secker & Warburg, 1949), 103.

2 Stefan Halper and Jonathan Clarke, *America Alone: The Neo-Conservatives and the Global Order* (Cambridge: Cambridge University Press, 2004), jacket.

3 "Basic Provisions of the Foreign Policy Concept of the Russian Federaltion," approved by presidential decree April 23, 1993, trans. Rebecca Koffler.

4 "National Security Concept of the Russian Federation," approved by Presidential Decree No. 1300 of December 17, 1999, given in the wording of Presidential Decree No. 24 of January 10, 2000. English translation in *Rossiskaya Gazeta*, January 18, 2000, accessed online at the Federation of American Scientists, https://nuke.fas.org/guide/russia/doctrine/gazeta012400.htm.

5 Luke Harding and Ian Traynor, "Obama Abandons Missile Defence Shield in Europe," *The Guardian*, September 17, 2009, https://www.theguardian.com/world/2009/sep/17/missile-defence-shield-barack-obama.

6 Seth Elan, *Russia's Skolkovo Innovation Center*, EUCOM Strategic Foresight, July 29, 2013, https://community.apan.org/cfs-file/___key/docpreview-s/00-00-00-84-84/20130805-Allen-__2D00__-Russias-Skolkovo-Innovation-Center.pdf.

7 Elan, *Russia's Skolkovo Innovation Center*, 5.

8 "The Foreign Policy Concept of the Russian Federation, Approved by the President of the Russian Federation, V. Putin," June 28, 2000, Berlin Information-Center for Transatlantic Security, https://www.bits.de/EURA/russia052800.pdf.

9 The official justification of Obama's military-intelligence-sharing with a U.S. enemy was to help Putin battle ISIS. Yet Obama famously ridiculed ISIS, in public and private, by calling it the "JV team." Thus, one must conclude that Obama's unprecedented sharing of battlefield intelligence with Putin was driven not by military necessity, but rather to strengthen the Russian empire. See Karen De Young, "U.S. Offers to Share Syria Intelligence on Terrorists with Russia," *Washington Post*, June 30, 2016, https://www.washingtonpost.com/world/national-security/us-offers-to-share-syria-intelligence-on-terrorists-with-russia/2016/06/30/483a2afe-3eec-11e6-84e8-1580c7db5275_story.html.

10 Peter Baker, "A President Whose Assurances Have Come Back to Haunt Him," *New York Times*, September 8, 2014, https://www.nytimes.com/2014/09/09/us/politics/a-president-whose-assurances-have-come-back-to-haunt-him.html.

11 J. David Goodman, "Microphone Catches a Candid Obama," *New York Times*, March 26, 2012, https://www.nytimes.com/2012/03/27/us/politics/obama-caught-on-microphone-telling-medvedev-of-flexibility.html.

12 "Romney: Russia Is Our Number One Geopolitical Foe", CNN Pressroom, March 26, 2012, https://cnnpressroom.blogs.cnn.com/2012/03/26/romney-russia-is-our-number-one-geopolitical-foe.

13 Adam Martin, "Medvedev Mocks Romney in Obama's Place," *The Atlantic*, March 27, 2012, https://www.theatlantic.com/international/archive/2012/03/medvedev-mocks-romney-obamas-place/330075.

14 Barack Obama, "Remarks by the President to the White House Press Corps," The White House, August 20, 2012, https://obamawhitehouse.archives.gov/the-press-office/2012/08/20/remarks-president-white-house-press-corps.

15 Glenn Kessler, "Flashback: Obama's Debate Zinger on Romney's '1980s' Foreign Policy (Video)," *Washington Post*, March 20, 2014, https://www.washingtonpost.com/news/fact-checker/wp/2014/03/20/flashback-obamas-debate-zinger-on-romneys-1980s-foreign-policy.

16 The New York Times, "Election 2012 | Obama to Romney: Cold War Is Over —Third Presidential Debate," YouTube, October 22, 2012 1:40, https://www.youtube.com/watch?v=T1409sXBleg.

17 President Barack Obama, "Presidential Memorandum—National Insider Threat Policy and Minimum Standards for Executive Branch Insider Threat Programs," The White House, November 21, 2012, https://obamawhitehouse.archives.gov/the-press-office/2012/11/21/presidential-memorandum-national-insider-threat-policy-and-minimum-stand.

18 "Ninth Anniversary of the Ghouta, Syria Chemical Weapons Attack," U.S. Department of State, August 21, 2022, https://www.state.gov/ninth-anniversary-of-the-ghouta-syria-chemical-weapons-attack.

19 Babar Baloch, "Refugees Bear Cost of Massive Underfunding," The United Nations Refugee Agency, October 9, 2018, https://www.unhcr.org/us/news/briefing-notes/refugees-Bear-Cost-massive-underfunding.

20 John Hudson, "U.N. Envoy Revises Syria Death Toll to 400,000," *Foreign Policy*, April 22, 2016, https://foreignpolicy.com/2016/04/22/u-n-envoy-revises-syria-death-toll-to-400000.

21 This is the term used by the United States Holocaust Memorial Museum in its "Syria Research Project," accessed May 6, 2024, https://www.ushmm.org/genocide-prevention/simon-skjodt-center/work/research/syria-research/project.

22 Samantha Power, quoted in "U.N. Ambassador Samantha Power on Slow Aid to Syria, N. Korea Nuke Threats," interview with CBS news, September 16, 2016, https://www.cbsnews.com/news/samantha-powers-united-nations-us-ambassador-syria-russia-cease-fire-north-korea-nuclear-threats.

23 Hillary Clinton, "Interview with Vladimir Pozner of First Channel Television," March 19, 2010, accessed at U.S. Department of State, https://2009-2017.state.gov/secretary/20092013clinton/rm/2010/03/138712.htm.

24 Maggie Haberman, "Hillary Clinton Calls Romney's Russia Comments 'Dated,'" *Politico*, April 1, 2012, https://www.politico.com/blogs/burns-haberman/2012/04/hillary-clinton-calls-romneys-russia-comments-dated-updated-119292.

25 "Russia Moving into High Gear on Nanotechnology; Actively Seeking Cooperation with U.S.," U.S. State Department Cable, February 11, 2009.

26 "Russia Moving into High Gear on Nanotechnology."

27 Jo Becker, and Mike McIntire. "Cash Flowed to Clinton Foundation amid Russian Uranium Deal," *New York Times*, April 23, 2015, https://www.nytimes.com/2015/04/24/us/cash-flowed-to-clinton-foundation-as-russians-pressed-for-control-of-uranium-company.html.

28 Hunter Walker, "The Billionaire Linked to the 'Clinton Cash' Scandals Once Said Something Amazing about Doing Business with Bill Clinton," Business Insider, April 24, 2015, https://www.businessinsider.com/frank-giustras-amazing-comment-about-bill-clinton-2015-4. See also Jo Becker and Don Van Natta Jr., "After Mining Deal, Financier Donated to Clinton," *New York Times*, January 31, 2008, https://www.nytimes.com/2008/01/31/us/politics/31donor.html.

29 The roles that Robert Mueller and Andrew McCabe played in this affair are recounted in House Resolution 606, November 3, 2017, https://www.congress.gov/115/bills/hres606/BILLS-115hres606ih.pdf.

30 These included Viktor Vekselberg, a billionaire Putin confidant, and his company, Renova Group, as well as Andrey Vavilov, a businessman and former Russian secretary of state. See Philip Bump, "A Searchable Index of Clinton Foundation Donors," *Washington Post*, February 26, 2015, https://www.washingtonpost.com/news/the-fix/wp/2015/02/26/a-searchable-index-of-clinton-foundation-donors.

31 Becker and McIntire, "Cash Flowed to Clinton Foundation."

32 Missy Ryan, "Russia Spent Millions on Secret Global Campaign, U.S. Intelligence Finds," *Washington Post*, September 13, 2022, https://www.washingtonpost.com/national-security/2022/09/13/united-states-russia-political-campaign.

33 David E. Sanger and William J. Broad, "In Hacked Audio, Hillary Clinton Rethinks Obama's Nuclear Upgrade Plan," *New York Times*, September 29, 2016, https://www.nytimes.com/2016/09/30/us/politics/hillary-clinton-obama-nuclear-policy.html.

34 S. E. Cupp, "Hillary Clinton's Depressing Defeatism," CNN, August 19, 2015, https://www.cnn.com/2015/08/19/opinions/cupp-hillary-clinton-defeatist-mindset/index.html.

35 Hillary Clinton, "Mueller Documented a Serious Crime against All Americans. Here's How to Respond," opinion, *Washington Post*, April 24, 2019, https://www.washingtonpost.com/opinions/hillary-clinton-mueller-documented-a-serious-crime-against-all-americans-heres-how-to-respond/2019/04/24/1e8f7e16-66b7-11e9-82ba-fcfeff232e8f_story.html.

CHAPTER 13: THE NET ASSESSMENT DOSSIER

1 U.S. Government reports of investigation refer to a collection of memos Christopher Steele produced in the summer and fall of 2016 as the Steele Dossier. This term encompasses twenty memos—seventeen of them have been publicly released—that the FBI received from Steele. See *Report of the Select Committee on Intelligence, United States Senate, on Russian Active Measures Campaigns and Interference in the 2016 U.S. Election, Volume 5: Counterintelligence Threats and Vulnerabilities*, Report 116-XX, 116th Congress, 1st Session, August 18, 2020, 846 n5650, https://www.intelligence.senate.gov/sites/default/files/documents/report_volume5.pdf.

2 Valery Gerasimov, "The Value of Science Is in the Foresight," *Military Review*, January-February 2016, https://www.armyupress.army.mil/portals/7/military-review/archives/english/militaryreview_20160228_art008.pdf.

3 John Durham, *Report on Matters Related to Intelligence Activities and Investigations Arising out of the 2016 Presidential Campaigns*, May 12, 2023, 81, at https://www.justice.gov/storage/durhamreport.pdf.

4 "Chairman Graham Releases Information from DNI Ratcliffe on FBI's Handling of Crossfire Hurricane," press release, U.S. Senate Committee on the Judiciary, September 29, 2020, https://www.judiciary.senate.gov/press/rep/releases/chairman-graham-releases-information-from-dni-ratcliffe-on-fbis-handling-of-crossfire-hurricane.

5 Durham, *Report*, 88.

6 Hillary Clinton, "The man who could be your next president....," Twitter, September 22, 2016, 4:30 p.m., https://twitter.com/HillaryClinton/status/77905 5195607166977?lang=en.

7 Paul Sperry, "What Did Clinton Know and When Did She Know It? The Russiagate Evidence Builds," Real Clear Investigations, January 27, 2022, https://www.realclearinvestigations.com/articles/2022/01/27/what_did_clinton_know_about_the_russiagate_smear_and_when_did_she_know_it_the_evidence_builds_813739.html.

8 Mark Leibovich, "I'm the Last Thing Standing between You and the Apocalypse,"

New York Times Magazine, October 11, 2016, https://www.nytimes.com/2016/10/16/magazine/hillary-clinton-campaign-final-weeks.html.

9   Sperry, "What Did Clinton Know?"

10 Hillary Clinton, "Interview with Vladimir Pozner of First Channel Television," March 19, 2010, accessed at U.S. Department of State, https://2009-2017.state.gov/secretary/20092013clinton/rm/2010/03/138712.htm.

11 The Global Magnitsky Act of 2016 authorizes the U.S. Government to sanction, freeze the assets, and bar from entering the U.S. foreign government officials who commit human-rights abuses. See "S.284—Global Magnitsky Human Rights Accountability Act," 114th U.S. Congress, April 18, 2016, https://www.congress.gov/bill/114th-congress/senate-bill/284/text.

12 Edward Malnick, "Exclusive: £6.6m Linked to Death of Lawyer 'Traced to Russian Firm's UK Account'," *The Telegraph*, April 13, 2017, https://www.telegraph.co.uk/news/2017/04/13/exclusive-66m-linked-death-lawyer-traced-russian-firms-uk-account.

13 Charles Grassley, "Complaint: Firm Behind Dossier & Former Russian Intel Officer Joined Lobbying Effort to Kill Pro-Whistleblower Sanctions For Kremlin," press release, March 31, 2017, https://www.grassley.senate.gov/news/news-releases/complaint-firm-behind-dossier-former-russian-intel-officer-joined-lobbying-effort. See also the description of the role of Prevezon Holdings Limited in Hermitage Capital Management, email to Heather H. Hunt, FARA Registration Unit, Counterintelligence and Export Control Section, National Security Division, U.S Department of Justice, July 15, 2016, https://www.grassley.senate.gov/imo/media/doc/judiciary/upload/Russia%2C%2003-31-17%2C%20Magnitsky%20Act%20-%202016-%2007-15%20HCM%20Complaint%20to%20FARA%20%28003%29_Redacted.pdf.

14 Kim Sengupta, "Former MI6 Agent Christopher Steele's Frustration as FBI Sat on Donald Trump Russia File for Months," *The Independent*, January 14, 2017, https://www.independent.co.uk/news/world/americas/donald-trump-russia-dossier-file-investigation-hacking-christopher-steele-mi6-a7526901.html.

15 Howard Blum, "How Ex-Spy Christopher Steele Compiled His Explosive Trump-Russia Dossier," *Vanity Fair,* March 30, 2017, https://www.vanityfair.com/news/2017/03/how-the-explosive-russian-dossier-was-compiled-christopher-steele.

16 Kathleen Kavalec, "Notes from Meeting with Chris Steele and Tatyana Duran of Orbis Security, October 11, 2016," https://www.scribd.com/document/409364009/Kavalec-Less-Redacted-Memo.

17 Eric Felten, "Was Christopher Steele Disseminating Russian Disinformation to the State Department?," *Washington Examiner*, September 14, 2018, https://www.washingtonexaminer.com/politics/2631472/was-christopher-steele-disseminating-russian-disinformation-to-the-state-department.

18 "Transcript of George Papadopoulos and a Confidential Human Source," Federal Bureau of Investigation, United States Department of Justice, declassified March 13, 2020, of a confidential human source, FBI, United States Department of Justice, FISA202000413–202000447, https://www.judiciary.senate.gov/

imo/media/doc/2020-3-13%20FISA%20Senate%20-%20Transcript%20of%20 George%20Papadopoulos%20and%20FBI%20Confidential%20Human%20 Source%20declassified%20March%2013%202020.pdf.

19 Durham, *Report*, 49.

20 John Solomon, "From Durham to CIA, Evidence Mounts FBI Was Warned Russia Collusion Story Might Be Disinformation," Just the News, October 15, 2022, https://justthenews.com/accountability/russia-and-ukraine-scandals/ sunfrom-durham-cia-evidence-mounts-fbi-told-steele.

21 Bruce Ohr, testimony, U.S. House of Representatives Committee on the Judiciary, Joint with the Committee on Government Reform and Oversight, August 28, 2018.

22 Sergey Ledbedev, the only other living SVR head, had never been a "former Russian Foreign Ministry official."

23 *Review of Four FISA Applications and Other Aspects of the FBI's Crossfire Hurricane Investigation*, U.S. Department of Justice, Office of the Inspector General, declassified April 15, 2020, footnotes available online at https://www.grassley. senate.gov/imo/media/doc/2020-04-15%20ODNI%20to%20CEG%20RHJ%20 (FISA%20Footnote%20Declassification).pdf.

24 *Review of Four FISA Applications*, n350.

25 Sam Jones, "Cambridge Espionage Experts Review Funding after Russia Link Claim," *Financial Times*, December 21, 2016, https://www.ft.com/content/ ee2ccde2-c775-11e6-9043-7e34c07b46ef.

26 John Brennan, testimony, U.S. House of Representatives Permanent Select Committee on Intelligence, May 23, 2017, https://www.c-span.org/video/?c4670890/ cia-director-brennan-russia-brazenly-interfered-us-election.

27 "Think Tank Analyst Acquitted in Trial over Discredited Donald Trump Dossier," NPR, October 18, 2022, https://www.pbs.org/newshour/politics/think-tank-analyst-acquitted-in-trial-over-discredited-donald-trump-dossier.

28 *Overview of the Counterintelligence Investigation of Christopher Steele's Primary Sub-source*, Federal Bureau of Investigation, declassified September 23, 2020, https://www.judiciary.senate.gov/imo/media/doc/AG%20Letter%20to%20Chairman%20Graham%209.24.2020.pdf.

29 *Overview of the Counterintelligence Investigation.*

30 "Soviet Active Measures in the United States—an Updated Report by the FBI," Congressional Record, December 9, 1987, accessed online at the Central Intelligence Agency, https://www.cia.gov/readingroom/docs/CIA-RDP11M01338R000400470089-2.pdf.

31 Durham, *Report*, 14.

32 Durham, *Report*, 130.

33 *Overview of the Counterintelligence Investigation.*

34 Fiona Hill, testimony, the House of Representatives Permanent Select Committee on Intelligence, October 14, 2019, https://d3i6fh83elv35t.cloudfront.net/ static/2019/11/FionaHill-compressed.pdf.

35 "Opening Statement of Dr. Fiona Hill to the House of Representatives Permanent Select Committee on Intelligence," November 21, 2019, https://www.congress.gov/116/meeting/house/110235/witnesses/HHRG-116-IG00-Wstate-HillF-20191121.pdf.

36 "VI Moscow Conference on International Security," Russian Ministry of Defence, April 26–27, 2017, https://eng.mil.ru/en/mcis/2017.htm.

37 Foreign Agent Registration Act filing for Ketchum Inc., naming Charles Dolan as foreign agent recipient of monies from the Russian Federation, U.S. Department of Justice, accessed June 22, 2024, at https://efile.fara.gov/docs/5758-Supplemental-Statement-20120905-18.pdf.

38 Durham, *Report*, 142. See also Indictment, United States of America v. Igor Y. Danchenko, United States District Court for the Eastern District of Virginia, November 3, 2021, at https://www.justice.gov/sco/press-release/file/1446386/dl.

39 Durham, *Report*, 143.

40 *Review of Four FISA Applications*, n334. See William Barr to Lindsey Graham, September 24, 2020, https://www.judiciary.senate.gov/imo/media/doc/AG%20Letter%20to%20Chairman%20Graham%209.24.2020.pdf.

41 Steven Pifer, "President Medvedev Rocks at Brookings," Brookings Commentary, April 15, 2010, https://www.brookings.edu/articles/president-medvedev-rocks-at-brookings.

42 Hillary Clinton, "Remarks and a Question and Answer Session at the Brookings Institution in Washington, DC," The American Presidency Project, September 9, 2015, https://www.presidency.ucsb.edu/documents/remarks-and-question-and-answer-session-the-brookings-institution-washington-dc.

43 "Transcript: Fiona Hill and David Holmes Testimony in Front of the House Intelligence Committee," *Washington Post*, November 21, 2019, https://www.washingtonpost.com/politics/2019/11/21/transcript-fiona-hill-david-holmes-testimony-front-house-intelligence-committee.

44 Ladislav Bittman, *The KGB and Soviet Disinformation: An Insider's View* (Washington, DC: Pergamon-Brassey's, 1985), 49.

45 *Review of Four FISA Applications*, 188.

46 Durham, *Report*, 80.

47 "Former Special Agent in Charge of the New York FBI Counterintelligence Division Pleads Guilty to Conspiring to Violate U.S. Sanctions on Russia," press release, U.S. Department of Justice, August 15, 2023, https://www.justice.gov/opa/pr/former-special-agent-charge-new-york-fbi-counterintelligence-division-pleads-guilty.

48 Kimberly A. Strassel, "Hillary Clinton's Russian Helpers," *Wall Street Journal*, November 11, 2021, https://www.wsj.com/articles/hillary-clinton-russia-trump-2016-election-collusion-russiagate-durham-danchenko-steele.

49 Durham, *Report*, 8.

50 Brennan, testimony.

51 Durham, *Report*, 85.

52 These would include, among other inquiries, the Halper investigation, Crossfire Hurricane, Crossfire Fury, Crossfire Dragon and Foreign Intelligence Surveillance Act surveillance operations, Crossfire Razor, Crossfire Typhoon, Cross Wind, Alfa Bank New York Field Office, Alfa Bank Chicago Field Office, Trump counterintelligence, and Trump Obstruction.

53 *Review of Four FISA Applications,* iii.

54 Durham, *Report,* 106.

55 *Review of Four FISA Applications,* 314.

56 *Review of Four FISA Applications,* 313–14.

57 United States v. Halper, 1:94-po-00199, District Court for the Eastern District of Virginia, July 11, 1994, https://www.courtlistener.com/docket/6345826/parties/united-states-v-halper.

58 James Comey, testimony, U.S. Senate Select Committee on Intelligence, June 8, 2017, https://www.intelligence.senate.gov/hearings/open-hearing-former-fbi-director-james-comey.

59 Chuck Grassley, "FBI Ignored Early Warnings That Debunked Anti-Trump Dossier Was Russian Disinformation," Chuck Grassley, press release, April 10, 2020, https://www.grassley.senate.gov/news/news-releases/fbi-ignored-early-warnings-debunked-anti-trump-dossier-was-russian-disinformation.

60 Kevin Brock, prepared statement for the record, U.S. Senate Committee on Homeland Security and Governmental Affairs Hearing on "Congressional Oversight in the Face of Executive Branch and Media Suppression: The Case Study of Crossfire Hurricane," December 3, 2020, https://www.hsgac.senate.gov/wp-content/uploads/imo/media/doc/Testimony-Brock-2020-12-03.pdf.

61 *Review of Four FISA Applications,* 82.

62 *Report of Investigation of Former Federal Bureau of Investigation Director James Comey's Disclosure of Sensitive Information and Handling of Certain Memoranda,"* U.S. Department of Justice, Office of the Inspector General, August 2019, https://oig.justice.gov/reports/2019/o1902.pdf.

CHAPTER 14: RUSSIAN DISINFORMATION BECOMES A U.S. INTELLIGENCE PRODUCT

1 Max Farrand, *Records of the Federal Convention of 1787,* (New Haven: Yale University Press, 1911), vol. 1, 465.

2 Conor Friedersdorf, "A Brief History of the CIA's Unpunished Spying on the Senate," *The Atlantic,* December 23, 2014, https://www.theatlantic.com/politics/archive/2014/12/a-brief-history-of-the-cias-unpunished-spying-on-the-senate/384003/.

3 Sharyl Attkisson, "CIA's 'Surveillance State' is Operating against Us All," *The Hill,* November 5, 2018, https://thehill.com/opinion/national-security/414804-surveillance-state-is-alive-well-and-operating-against-us-all/.

4 Aaron Blake, "Harry Reid's Incendiary Claim about 'Coordination' between Donald Trump and Russia," *Washington Post,* October 31, 2016, https://www.washingtonpost.com/news/the-fix/wp/2016/10/31/harry-reid-just-made-a-huge-incendiary-evidence-free-claim-about-trump-and-russia.

5 According to the *Washington Post*, Brennan's information came from a high-level Russian government source who confirmed that Putin had sought to "defeat or at least damage the Democratic nominee, Hillary Clinton, and help elect her opponent, Donald Trump." That tracks the language from the Steele Dossier sourced from a "former senior [Russian] intelligence officer," which details a Russian Foreign Intelligence Service operation "supported and directed by Russian President Vladimir Putin" to harm Clinton and help Trump. Gregg Miller, Ellen Nakashima, and Adam Entous, "Obama's Secret Struggle to Punish Russia for Putin's Election Assault," *Washington Post*, June 23, 2017, accessed at https://www.washingtonpost.com/graphics/2017/world/national-security/obama-putin-election-hacking.

6 Miller, Nakashima, and Entous, "Obama's Secret Struggle."

7 "Interview: Susan Rice," U.S. House of Representatives Permanent Select Committee on Intelligence, September 8, 2017, https://www.dni.gov/files/HPSCI_Transcripts/2020-05-04-Susan_Rice-MTR_Redacted.pdf, 27–28.

8 Greg Miller, "CIA Director Alerted FBI to Pattern of Contacts between Russian Officials and Trump Campaign Associates," *Washington Post*, May 23, 2017, https://www.washingtonpost.com/world/national-security/cia-director-warned-russian-security-service-chief-about-interference-in-election/2017/05/23/ebff2a7e-3fbb-11e7-adba-394ee67a7582_story.html.

9 Jerry Dunleavy, "'Completely Untrustworthy': FBI Agent Trashed Christopher Steele for Leaking to the Media," *Washington Examiner*, January 18, 2021, https://www.washingtonexaminer.com/news/1126237/completely-untrustworthy-fbi-agent-trashed-christopher-steele-for-leaking-to-the-media.

10 *Assessing Russian Activities and Intentions in Recent US Elections, Annex A*, Intelligence Community Assessment, 2017, https://www.grassley.senate.gov/imo/media/doc/2020-06-10%20ODNI%20to%20CEG,%20RJ%20-%20ICA%20Annex.pdf.

11 Brennan's denial was reported in U.S. House Resolution 844, December 8, 2021, https://www.congress.gov/117/bills/hres844/BILLS-117hres844ih.pdf.

12 James Clapper, interview with CNN's Erin Burnett, *Erin Burnett OutFront* October 25, 2017, http://www.cnn.com/TRANSCRIPTS/1710/25/ebo.01.html.

13 "Full Transcript: Sally Yeats and James Clapper Testify on Russian Election Interference," *Washington Post*, May 8, 2017, https://www.washingtonpost.com/news/post-politics/wp/2017/05/08/full-transcript-sally-yates-and-james-clapper-testify-on-russian-election-interference/?utm_source=substack&utm_medium=email.

14 "Full Transcript: Sally Yeats and James Clapper Testify."

15 As the longtime diplomat and the last U.S. ambassador to the Soviet Union, Jack Matlock Jr. would write: "During my time in government a judgement regarding national security would include reports from, as a minimum, the CIA, the Defense Intelligence Agency (DIA), and the Bureau of Intelligence and Research (INR) of the State Department. The FBI was rarely, if ever included unless the principal question concerned law enforcement within the United States." Jack Matlock, "Former US Envoy to Moscow Calls Intelligence Report on Alleged Russian Interference 'Politically Motivated,'" *Consortium News* 29, no. 132 (May

14, 2024), https://consortiumnews.com/2018/07/03/former-us-envoy-to-moscow-calls-intelligence-report-on-alleged-russian-interference-politically-motivated.

16 Federal Bureau of Investigation spreadsheet of Strzok-Page texts, furnished to U.S. Senate Committee on Homeland Security and Governmental Affairs, October 23, 2020, https://www.grassley.senate.gov/imo/media/doc/lync_text_messages_of_peter_strzok_from_2-13-16_to_12-6-17.pdf.

17 Peter Strzok, quoted in letter from Charles Grassley to Rod Rosenstein, December 13, 2017, https://www.grassley.senate.gov/news/news-releases/grassley-seeks-clarity-justice-depts-response-political-texts.

18 Report: A Review of Various Actions by the Federal Bureau of Investigation and Department of Justice in Advance of the 2016 Election," Office of the Inspector General, U.S. Department of Justice, June 2018, 190, https://www.oversight.gov/sites/default/files/oig-reports/o1804.pdf.

19 Michael E. Horowitz, "Oversight of the FBI and DOJ Actions in Advance of the 2016 Election,", statement before the U.S. House of Representatives Committees on Oversight and Government Reform and the Judiciary, June 19, 2018, https://oig.justice.gov/node/640.

20 Horowitz, "Oversight of the FBI and DOJ."

21 District Judge Royce C. Lamberth, Memorandum Opinion, Judicial Watch, Inc. v. U.S. Department of State, December 6, 2018, https://www.casemine.com/judgement/us/5cob6d7b342cca09de3cfc1f.

22 Paul Sperry, "Secret Report: How CIA's Brennan Overruled Dissenting Analysts Who Concluded Russia Favored Hillary," Real Clear Investigations, September 24, 2020, https://www.realclearinvestigations.com/articles/2020/09/24/secret_report_how_cias_brennan_overruled_dissenting_analysts_who_thought_russia_favored_hillary_125315.html.

23 Background to "Assessing Russian Activities and Intentions in Recent U.S. Elections": The Analytic Process and Cyber Incident Attribution, Office of the Director of National Intelligence, January 6, 2017, ii–iii, https://www.dni.gov/files/documents/ICA_2017_01.pdf.

24 Report on Russian Active Measures, U.S. House of Representatives Permanent Select Committee on Intelligence, March 22, 2018, 42, https://docs.house.gov/meetings/IG/IG00/20180322/108023/HRPT-115-1_1-p1-U3.pdf.

25 Report of the Select Committee on Intelligence, United States Senate, on Russian Active Measures Campaigns and Interference in the 2016 U.S. Election Volume 5: Counterintelligence Threats and Vulnerabilities, 116th Congress, 1st Session, Report 116-XX, August 18, 2020, https://www.intelligence.senate.gov/sites/default/files/documents/report_volume5.pdf.

26 Report on Active Russian Measures, 6.

27 Paul Sperry, "Secret Report."

28 NSA hedged its bets by declaring only "moderate confidence." IC insiders deem this to mean that "some of our analysts could believe this may be true." By contrast, "high confidence" is known as a "best guess."

29 Report on Active Russian Measures.

CHAPTER 15: AN EXISTENTIAL THREAT TO THE DEEP STATE

1 Stefan Becket, "Intel Chief Reveals Obama Officials Who Requested 'Unmasking' of Michael Flynn," CBS News, May 13, 2020, https://www.cbsnews.com/news/michael-flynn-unmasking-list-richard-grenell.

2 On account of security and privacy considerations and laws, U.S. intelligence agencies are required to "mask" or "minimize" the identities of U.S. persons intercepted in the course of spying on foreign entities or persons. "Unmasking" is the process of revealing the identity of that U.S. citizen.

3 Susan E. Rice, "Note to File [TOP SECRET: RECORD]," declassified, email to self, January 20, 2017, https://www.grassley.senate.gov/imo/media/doc/2017-01-20%20Susan%20Rice%20Note%20to%20File%20-%2001-05-17%20Oval%20Office%20Meeting.pdf.

4 According to an "Electronic Communication" document from an FBI field office dated January 4, 2017, there was "NO DEROGATORY info on him [Flynn] in FBI files. NO DEROGATORY info on him in [redacted: likely DIA] files. NO DEROGATORY information on him in [redacted: likely CIA] files." Flynn "was no longer a viable candidate as part of the large CROSSFIRE HURRICANE umbrella case." See United States of America v. Michael T. Flynn, Crim.No.17-232 (EGS), Exhibit 1, 1–3, https://int.nyt.com/data/documenthelper/6936-michael-flynn-motion-to-dismiss/fa06f5e13a0ec71843b6/optimized/full.pdf.

5 Kimberley A. Strassel, "The FBI's Flynn Outrage," *Wall Street Journal*, April 30, 2020, https://www.wsj.com/articles/the-fbis-flynn-outrage-11588288438.

6 "The FBI claims the counterintelligence investigation of the Trump campaign began on July 31, 2016. But in fact, it began before that. In June 2016 before the investigation officially opened, Trump campaign associates...were invited to attend a symposium at Cambridge University in July 2016." Devin Nunes, "Full Transcript: Mueller Testimony before House Judiciary, Intelligence Committees," NBC News, July 24, 2019, https://www.nbcnews.com/politics/congress/full-transcript-robert-mueller-house-committee-testimony-n1033216.

7 Devin Nunes, interview with Maria Bartiromo, Fox News Channel, July 28, 2019, https://www.realclearpolitics.com/video/2019/07/28/nunes_its_clear_that_mueller_didnt_write_the_report.html.

8 Andrew G. McCabe, "Midyear Exam—Unclassified," email to E. W. Priestap, May 11, 2016, U.S. Senate Homeland Security and Governmental Affairs Committee DOJ-PROD-0000041, June 4, 2018, 53, https://www.hsgac.senate.gov/wp-content/uploads/imo/media/doc/Appendix%20C%20-%20Documents.pdf.

9 "Net Neutrality," *Congressional Record*, vol. 165, no. 62, April 10, 2019, https://www.govinfo.gov/content/pkg/CREC-2019-04-10/html/CREC-2019-04-10-pt1-PgH3243-6.htm.

10 "In Re Accuracy Concerns Regarding FBI Matters Submitted To The FISC," United States Foreign Intelligence Surveillance Court, Docket No. Misc. 19-02, December 17, 2019, https://www.fisc.uscourts.gov/sites/default/files/MIsc%2019%2002%20191217.pdf.

11 Christopher Andrew, "Impulsive General Misha Shoots Himself in the Foot," *The Times* (of London), February 19, 2017, https://www.thetimes.com/world/article/impulsive-general-misha-shoots-himself-in-the-foot-l7gfpbghr.

CHAPTER 16: THE KILL SHOT

1 Brooke Singman, "House Intel Transcripts Show Top Obama Officials Had No 'Empirical Evidence' of Trump-Russia Collusion," Fox News, May 7, 2020, https://www.foxnews.com/politics/intel-transcripts-obama-officials-no-empirical-evidence-trump-russia-collusion.

2 *United States of America v. Michael T. Flynn*, Crim.No.17-232 (EGS), Exhibit 4, 1, https://int.nyt.com/data/documenthelper/6936-michael-flynn-motion-to-dismiss/fa06f5e13a0ec71843b6/optimized/full.pdf.

3 Glenn Kessler, "Michael Flynn, Barack Obama and Trump's Claims of 'Treason,'" *Washington Post*, June 26, 2020, https://www.washingtonpost.com/politics/2020/06/26/michael-flynn-barack-obama-trumps-claims-treason.

4 David Ignatius, "Why Did Obama Dawdle on Russia's Hacking?," *Washington Post*, January 12, 2017, https://www.washingtonpost.com/opinions/why-did-obama-dawdle-on-russias-hacking/2017/01/12.

5 Kerry Picket, "Pentagon Official Denies ONA Director Named by Flynn Lawyer Is Leaker to Washington Post," *Washington Examiner*, May 18, 2020, https://www.washingtonexaminer.com/news/pentagon-official-denies-ona-director-named-by-flynns-lawyer-is-leaker-to-washington-post.

6 James H. Baker, "Rise of Eurasian Revisionist Powers (Iran, Russia, China) and the Implications for the Japan-U.S. Alliance," July 2017.

7 Baker, "Rise of Eurasian Revisionist Powers."

8 David Ignatius, "Obama's Diplomatic Opportunity," *Washington Post*, October 4, 2013, https://www.washingtonpost.com/opinions/david-ignatius-obamas-diplomatic-opportunity/2013/10/04.

9 Jeremy Herb et al., "James Comey Defends FBI's Interview of Michael Flynn, Transcript Shows," CNN, December 18, 2018, https://www.cnn.com/2018/12/18/politics/james-comey-congress-interview/index.html.

10 Government's Motion to Dismiss the Criminal Information, May 7, 2020, *United States of America v. Michael T. Flynn*, United States District Court for the District of Columbia, accessed online at the *New York Times*, June 23, 2024, https://int.nyt.com/data/documenthelper/6936-michael-flynn-motion-to-dismiss.

11 Marshall Cohen, "The Steele Dossier: A Reckoning," CNN, November 18, 2021, https://www.cnn.com/2021/11/18/politics/steele-dossier-reckoning/index.html.

12 "Did Obama, Brennan and Clinton Illegally Collude to Take Trump Down?," editorial, *Investor's Business Daily*, July 23, 2018, https://www.investors.com/politics/editorials/russia-trump-collusion-investigation.

13 Hillary Clinton, "Mueller Documented a Serious Crime against All Americans. Here's How to Respond," *Washington Post*, April 24, 2019, https://www.washingtonpost.com/opinions/hillary-clinton-mueller-documented-a-serious-crime-against-all-americans-heres-how-to-respond/2019/04/24.

14 Clinton, "Mueller Documented."

15 Mary Louise Kelly, "Russia's Ex-Spy Chief Shares Opinions of His American Counterparts," NPR, June 28, 2016, https://www.npr.org/transcripts/483734866.

16 Mary Louise Kelly, "Russia Meddled in U.S. Election, Comey Says During Sen-

ate Testimony," NPR, June 9, 2017, https://www.npr.org/2017/06/09/532208376/russia-meddled-in-u-s-election-comey-says-during-senate-testimony.

17 Missy Ryan, "Russia Spent Millions on Secret Global Campaign, U.S. intelligence Finds," *Washington Post*, September 13, 2022, https://www.washingtonpost.com/national-security/2022/09/13/united-states-russia-political-campaign.

CHAPTER 17: DEVIL'S ISLAND

1 The Complete Tanakh (Tanach)—Hebrew Bible, trans. A. J. Rosenberg (Judaica Press, 1998), https://www.chabad.org/library/bible_cdo/aid/15936/jewish/Chapter-5.htm.

2 District Judge Royce C. Lamberth, Memorandum Opinion, *United States of America v. Michael T. Flynn*, December 6, 2018, https://www.casemine.com/judgement/us/5c0b6d7b342cca09de3cfc1f.

3 "JW v DoD Baker Ignatius Prod 1 03564," Judicial Watch, May 14, 2020, https://www.judicialwatch.org/documents/jw-v-dod-baker-ignatius-prod-1-03564-2.

CHAPTER 18: DISCOVERING THE DEEP STATE PLAYBOOK

1 Montesquieu, *The Spirit of Laws* (1758), trans. Thomas Nugent, Wikisource, accessed June 29, 2024, book 8, chapter 10, 169, https://en.wikisource.org/wiki/The_Spirit_of_Laws_(1758)/Book_VIII.

2 Armstrong v. Manzo, 380 U.S. 545 (1965).

3 Snyder v. Massachusetts, 291 U.S. 97, 105 (1934).

CHAPTER 19: LIE

1 Hal Brands, "Dealing with Allies in Decline: Alliance Management and U.S. Strategy in an Era of Global Power Shifts," Center for Strategic and Budgetary Assessments, 2017, https://csbaonline.org/uploads/documents/ALLIES_in_DECLINE_FINAL_b.pdf.

2 As quoted in Beth Weinhouse, "Trust Me, I'm a Doctor," *Columbia Magazine*, winter 2022–2023, https://magazine.columbia.edu/article/trust-me-im-doctor.

3 James H. Baker, "Memorandum for LT GEN (Ret) Flynn," January 17, 2017, 10:15 a.m. Emphasis added.

CHAPTER 20: LEAK

1 Bill Gertz, "Pentagon Pulls Clearance of Trump White House Aide," Washington Free Beacon, May 4, 2017, https://freebeacon.com/national-security/pentagon-pulls-security-clearance-trump-white-house-aide.

2 Bill Gertz, "Clearance of NSC Aide to Be Revoked," subsection of "Inside the Ring: Pacific Fleet Chief Headed to Pacom," *Washington Times*, September 13, 2017, https://www.washingtontimes.com/news/2017/sep/13/inside-the-ring-pacific-fleet-chief-headed-to-paco.

3 "Statement of Reasons (SOR) for Adam S. Lovinger," Washington Headquarters Services, December 8, 2017, Allegation (e), 4.

4 Thus the title of Gertz's subsection: "Clearance of NSC aide to Be *Revoked*" [emphasis added].

CHAPTER 21: INVESTIGATE

1   Rowan Scarborough, "Investigation Clears Analyst Accused of Leaking Data, but Officials Never Told Man's Defense Team," *Washington Times*, August 14, 2019, https://www.washingtontimes.com/news/2019/aug/14/investigation-clears-analyst-accused-of-leaking-da.

CHAPTER 22: THE DEEP STATE'S JUSTICE MACHINE

1   Julian E. Barnes, Adam Goldman, and Charlie Savage, "Blaming the Deep State: Officials Accused of Wrongdoing Adopt Trump's Response,' *New York Times*, December 18, 2018, https://www.nytimes.com/2018/12/18/us/politics/deep-state-trump-classified-information.html.

2   Adolph S. Ochs, "Business Announcement," *New York Times*, August 19, 1896, https://www.documentcloud.org/documents/2271357-business-announcement.html.

CHAPTER 23: WHO WATCHES THE WATCHERS?

1   Ronald Reagan, "The President's News Conference," The White House, January 29, 1981, https://www.reaganlibrary.gov/archives/speech/presidents-news-conference-1#:~:text=Now%2C%20as%20long%20as%20they,is%20moral%2C%20not%20immoral%2C%20and.

2   Like Baker, Westgate, and Finnegan-Myers, Fine had been appointed in the penultimate year of the Obama administration as "part of a wave of new Pentagon personnel moves in recent days, senior-level officials who will outlast President Obama's final term in office." Joe Gould, "New Face to Lead Pentagon Strategy Shop," *Defense News*, May 16, 2015, https://www.defensenews.com/pentagon/2015/05/16/new-face-to-lead-pentagon-strategy-shop.

3   Mandy Smithberger, "Pentagon Watchdog Changed Files Ahead of GAO Audit," Project on Government Oversight, March 8, 2016, https://www.pogo.org/analysis/pentagon-watchdog-changed-files-ahead-of-gao-audit.

4   "Grassley on a Case of Whistleblower Retaliation at the Pentagon: Floor Speech on Admiral Losey Whistleblower Investigation, " Chuck Grassley, press release, April 6, 2016, https://www.grassley.senate.gov/news/news-releases/grassley-case-whistleblower-retaliation-pentagon.

5   Amy MacKinnon, "Death of a Whistleblower," *Foreign Policy*, March 20, 2020, https://foreignpolicy.com/2020/03/20/death-of-a-whistleblower-suicide-pentagon-office-inspector-general.

6   MacKinnon, "Death of a Whistleblower."

7   MacKinnon, "Death of a Whistleblower."

8   MacKinnon, "Death of a Whistleblower."

9   Alexandria Police Department FOIA W018287-051722.

10 On June 24, 2024, the City of Alexandria FOIA bureau authenticated that report. Alexandria Police Department FOIA Request W018287-051722.

11 Michael J. Buxton, email to Milton Barnes et al., "RE: Assist Alexandria PD and PFPA," January 30, 2019, FOIA Request W018287-051722.

12 Buxton, email to Milton Barnes et al.

13 "Grassley on a Case of Whistleblower Retaliation."

14 Philip Hamburger, *Is Administrative Law Unlawful?* (Chicago: University of Chicago Press, 2014), 496.

CHAPTER 24: DEEP STATE END GAME

1 George Orwell, *1984* (London: Secker & Warburg, 1949), 95.

2 "Whistleblower and Reprisal Investigation Mr. Adam S. Lovinger Office of Net Assessment, Office of the Secretary of Defense, Pentagon, Arlington, Virginia," CASE 20170914-046986-CASE-02, Inspector General, Department of Defense, January 13, 2021, 12.

CHAPTER 25: A WARNING FROM HISTORY

1 Donald Kagan, quoted in Maureen Dowd, "How We're Animalistic—in Good Ways and Bad," *New York Times*, May 30, 2007, https://www.nytimes.com/2007/05/30/opinion/30dowd.html.

2 Ernst Fraenkel, *The Dual State: A Contribution to the Theory of Dictatorship* (Clark, New Jersey: Lawbook Exchange Ltd., 2006), xiii.

3 "Statement of Reasons (SOR) for Adam S. Lovinger," Washington Headquarters Services, December 8, 2017, Allegation (e), 4.

4 Stefan Zweig, *The Tide of Fortune* (London: Ebenezer Baylor & Sons, 1955), 17–19.

5 Ronald Reagan, "Encroaching Control," speech given before the Phoenix Chamber of Commerce, March 30, 1961, audio and transcript accessed at https://archive.org/details/RonaldReagan-EncroachingControl.

6 Brandon Brockmyer, "Corruption Is Public Enemy Number 1," Project on Government Oversight, October 12, 2021, https://www.pogo.org/analysis/corruption-is-public-enemy-number-1.

7 "Public Trust in Government: 1958–2023," Pew Research Center, September 19, 2023, https://www.pewresearch.org/politics/2023/09/19/public-trust-in-government-1958-2023.

8 Meryl Kornfield and Mariana Alfaro, "1 in 3 Americans Say Violence against Government Can Be Justified, Citing Fears of Political Schism, Pandemic," *Washington Post*, January 1, 2022, https://www.washingtonpost.com/politics/2022/01/01/1-3-americans-say-violence-against-government-can-be-justified-citing-fears-political-schism-pandemic.

9 Zweig, *The Tide of Fortune*, 16.

CHAPTER 26: A CALL TO ACTION

1 Montesquieu, *The Spirit of Laws* (1758), trans. Thomas Nugent, Wikisource, accessed June 29, 2024, book 8, chapter 12, 172, https://en.wikisource.org/wiki/The_Spirit_of_Laws_(1758)/Book_VIII.

2 Thomas Mann, *The Magic Mountain*, trans. John E. Woods (New York: Alfred A. Knopf, 1996), 506.

3 Elie Wiesel, "Oprah Talks to Elie Wiesel," interview, *O: The Oprah Magazine*, November 2000, accessed online at: https://www.oprah.com/omagazine/oprah-interviews-elie-wiesel/all.

4 Alexis de Tocqueville, *Democracy in America*, trans. Harvey C. Mansfield and Delba Winthrop (Chicago: University of Chicago Press, 2000), 275.

5 Tocqueville, *Democracy in America*, 275.

6 Frank J. Smist Jr., *Congress Oversees the United States Intelligence Community: Second Edition 1947–1994* (Knoxville: University of Tennessee Press, 1994), 35.

7 Daniel Immerwahr, "When the C.I.A. Messes Up," *New Yorker*, June 10, 2024, https://www.newyorker.com/magazine/2024/06/17/the-cia-an-imperial-history-hugh-wilford-book-review.